Focus on Developmentally
Appropriate Practice

Equitable & Joyful
Learning in Preschool

Iliana Alanís & Toni Sturdivant, EDITORS

Susan Friedman, SERIES EDITOR

National Association for the Education of Young Children

Washington, DC

National Association for the Education of Young Children

1401 H Street NW, Suite 600
Washington, DC 20005
202-232-8777 • 800-424-2460
NAEYC.org

NAEYC Books

Senior Director, Publishing & Content Development
Susan Friedman

Director, Books
Dana Battaglia

Senior Editor
Holly Bohart

Editor II
Rossella Procopio

Senior Creative Design Manager
Charity Coleman

Senior Creative Design Specialist
Gillian Frank

Publishing Business Operations Manager
Francine Markowitz

Through its publications program, the National Association for the Education of Young Children (NAEYC) provides a forum for discussion of major issues and ideas in the early childhood field, with the hope of provoking thought and promoting professional growth. The views expressed or implied in this book are not necessarily those of the Association.

We would like to thank our funder for their generous support for NAEYC equity initiatives, including the development of this book.

The following chapters were previously published in the specified issues of *Teaching Young Children:* December 2018/January 2019—Chapter 11; August/September 2019—Chapter 9; October/November 2019—Chapters 7 and 13; December 2019/January 2020—Chapters 26 and 29; April/May 2020—Chapter 3; August/September 2020—Chapter 20; October/November 2020—Chapters 1 and 12; Winter 2021—Chapter 32; Summer 2021—Chapters 4, 22, and 25; Fall 2021—Chapter 21; Winter 2022—Chapter 6; Spring 2022—Chapter 19; Fall 2022—Chapter 15.

The following chapters are adapted from the specified issues of *Young Children:* September 2015—Chapter 14; March 2019—Chapter 18; May 2019—Chapter 17; September 2019—Chapter 30; November 2019—Chapter 24; July 2020—Chapter 5; December 2020—Chapter 23; Fall 2021—Chapter 27.

Chapter 2 is adapted from P. Brillante, *The Essentials: Supporting Young Children with Disabilities in the Classroom* (Washington, DC: NAEYC, 2017).

Chapter 16 and Chapter 16 appendix are adapted from I.M. Escamilla, L.R. Kroll, D.R. Meier, & A. White, *Learning Stories: A Framework for Authentic Assessment and Critical Pedagogy* (Washington, DC: NAEYC, 2021).

Permissions

NAEYC accepts requests for limited use of our copyrighted material. For permission to reprint, adapt, translate, or otherwise reuse and repurpose content from this publication, review our guidelines at NAEYC.org/resources/permissions.

Photo Credits

Copyright © Getty Images: cover, xii, 17, 21, 28, 41, 47, 61, 91, 97 (center), 112, 147, 150

Copyright © NAEYC: 100

Courtesy of the authors: 9, 13, 33, 34, 56, 60, 72, 74, 81, 86, 97 (left and right), 124

Courtesy of Tiny Trees Preschool: 116

Courtesy of Robin Koetting: 118

Library of Congress Control Number: 2022935929

ISBN: 978-1-952331-10-7

Item: 1162

Contents

About the Editors

Volume Editors

Iliana Alanís, PhD, a native of South Texas, is professor of early childhood and elementary education in the Department of Interdisciplinary Learning and Teaching at the University of Texas at San Antonio. With over 20 years in the early childhood field, her work focuses on teaching practices in culturally and linguistically diverse early childhood contexts with an emphasis on the effect of schooling for language minority children in Spanish/English dual language programs. She is especially interested in forms of teaching that promote native language development and its correlation to second language acquisition. With more than 48 refereed publications related to dual language education, her recent research focuses on higher-order cognitive and linguistic interaction found in student–student exchanges. Dr. Alanís is former president of the Texas Association for Bilingual Education and former board member for the National Latino Children's Institute. She has served as a NAEYC Governing Board member and an Early Childhood Advisory Board member for Scholastic Education. As a member of the Dual Language Training Institute, she facilitates professional development for teachers in dual language classrooms across the country. Dr. Alanís is coauthor of *The Essentials: Supporting Dual Language Learners in Diverse Environments in Preschool and Kindergarten.*

Toni Sturdivant, PhD, is the vice president of early education at Camp Fire First Texas. She earned a PhD in interdisciplinary learning and teaching with a cognate in early childhood education. In addition, she has a master's degree in early childhood and elementary education with a specialization in child development. She earned a BA in linguistics with a minor in African and African American studies. Dr. Sturdivant has taught prekindergarten in both an urban school district and a center-based setting, as well as kindergarten. She has served as a trainer for practicing early childhood teachers and taught preservice teachers in various institutions of higher education. Her research, which focuses on issues of racial learning and racial identity with young children and culturally relevant teaching practices, has been published in several scholarly journals, such as *Early Childhood Education Journal, The Journal for Multicultural Education, International Journal of Early Childhood,* and *Young Children.*

Series Editor

Susan Friedman is senior director of publishing and content development at NAEYC. In this role, she leads the content development work of NAEYC's books and periodicals teams. Ms. Friedman is coeditor of *Each and Every Child: Teaching Preschool with an Equity Lens.* She has extensive prior experience creating content on play, developmentally appropriate uses of media, and other topics for educators and families. She has presented at numerous educational conferences, including NAEYC's Professional Learning Institute and Annual Conference, the South by Southwest Education (SXSW EDU) Conference & Festival, and the School Superintendents Association's Early Learning Cohort. She began her career as a preschool teacher at City and Country School in New York City. She holds degrees from Vassar College and the Harvard Graduate School of Education.

Focus on Developmentally Appropriate Practice
Equitable and Joyful Learning Book Series

In this series, each book presents essential, foundational information from both NAEYC's position statement on developmentally appropriate practice and the fourth edition of *Developmentally Appropriate Practice in Early Childhood Programs Serving Children from Birth Through Age 8*. The books provide early childhood educators with the context and tools for applying developmentally appropriate practice in their work with specific age groups: infants and toddlers, preschoolers, kindergartners, and children in the primary grades. The foundational content is supported by examples of developmentally appropriate practice in real classrooms, illustrated through articles from NAEYC's periodicals, *Young Children* and *Teaching Young Children,* and through new material.

Developmentally Appropriate Practice

An Introduction

What Is Developmentally Appropriate Practice?

Developmentally appropriate practice is about effective teaching and joyful, engaged learning. It is a framework that guides the thinking and work of early childhood educators to create healthy, respectful, and responsive learning environments in which children thrive. It requires both meeting children where they are—which means that teachers must get to know them well—and helping them reach goals that are both challenging and achievable.

NAEYC defines developmentally appropriate practice as "methods that promote each child's optimal development and learning through a strengths-based, play-based approach to joyful, engaged learning" (NAEYC 2020, 5). But no single method is appropriate in all settings or with all children. Educators use several sources of information to make intentional decisions about what's developmentally appropriate for *this* child at *this* time. These sources include what is known from research about child development, each child's individual characteristics, and each child's and family's context. Applying developmentally appropriate practice, then, means gaining the tools to build on children's strengths and knowledge so you can set goals and provide experiences that are suited to their learning and development.

Besides being an approach to teaching, developmentally appropriate practice is a position statement. Developed in the mid-1980s, NAEYC's original position statement on developmentally appropriate practice was a response to inappropriate teaching practices and expectations for preschool and kindergarten children. The statement has since been expanded to include children from birth through age 8. It remains focused on supporting equitable, high-quality learning experiences for all young children. The position statement emphasizes the need for teachers to have a foundational knowledge of child development and a wide set of skills to support children's learning. The position statement also calls for teachers to embrace children's cultural, linguistic, and racial and ethnic diversity as well as individual learning needs and development. Effective educators learn who their children and families are and recognize the unique, multiple assets each brings to the learning community.

The fourth edition of *Developmentally Appropriate Practice in Early Childhood Programs Serving Children from Birth Through Age 8* examines developmentally appropriate practice in more detail. That book expands on the important concepts of the position statement with contributions from early childhood experts and champions of high-quality early learning experiences. The book and position statement, along with the advancing equity position statement and the book *Advancing Equity and Embracing Diversity in Early Childhood Education: Elevating Voices and Actions*, present integrated resources for all early childhood educators, regardless of their role or the ages of the children they serve.

As an educator, use the position statement on developmentally appropriate practice and the accompanying resources to get an overview of the ideas and components of developmentally appropriate practice. Reflect on your current practice and develop goals to improve your practice so that you are responding to children's learning needs within the larger context of their culture, language, racial identity, and other social identities.

Using the Three Core Considerations to Make Teaching Decisions

Effective early childhood educators use three core considerations to make decisions about curriculum and teaching: commonality, individuality, and context. Here we briefly outline each of these and provide some examples to help you connect the core considerations to your work.

Commonality

Research on how children learn and develop provides several principles of human development and learning that are true for all children (see "Principles of Child Development and Learning," below). Teachers need a clear understanding both of how children learn and develop and what teaching practices are effective. However, learning is also greatly influenced by culture, experience, and individual characteristics. Within general progressions, development will look different for each child. For example, play is a foundational way children learn, but it can look different based on a child's culture and experiences. While children of various social, cultural, and linguistic backgrounds develop similarly in many ways, their specific identities and the history around those identities help shape their development and learning. It is important to understand the common characteristics of children's development and learning and how they may take unique forms.

Individuality

Each child is a unique individual but also a member of a family and community. Effective educators get to know each child and family. They see individual differences—including children's personalities, abilities, knowledge, interests, cultural and social identities, home languages, and approaches to learning—as assets to build on. For example, Francisco is a dual language learner who speaks Mixtec and Spanish. He is learning English as a third language. Knowing this about Francisco helps his teacher make decisions about how to effectively support his learning. Understanding each child and their individual characteristics will influence your planning, instruction, and assessment.

Context

To fully support each child's development and learning, teachers consider the children's and families' social and cultural contexts, as well as their own. As an educator, you might hold certain biases (whether known or unknown) based on your own upbringing, your personal experiences, and your identities.

Be reflective about your practices to ensure that you are not teaching and making decisions from a deficit perspective based on stereotypes and misinformation about certain groups. For example, Bre might arrive in your preschool program speaking a common dialect of English called African American Vernacular English (AAVE), sometimes negatively referred to as Ebonics or even "bad English." Although Bre's standard English skills are still developing, her AAVE skills are strong. Educators should not let deficit assumptions about home language and other characteristics influence their beliefs about children's behavior or their emerging skills.

As you learn more about each of these core considerations, you will understand how they work together and how to balance them as you plan and teach. You will begin to make decisions based on your knowledge of child development; effective educational practices; and the family, societal, and cultural values and priorities in your program's community.

Principles of Child Development and Learning

Developmentally appropriate practice is based on several principles of child and family development that have emerged from decades of research. The principles inform teachers' planning, instruction, and assessment. They also describe the importance of culture, context, and relationships for children's development.

1. Development and learning are dynamic processes that reflect the complex interplay between a child's biological characteristics and the environment, each shaping the other as well as future patterns of growth.

2. All domains of child development—physical development, cognitive development, social and emotional development, and linguistic development (including bilingual or multilingual development), as well as approaches to learning—are important; each domain both supports and is supported by the others.

3. Play promotes joyful learning that fosters self-regulation, language, cognitive, and social

competencies as well as content knowledge across disciplines. Play is essential for all children, birth through age 8.

4. Although general progressions of development and learning can be identified, variations due to cultural contexts, experiences, and individual differences must also be considered.

5. Children are active learners from birth, constantly taking in and organizing information to create meaning through their relationships, their interactions with their environment, and their overall experiences.

6. Children's motivation to learn is increased when their learning environment fosters their sense of belonging, purpose, and agency. Curricula and teaching methods build on each child's assets by connecting their experiences in the school or learning environment to their home and community settings.

7. Children learn in an integrated fashion that cuts across academic disciplines or subject areas. Because the foundations of subject-area knowledge are established in early childhood, educators need subject-area knowledge, an understanding of the learning progressions within each subject area, and pedagogical knowledge about teaching each subject area's content effectively.

8. Development and learning advance when children are challenged to achieve at a level just beyond their current mastery and when they have many opportunities to reflect on and practice newly acquired skills.

9. Used responsibly and intentionally, technology and interactive media can be valuable tools for supporting children's development and learning.

Guidelines for Developmentally Appropriate Practice in Action

These three core considerations and nine principles are a foundation for six guidelines for putting developmentally appropriate practice into action. The guidelines lead teachers as they make decisions in these areas:

1. Creating a caring, equitable community of learners

2. Engaging in reciprocal partnerships with families and fostering community connections

3. Observing, documenting, and assessing children's development and learning

4. Teaching to enhance each child's development and learning

5. Planning and implementing an engaging curriculum to achieve meaningful goals

6. Demonstrating professionalism as an early childhood educator

These guidelines are the principles in practice and form the structure of each book in the series. The star graphic below illustrates how each guideline represents one aspect of what teachers do to effectively support children's learning. Each guideline is critical to the overall practice of teachers. The guidelines all work together to create practices that are developmentally, culturally, and linguistically appropriate for all children. They are described in greater detail throughout each book.

1 Creating a Caring, Equitable Community of Learners

2 Engaging in Reciprocal Partnerships with Families and Fostering Community Connections

3 Observing, Documenting, and Assessing Children's Development and Learning

4 Teaching to Enhance Each Child's Development and Learning

5 Planning and Implementing an Engaging Curriculum to Achieve Meaningful Goals

6 Demonstrating Professionalism as an Early Childhood Educator

Developmentally Appropriate Practice in Preschool

Preschool children are engaged by playful learning experiences and learning routines that make them feel safe, valued, and important. This book focuses on the unique joys, needs, challenges, and opportunities that occur in working with children ages 3 to 5. It shares ideas and key concepts outlined in the position statement on developmentally appropriate practice through a preschool lens.

Often, teachers feel ongoing pressure to prepare preschoolers for elementary school by focusing on academic skills. This limits opportunities for play, joy, and supporting preschoolers' physical, social, and emotional needs. In contrast, the chapters in this book present practical ideas and strategies from a variety of programs that honor the ways preschoolers learn. By showing developmentally appropriate practice in action, this book models practices that preschool educators can adapt to use in their own programs to enhance learning.

Each of the six parts of this book highlights one of the guidelines for developmentally appropriate practice. In each part, you'll find chapters from teachers like you who are working toward developmentally appropriate practice every day. These chapters have been carefully selected to reflect various aspects of the guidelines, including equity, inclusion, and instruction that is culturally responsive. The educators featured in the chapters have successfully implemented or strive to implement various components of the guidelines for developmentally appropriate practice in their classrooms. Although these chapters don't cover every topic in the position statement on developmentally appropriate practice, you'll find many ideas and strategies that you can integrate into your work as you support children and their families.

The introduction to each part discusses the guideline addressed in that part and includes overviews of each chapter. While the practices described in each chapter work well for the children in those particular settings, remember that developmentally appropriate practice is not a scripted, one-size-fits-all approach to early learning. Instead, use the chapters to reflect on the practices and approaches that could be effective with the preschoolers you work with. Be inspired to think about ways you create goals and experiences that fit who and where the children are and that are challenging enough to promote their progress and interests.

Each chapter includes sidebars (identified by an icon) that connect to one of the position statements on developmentally appropriate practice and advancing equity. Focusing on a certain aspect of developmentally appropriate practice and equity, these sidebars are intended to support your reflection on how that aspect relates to the chapter.

Throughout the book, we note the use of the principles in action to illustrate how preschool educators can apply what is known about child development and learning to actual classroom practice. You will, however, want to spend some time reading more about the principles in the fourth edition of *Developmentally Appropriate Practice in Early Childhood Programs Serving Children from Birth Through Age 8*. This will give you a richer understanding of child development and how you can best nurture and support children.

Part 1: Creating a Caring, Equitable Community of Learners illustrates ways preschool educators can build a supportive learning community—a classroom that provides a physical, emotional, and cognitive environment that is appropriate for the development and learning of each child. This environment is built on consistent, positive, caring relationships between teachers, children, and families. The chapters in this section describe how you can develop this community through your daily routines, practices, and actions. They highlight the need to recognize children's strengths as you help them develop identity, purpose, and agency. They remind you to consider children's developmental levels as you provide support that will guide children's interactions and help them gain language and self-regulation skills.

Part 2: Engaging in Reciprocal Partnerships with Families and Fostering Community Connections demonstrates the opportunities preschool educators create to welcome families as collaborative partners and first teachers for children's development and learning. The chapters in this section provide examples of ways to involve families in daily learning experiences, learn about your program's community so you get to know children and families better, and understand families' funds of knowledge to strengthen your curriculum and foster children's success.

Part 3: Observing, Documenting, and Assessing Children's Development and Learning illustrates the process of authentic assessment in preschool. Assessment methods that are appropriate for young children are tied to the activities and daily routines they engage in. They include observation, anecdotal note taking, children's work samples, and Learning Stories (see Chapter 16). Appropriate assessment also includes the awareness of your own explicit and implicit bias and how these can affect your perception of children's capabilities. The chapters in Part 3 focus on assessment tools that are tied to what children are actually doing and learning in the classroom. With an understanding of where children are, you can plan curriculum and implement learning experiences that build on children's current knowledge to further their learning. The authors of these chapters urge you to consider children's developmental and linguistic levels but also their individual experiences and family contexts when choosing assessment tools and interpreting the outcomes.

Part 4: Teaching to Enhance Each Child's Development and Learning discusses approaches and techniques that preschool teachers use to engage children in joyful, relevant, and appropriately challenging lessons across learning domains. In the chapters in Part 4, you'll see creative, supportive ways teachers make learning relevant to preschoolers' needs and identities to support their physical, academic, social, emotional, cognitive, and linguistic growth.

Part 5: Planning and Implementing an Engaging Curriculum to Achieve Meaningful Goals highlights teachers' curriculum choices that have made meaningful connections with the children in their settings. You'll read about teachers integrating learning to target social justice aims. You'll also see how educators have expanded their program's curricula to be more responsive to the cultural and linguistic backgrounds of the children and their communities. The chapters in Part 5 demonstrate making goal-oriented, relevant curricular choices for preschoolers.

Part 6: Demonstrating Professionalism as an Early Childhood Educator suggests steps that preschool educators can take to improve their practice, advocate for children and families, and represent the dignity and importance of the profession. The chapters in the section discuss ways for you to reflect on your practice to better meet the needs of children and families. They also emphasize your responsibility to advocate for equitable, child-centered practices as you support other preschool educators.

Although the guidelines are addressed in separate parts, you will find common themes across the six parts. This is because children are whole beings. They arrive at our doors with individual experiences that have shaped their development. They are members of families and communities that carry multiple social identities. While you are developing two-way partnerships with families, you are also building a caring, equitable community of learners. As you use authentic assessments that capture what children know and can do, you are also teaching to enhance each child's development. As you include family members in setting goals for their children and making curricular decisions, you are demonstrating professionalism. The guidelines work together to support your use of developmentally appropriate practice.

We would be remiss if we did not stress the critical role of reflection in your daily practice. As you read and reread these chapters, use the reflection questions in each part's introduction to engage in conversations with colleagues and families. Consider how your work is developmentally, culturally, and linguistically appropriate for each child in your learning environment. In what areas do you excel? What areas can be improved? As a lifelong learner, use the many tools and resources NAEYC offers and encourage others to do the same so that you support each and every child to achieve their full potential. (Visit NAEYC.org/dap-focus-preschool for additional material related to this book.)

Creating a Caring, Equitable Community of Learners

RECOMMENDATIONS FROM THE DAP POSITION STATEMENT

Because early childhood education settings are often among children's first communities outside the home, the character of these communities is very influential in children's development. Through their interactions, children learn how to treat others and how they can expect to be treated. In developmentally appropriate practice, educators create and foster a community of learners. The role of the community is to provide a physical, emotional, and cognitive environment conducive to development and learning for each child. The foundation for the community is consistent, positive, caring relationships between educators and other adults and children, among children, among educators and colleagues, and between educators and families. Each member of the learning community is valued for what they bring to the community; all members are supported to consider and contribute to one another's well-being and learning.

At the beginning of the year, Nathaniel often arrived at school late and either crying or concealing outward signs of emotion. I had worked to establish a predictable morning routine to help children adjust to coming into school, but it was clear that Nathaniel struggled with big emotions. As Nathaniel's first teacher, I had an important job. I needed to create a secure relationship with him and find ways to be responsive to his individual strengths and challenges, his interests, and his approaches to learning and interacting with others. With his trust in me, Nathaniel could feel comfortable exploring the environment and curriculum of his new classroom community. (From "The Power of 'Good Morning,'" page 6)

This excerpt illustrates an educator aware of the power of positive adult–child relationships for children's development and their potential to impact children's social and emotional well-being. All children come into our educational spaces with the need to connect with others, to feel cared for, and to belong, and all educators have the power to build supportive, caring, and positive relationships with the children they serve. In "The Power of Good Morning," the author describes how she and Nathaniel developed a strong and caring connection over time. Nathaniel's smile, and the pride he showed in sharing with his mom the special tradition he and his teacher developed, speaks volumes about the effectiveness of the teacher's efforts.

Developing a caring, equitable community of learners involves intentionally building relationships among all members of the community—between teacher and child, between teacher and families, and among children. Providing children with multiple opportunities to play, interact with peers, and problem-solve with others through culturally and linguistically appropriate experiences is key to a welcoming, inclusive community. An important part of your role as a preschool teacher is to scaffold these experiences for children's varying levels of development and provide meaningful feedback to make their interactions more cooperative and effective. This includes modeling prosocial behaviors such as sharing and turn taking as well as using guidance strategies when conflict occurs. As you model the expressive language and other tools for children to problem-solve on their own, they gradually strengthen their self-regulation skills. These opportunities also lead to the development of children's agency and lay the groundwork for important lifelong social and emotional skills.

Within your learning community, recognize children's need for physical movement and organized spaces. Carefully choose the most appropriate learning format based on the children's characteristics and the learning goals. Formats include large and small group activities as well as play-based learning centers, in both indoor and outdoor spaces. Some of these experiences involve child-initiated play; others are most effective within guided play. Ultimately, provide children with choices in learning materials and activities within an environment that supports flexibility, responsibility, and freedom of movement.

As you create these supportive spaces, consider your own implicit biases about children's and families' race and ethnicity, home language, ability, and other characteristics. Preschoolers are in the process of developing their identity. Including their language and culture within your learning environment will help them develop that identity. In addition, support children's expression of gender and avoid engaging in gender stereotypes. This requires reflective practices about your interactions with children and families and intentional actions to counter stereotypical thinking.

Recognize that 3- and 4-year-olds are still learning and refining their behavior regulation. When children behave in a manner that is not conducive to the learning and well-being of all, first reflect on what might be causing the behavior. Then, consider what changes you might need to make to your learning environment or instruction. For example, creating predictable routines, crafting classroom rules with children, and having developmentally appropriate transitions go a long way toward setting children up for success and preventing challenging behaviors because the children know what to expect. When needed, do not hesitate to call on additional resources for support. These might be family members, but they might also be colleagues who specialize in bilingual or special education or mental health experts who can provide you with strategies to ensure that the children receive appropriate support.

While each early learning setting looks different, reflecting the particular children, families, communities, and educators in it, all caring and equitable communities of preschool learners share important characteristics. Children "see themselves and each other—their social and cultural identities—reflected and respected" (Wright 2022, 112). This means building on children's cultural and linguistic wealth through environments and activities that connect to children's funds of knowledge, incorporate children's strengths, and foster joyful learning. Educators also respond to individual strengths and approaches to learning as they develop secure relationships with children and their families.

Part 1 features educators who develop caring and equitable learning communities where children are valued and recognized for their strengths. These educators promote social and emotional competence as they nurture relationships with families and children and create environments for learning and development that reflect children's language and cultural experiences.

READ AND REFLECT

As you read the chapters in this section, consider and evaluate your own classroom practices using these reflection questions.

"The Power of 'Good Morning'" highlights the importance of fostering secure, trusting relationships with children throughout the school day. Such relationships support children to freely and safely explore, learn, and build resilience. **Consider:** How do you respond to children's need for secure and positive relationships? How do you nurture children's relationships with each other?

Differentiating support for children using a strengths-based approach is the most equitable way to meet children's needs. "Every Child Belongs: Welcoming a Child with a Disability" provides ideas and tips to help educators do just that. **Consider:** How do you show different levels of support for individual children? How do you involve families in the process?

"Will You Pass the Peas, Please?" outlines the benefits of sitting down with children and engaging in family-style mealtimes together. Children have opportunities to develop their social and emotional competence as well as their communication and coordination skills. **Consider:** How can you use mealtimes to support children in contributing to each other's well-being?

"Instead of Discipline, Use Guidance" illustrates processes educators use with children in conflict to help each child develop their own perspective taking, self-regulation skills, and agency. **Consider:** What opportunities do you give children to make choices in planning and carrying out their activities? How do you encourage children to work together to resolve problems or challenges?

In "Preventing Exclusionary Discipline Practices in Early Childhood," the authors highlight that children are often excluded from learning opportunities even without official suspensions or expulsions. They offer steps for addressing implicit biases and implementing positive behavioral interventions. **Consider:** How might your own personal biases contribute to your understanding of a situation involving a child? How might these biases be affecting your assessment of the child's behavior?

CHAPTER 1

The Power of "Good Morning"

Sarah Calzone

It's 3:30 a.m., and Nathaniel, a 3-year-old in my preschool classroom, is awoken by a familiar hand. As Nathaniel's mother does each weekday morning, she wakes him and his 1-year-old sister so they can get ready for their day. Nathaniel and his sister will spend the morning at their grandmother's house until school starts, and Nathaniel's mother will head to work as an EMT (while balancing schoolwork of her own).

Once Nathaniel and his sister arrive at their grandmother's house, they usually fall back asleep until it's time to leave for school. Their grandmother drops off Nathaniel's sister at a child care center and then Nathaniel at our preschool before she goes to work.

At the beginning of the year, Nathaniel often arrived at school late and either crying or concealing outward signs of emotion. As the weeks passed, he took a long time to warm up and generally kept to himself. It was clear that Nathaniel struggled with big emotions. I was concerned that he continued to engage in solitary activities; he often stayed alone in the cozy corner of the classroom instead of interacting with his peers.

As Nathaniel's first teacher, I had an important job. I needed to create a secure relationship with him and find ways to be responsive to his individual strengths and challenges, his interests, and his approaches to learning and interacting with others. With his trust in me, Nathaniel could feel comfortable exploring the environment and curriculum of his new classroom community.

I engaged with Nathaniel during different activities, and I observed and took notes throughout the day. I talked with his mother to learn more about their family life and routines, her hopes for Nathaniel, and the challenges facing her family. As I got to know Nathaniel and his family more, I decided that I needed to change my actions as a teacher. Even in my intentional practices, there was more for me to do. I made the conscious and deliberate effort to be right at the door each day when Nathaniel arrived at school.

Intentional Morning Greetings

At the beginning of the school year, I had worked to establish a predictable morning routine to help children adjust to coming into school. I used pictures for instructions, and I talked about arrival time during our first circle time. Many children were able to come into the classroom, hang up their belongings, wash their hands, and engage in free play with ease. However, I noticed that some children struggled during this period of transition and needed more support. When the struggles continued after the first two months of school, I realized that I needed to change my intentional practices in order to meet the needs of all of the children.

Upon making the decision to adjust my morning greetings, I changed where I positioned myself and the words I used. For Nathaniel, I got down on his level and said greetings like, "Good morning, Nathaniel, I'm so glad you're here!" or "Good morning, Nathaniel, I've been waiting to see you!" At first, Nathaniel did not respond to my attempts to make a connection. Knowing that building a strong relationship takes time and consistency, I maintained my new morning greetings. After a few months of this new approach, Nathaniel smiled; soon, he was comfortable responding to me in different ways and, in time, our morning greeting consisted of a hug and a cross-handed high five, a greeting Nathaniel chose.

During our more intentional morning greetings, Nathaniel began to open up and share parts of his world with me. He told me that he loves dinosaurs, especially pterodactyls, and he wonders what it must be like to fly like one. He mentioned that his sister loves her teddy bear and that she had recently been sick. The morning greeting took only a few minutes, but in that time, I learned about what interested and concerned Nathaniel and about the people who are most important to him. Had our greeting remained the same as it was at the beginning of the year, I would have missed valuable moments to learn about and be responsive to Nathaniel.

 Educators use their knowledge of each child and family to make learning experiences meaningful, accessible, and responsive. They plan the environment, schedule, and daily activities to promote each child's development and learning.

One morning in early spring, Nathaniel arrives with a wide-eyed smile on his face. I realize that his mother has come to drop him off today. Nathaniel and I go about our now well-established morning greeting. Nathaniel looks up at his mother and says, "See, Mom—I told you our 'good morning' would make you smile."

As Nathaniel continues his morning routine, his mother tells me that Nathaniel is more talkative at home and shares more about his school day. He has told his mother that he and I have a time set aside to say "good morning" when he arrives, and it makes him feel special. He has also told his mother that he feels excited to come to school and share a smile with me. His mother says, "Thank you. You have made him excited to learn and to come to school. He is smiling so much now."

This conversation gave me insights into the power of morning greetings. By being intentional, I was able to connect with and respond to Nathaniel, and this intentional morning greeting offered connections with the important people in his life. Nathaniel's mother began to trust me and share her struggles and difficulties, which allowed me opportunities to share helpful resources with her.

Planning for and Carrying Out Intentional Morning Greetings

The practice of an intentional morning greeting can empower young children to embrace their day and their learning. Young children may be experiencing challenges or anxieties beyond the classroom, whether their teachers are aware of them or not. Classrooms must be safe and secure environments where children are free to explore and learn and are able to build and practice resilience.

Here are four effective ways to plan for and carry out individualized morning greetings in your program:

> **Greet each child with a smile.** You help set the tone for the day. A smile signals to each child that they are in a safe place and that they belong there.

> **Use each child's name.** When a child hears their name, not only do they realize that the greeting is for them, they also understand that the teacher is thinking about them.

> **Include personalized information.** Use statements such as "Jordan, I remember you had swim class last night. I can't wait to hear all about it!" and "Jada, you were excited to watch a movie with your family last night. Tell me more about it during breakfast." "Sofia, I noticed you brought a toy dog with you today. Is that dog similar to your dog at home?" or "Antonio, I remember you wanted to play with the blocks today, so I put them out for free play. I can't wait to see what you are going to build!" Statements like these show each child that you pay attention to their interests and look forward to learning more about them.

> **Offer options for morning greetings.** Some children need physical touch and support to start their day: handshakes, hugs, high fives, or other movements can help you greet each child when they arrive. Other children prefer a wave, facial expressions, or words rather than physical touch. Introducing these options, providing pictures that model various greetings, and asking for a child's preference give children the sense that they belong and are cared for and enable them to be comfortable with their individual morning greeting.

Although Nathaniel has since moved on from my classroom, his mother still keeps in touch. Nathaniel and his sister are both doing well in and outside of school, and their mother has completed her degree program and is thriving in her work as a nurse. While I won't forget Nathaniel's start of the year, I cherish the smile Nathaniel gained from the power of "good morning" and the lessons I learned moving forward as an intentional teacher.

SARAH CALZONE, MEd, is a special education preschool teacher for Stratford Public Schools in Stratford, Connecticut.

CHAPTER 2

Every Child Belongs
Welcoming a Child with a Disability

Pamela Brillante

In any group of preschoolers, the children have a variety of experiences, strengths, and challenges. For some, it is their first time in a classroom, and they may struggle to follow routines and grasp concepts. Others arrive having a lot of experience with books and language. Some may be dual language learners. A few children might have disabilities or developmental delays that impact their learning, social skills, or behavior.

You may be wondering how to support children with disabilities or developmental delays if you don't have any training to do so. First things first: all children learn best in developmentally appropriate programs that offer them the supports they need to participate successfully alongside their classmates. Many children with disabilities benefit from simple accommodations and modifications, while other children may need more specialized, individualized supports provided by special education professionals. These professionals will work with you, the children, and their families to help the children learn and thrive.

To be an effective teacher, remember that regardless of individual needs, children are first and foremost children—and best practices for young children are best practices for *all* young children. Here are some ideas to help you set the stage for success for everyone.

See the Child as a Child First

Each child is unique, and every child can learn. Look beyond a child's disability, medical diagnosis, or label and get to know each one as a person. Observe children to discover what interests and motivates them. Talking and playing with children provides important opportunities for building trusting relationships. Engage families in setting learning goals, choosing

relevant strategies, and assessing children's progress. And just as you do for all children, have high—but realistic—expectations for children with disabilities or developmental delays.

Reexamine Your Beliefs and Knowledge

To be an excellent educator for all the children in your classroom, stay in touch with your inner teacher. Review both your understanding of child development and your toolkit of practices. Honestly examine your beliefs about children and families. Then think deeply about your responsibility to make learning—and the physical environment—engaging, accessible, and developmentally, culturally, and linguistically appropriate for all children.

Tap into the Expertise of Other Professionals

A child who has an identified disability or developmental delay may receive services that are specified in their Individualized Education Program (IEP). The classroom teacher must have access to a copy of this document. Don't hesitate to ask the special education teacher, early intervention coordinator, or administrator to explain anything in the IEP that may be confusing. They can help you adapt and modify your curriculum, physical space, materials, and educational expectations so the child can participate as fully as possible in classroom routines and activities. These professionals can also support you in identifying the child's strengths and interests, helping you find relevant ways to connect your teaching to each child.

Speech, physical, and occupational therapists who work directly with a child can also brainstorm adaptations and modifications with you. For example, a child who uses a wheelchair for mobility may benefit from a specialized classroom chair so they can participate at the table at the same eye level as their peers, and a physical therapist will help decide which chair is best for that. Bilingual education professionals can help you distinguish between typical second language acquisition behaviors and a language delay or disability if you are unsure about a child's progress (Alanís, Arreguín, & Salinas-González 2021).

Make Simple Changes

Proactively design the classroom space, routines, and activities so they can be used by the children in a variety of ways right from the start. This proactive approach supports children's strengths and can be modified to address children's needs. Plan activities that require peer interaction to accomplish a task. For example, provide dress-up items with multiple ways to fasten them. Instead of an adult always working with a child with a disability, pair the child with a peer buddy.

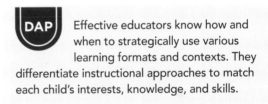

DAP Effective educators know how and when to strategically use various learning formats and contexts. They differentiate instructional approaches to match each child's interests, knowledge, and skills.

Strategies to Try

Here are a few strategies to support children.

Environment: Arrange the classroom furnishings so all children—including children with visual or physical disabilities—can move and maneuver around the room and learning centers by themselves. Make sure materials are within reach. Watch for classroom clutter and unstable flooring, like throw rugs that move easily, that make the classroom space inaccessible for some children. Managing noise in the classroom is also important for supporting both learning and behavior. Loud environments affect a child's ability to understand increasingly complex language. Carpets and other sound-absorbing materials, like wall hangings, heavy drapes, felt, and chairs with tennis balls on the bottom of metal legs all help reduce classroom noise.

Commonly Used Special Education Terms

When there is a child with a disability or developmental delay in your class, you're likely to hear a dizzying variety of terms from special education professionals. Here are a few helpful definitions.

Assistive technology (AT): any item, piece of equipment, software program, or product system that is used to increase, maintain, or improve the functional capabilities of children with disabilities. Assistive technology helps with speaking, seeing, hearing, learning, walking, and many other functions. Different disabilities require different assistive technologies (wheelchairs, walkers, braces, educational software, pencil holders, communication boards).

Developmental delay: a significant lag in a child's achievement of developmental milestones in one or more areas of development (cognitive, language, motor, social, emotional).

Disability: a physical or mental condition—such as hearing loss, cerebral palsy, autism, or Down syndrome—that affects the way the body works or develops and that significantly limits a person's abilities in one or more major life activities, including walking, standing, seeing, hearing, speaking, and learning [Americans with Disabilities Act (ADA) of 1990 (Public Law 101-336)].

Inclusion: a part of the philosophy that people are more alike than different, that differences make classrooms and experiences richer, and that everyone—children with and without disabilities, families, educators, and communities—benefits when children are educated together.

Individualized Education Program (IEP): a written plan for a child between the ages of 3 and 21 that outlines the child's learning goals and the services to be provided to meet their educational needs.

Individuals with Disabilities Education Act (IDEA) of 2004 (Public Law 108-446): the law that governs how states and agencies provide early intervention and special education services to children and young adults.

Interdisciplinary (or multidisciplinary) team: a team of professionals who evaluate a child to determine whether a delay or disability exists and whether the child qualifies for services.

Least restrictive environment (LRE): the educational setting that allows a child—to the maximum extent possible—to be educated with same-age peers who do not have disabilities.

Referral: a formal request that is often made by families, physicians, or teachers to begin the special education evaluation process.

Sensory processing issues: difficulty handling and responding to sensory input.

Note: While you may occasionally hear the older term *mainstreaming* used to mean inclusion, the two are not interchangeable. Mainstreaming describes a child with a disability participating in a program with peers for just part of the day or for specific activities where the child can participate without the teacher making any changes to the activity. Inclusion is the philosophy that children can engage in activities with their peers even if those activities need to be adapted or modified in some way for children to be successful.

Routines: Routines are useful for all children because they provide a sense of order to the schedule. The best routines have a predictable beginning, middle, and end. Use visual supports, such as pictures or props, to teach children routines, help them stay engaged, and aid them in transitioning between different activities. Provide children with verbal and nonverbal supports so that they understand what behaviors are expected at different times of the day (Alanís, Arreguín, & Salinas-González 2021).

Peers: Peers can model positive prosocial and communication skills and demonstrate everyday routines that young children with disabilities can imitate. Classmates can also help children develop social relationships and increase their motivation to be part of classroom activities.

Materials: Modifying materials in the classroom can have a big impact on independence. Working with occupational therapists to add pencil grips to crayons and markers can make them easier for children with motor difficulties to hold. Gluing small knobs to puzzle pieces make them easier to pick up. Some children have a hard time painting or drawing on a tabletop because it involves using very small muscles in the hands and wrists, which may not be developed yet. Try setting up easels, which allow children to stand and use bigger arm movements that originate from the shoulders, which often is easier. Make board books available and add jumbo paper clips to regular book pages to make them easier for children to turn. These modifications help children with motor delays but are also fun for everyone. Be sure to include books in children's home languages and pictures and graphics that reflect the children in your classroom. Make materials accessible so that all children see themselves as capable learners.

Determine Where Individual Children Need More Support

What do you expect children to do and learn during typical routines and activities? Consider this, then think about the supports you can provide to help a child with a disability be more independent and successful. Break down activities into smaller, more manageable tasks for the child, and teach the tasks one by one. To help the child transition to a new activity, give them a picture or symbol of the area to show where to go next. If a child uses a nonverbal mode of communication (picture symbols, sign language), teach all of the children to use it.

Finally, Trust Your Knowledge and Instincts

Whatever the needs of the children in your classroom, learn to trust your instincts and rely on your professional expertise and judgment. Be willing to seek help from others who have valuable experience and knowledge to share with you. These are important things you can do not just for children with disabilities but for *every* child in your classroom!

PAMELA BRILLANTE, EdD, professor of special education at William Paterson University, in Wayne, New Jersey. She does consulting work and has worked as a special education teacher and administrator.

CHAPTER 3

Will You Pass the Peas, Please?

Nikki Waldron

While I know that many of my fellow preschool teachers see the value of family-style dining, sometimes we may overlook the incredible learning that can take place during mealtimes. Through these interactions, children understand what it means to be in a community of learners where they learn from and respect each other (NAEYC 2020). These mealtimes create a space where children can extend their thinking, practice emerging language skills, and develop responsibility and self-regulation. Even in programs where children may not serve themselves or where they bring their food from home, many of these skills can still be practiced. By sharing what I've learned, I hope to encourage more teachers to use family-style dining as part of their daily intentional teaching. Every area of development can be expanded upon while the children are eating!

Motor and Coordination Skills

Mealtimes give children plenty of opportunities to build their motor skills. Providing appropriate serving dishes and utensils, such as small bowls, measuring cups, and clear pitchers, will help children successfully serve themselves. Having large plastic serving spoons ready for the children to scoop yogurt into their bowls can help build essential motor skills as well as hand–eye coordination. (It's also crucial to have extras on hand for children who decide to lick the spoon or who forget that the serving spoon is not their individual spoon.) When they serve themselves, children improve hand strength and dexterity. Plus, deciding which foods and how much of each they want helps give children the sense of autonomy they desire! When children pack their food from home, motor and coordination skills can be encouraged by having them open their own containers and wrappings, and it opens up an organic discussion about different types of foods. Mealtimes also offer a good opportunity to invite children's families to contribute foods they enjoy

eating and cooking at home. Integrating families' funds of knowledge and experiences fosters each child's enjoyment of and engagement in the mealtime process.

 DAP Effective educators strive to make sure that each child hears and sees their home language, culture, and family experiences reflected in the daily interactions, activities, and materials in the early learning setting.

When everything needed for a family-style meal is already on the table, you can sit down and enjoy the meal with the children. This provides time to observe the children's skills, note new developments ("Myla, you poured your glass of milk without spilling a single drop!"), and determine additional supports individual children may need.

Mathematics

Many building blocks of mathematics can be taught during family-style meals. Simple concepts like counting and one-to-one correspondence can be practiced by encouraging children to count out crackers during snack time. You can continue to build on those concepts with simple questions about addition and subtraction using food. For example, you can point out the two crackers that each child took and then ask how many they have if two more crackers are added.

Geometric concepts like shapes and their breakdown can also be discussed using peas, apples, and crackers. For example, a graham cracker is a large rectangle, but you can break it into two squares and then into four small rectangles. When children bring in foods from home, look for opportunities to discuss similar math concepts; for example, ask them how many cookies they packed or what shape their sandwich is. While preschoolers aren't likely to tell their families that they learned about fractions, they will begin to understand

shapes better. This also provides a space for children to engage in the language of mathematics.

Literacy, Science, and Social Studies

Sitting down with the children for mealtimes provides many opportunities for deeper and longer conversations than are normally possible during other parts of the day. It also allows for mealtimes to be unhurried as children engage in conversations. These conversations can be child driven, like when a child shares about taking the family's cat to the vet and it rolls into a 10-minute conversation about pets, shots, and doctors. When children participate in this kind of casual conversation, they are developing oral language and social skills, such as self-expression, listening, interpreting voice tones, taking turns, and respecting others. (This is important for all children but especially for emerging bilingual children, who need risk-free spaces to practice their new language skills.) You can further stimulate children's thinking by asking open-ended questions about the topic, such as "What kind of pet would you pick? Why?"

Use mealtimes to introduce new concepts or build on prior experiences. Conversations about the origins of food help children gain a basic understanding of the environment and the different roles people such as farmers, cooks, and truck drivers play in making food available to the community. It is also a good opportunity to ask children about the people within their own communities and neighborhoods. These conversations become important ways for you to identify community resources that can be incorporated into your curriculum.

Family-style meals are also good for discussing the nutritional value of different foods. Often, teachers say things like "You can't have more fruit until you eat your peas" without explaining the benefits of eating a variety of healthy foods. Explaining such benefits provides an intentional use of conversation that increases children's oracy as they attach vocabulary to objects and actions within their immediate experience. Young children love big words, so don't be afraid to talk about vitamins and nutrients!

One not-so-obvious benefit of engaging in conversation with children during meals is that they tend to eat at a slower pace. Eating too fast often leads to overeating, so children should be allowed to take their time at lunch (within reason, of course). As children finish eating, you can prompt them to understand their bodily cues by asking questions such as "Does your stomach feel full?" When a child says that they are finished eating, you should trust the child's judgment of their own body (again, within reason). I have heard teachers say some variation of "Eat your peas first and then you can get up." Although it is important to encourage children to eat vegetables, requirements like these can devalue children's autonomy and their understanding of their bodies.

Social and Emotional Skills

Because you are eating with the children, family-style dining is ideal for teaching and modeling social and emotional skills while also building strong, stable relationships with children.

Making a request such as "Will you pass the peas, please?" models a polite way to ask for something. Help children learn to start with small portions and ask for seconds (instead of taking too much initially and wasting food), encourage children to try new foods, and provide social cues and prompts. Having routines in place like a daily song for the children to sing at the start of each meal will help them learn to regulate themselves; the song provides a cue for children to adjust their behavior for what's going to happen next.

Encouraging children to clean up when they are finished eating will also give them a sense of responsibility and accomplishment while allowing you to focus more on interactions with and among the children. Young children love being independent and helping, so it's perfect!

Remember to engage in two-way conversations with families so that you learn what is appropriate within each home and culture. Acknowledge a family's choices and respond with sensitivity and respect to those preferences (NAEYC 2020).

Conclusion

If you intentionally integrate family-style dining into your curriculum, you will see how much both you and the children can learn during a simple meal. More important, you will foster a community of learners where all members are supported as they contribute to each other's well-being.

NIKKI WALDRON is the coordinator of curriculum and instruction for the Thrive to Five program of Community Action Partnership of Lancaster County, Pennsylvania.

CHAPTER 4

Instead of Discipline, Use Guidance

Dan Gartrell

Most—hopefully all—early childhood professionals know that we shouldn't punish young children when they exhibit challenging behaviors. The children in our preschool classrooms are just beginning to learn the complex skills of getting along with others. These are skills that we humans work on our entire lives.

Children are going to have disagreements—sometimes dramatic ones—as they interact with others. They really don't "know better" because they haven't learned the "better" yet. After all, a 4-year-old has only 48 months of on-the-ground experience! It's our job to help children develop emotional and social skills through appropriate learning situations. Cooperative activity represents the best of human behavior, and as they gain emotional and social skills, children feel safe, loved, valued and competent. Some examples of emotional and social competence include helping, sharing, cooperating, sympathizing, comforting, defending, and giving (Kostelnik et al. 2019). Most children will develop the necessary skills to interact with others. For example, expectations about sharing and actual sharing follow developmental pathways, and sharing expectations emerge around 4 years of age (Paulus & Moore 2014).

To support young children in gaining prosocial skills, instead of conventional discipline, early childhood professionals use *guidance*. Conventional discipline too easily slides into punishment. For example, if we embarrass children by singling them out as part of our discipline strategy, this is punishment. Punishment makes young children feel stressed, hurt, rejected, and angry; these feelings make it harder for children to learn emotional and social skills.

When we punish children, we are actually making life more difficult for

› The child, who feels rejected and unworthy and becomes more challenged in learning social skills

› Other children, who worry for themselves and the punished child

› Adults, who are not being the leaders they want to be

Using Guidance

Guidance is about building an encouraging community for every person in the group. To support children's learning, teachers create opportunities for children to interact and learn from each other. To give this help successfully, we need to build relationships with every child—especially with the children we find difficult to connect with and understand. We build these relationships from day one, outside of conflict situations. It is only when children know and trust us in day-to-day interactions that they will listen to us when conflicts happen (after we have helped everyone calm down).

So what do you do when conflicts arise and you want to use guidance? This chapter gives two illustrations of guidance at work. The first one might surprise you.

Illustration 1: Jeremiah Comes Through

This example comes from former preschool teacher Beth Wallace.

> When I first started working with Jeremiah, he had a lot of angry outbursts. The center used time-out at that point (the dreaded "green chair"), and Jeremiah spent considerable time there. While I was at the center, we moved away from using time-outs and introduced a system called peer problem solving. By the time Jeremiah graduated to kindergarten, we had been using the system for three years, and he was one of the experts.

One day, I overheard a fracas in the block corner. I stood up to see what was going on, ready to intervene. Jordan, just 26 months old and talking only a little bit, had a truck. Franklin, 50 months old, decided it was his turn to use the truck. I took a step forward, ready to go to their aid, but paused when I saw Jeremiah (then 60 months old) approach them.

"What's going on, guys?" Jeremiah asked (my standard opening line). He then facilitated a five-minute discussion between the two children. He made sure both got a chance to speak, interpreting for the little one. "Jordan, what do you think of that idea?" he asked. Jordan shook his head and clutched the truck tighter. "I don't think Jordan's ready to give up the truck yet," Jeremiah told Franklin.

After helping his classmates negotiate an agreement, Jeremiah's competence was without question, and his pride was evident.

On this day, Beth knew that three years of building relationships and teaching children how to resolve their conflicts through mediation was paying off.

DAP Understanding why a behavior is occurring helps you support the necessary skills. Always consider the context of what you know about the child as well as child development in general.

Illustration 2: Playdough Politics

In preschool, three common sources of conflicts are property, territory, and privilege. The following illustration is a combination of dozens of property-related conflicts I have worked with teachers to address. I put a magnifying glass to this one so you can see up close what guidance is and isn't, and how it teaches young children to learn from mistaken behavior.

Jason, age 42 months, is the only one at the playdough table. He gets a grin on his face and pulls the whole chunk of dough in front of him. He starts working the dough and mutters, "Makin' a dinosaur nest and eggs."

Daria, age 52 months, sits at the table and sees Jason has all the dough. She says, "Hey, give me some!" Jason hands Daria a tiny bit and circles

his arms around the big mound. Daria responds by grabbing a large handful of dough out from under Jason's arm. Jason screams. When he tries to grab the dough back, Daria pushes him and starts kneading the playdough. Teacher Kris sees Jason on the floor, yowling, and Daria using playdough as if nothing has happened.

Pause for a few minutes to think about how you would address this situation. Then read on to consider two possible intervention choices.

Conventional discipline: Kris walks over to Daria, stands above her, and says loudly, "You've taken something from another person again, Daria. You need to sit on the time-out chair so you will remember how to share." Kris takes Daria to the chair.

Daria is *not* thinking, "I am glad the teacher has temporarily prevented me from playing. Now I will be a better child and use friendly words instead of forcing my will on others." Instead, Daria is embarrassed, hurt, and angry. She feels rejected by Kris, dealt with unfairly, and unwelcome in the group. Daria *is* thinking how to get back at Jason.

Guidance: Kris moves between the two children, kneels down, and takes the following five firm, friendly actions:

1. **Describes** the scene in observable terms. "I see Jason on the floor very upset. I see Daria using a big bunch of playdough. We need to solve this problem."

2. **Calms** who needs calming. "Jason, we need to help you cool down so we can make this better. Let's get you back on the chair." Taking the playdough, Kris looks at Daria and says to both children, "I will hold the playdough. Take some deep breaths or just close your eyes to get calm."

3. **Leads** each child to describe the conflict, often starting with the younger child.

   Kris: Jason, what do you think happened?

   Jason: I was making a dinosaur nest and Daria took my playdough!

   Kris: Anything else?

   Jason: I gave her some, but she still took mine.

   Kris: Daria, what do you think happened?

   Daria: He had all the playdough and just shared a little. So I took some so I could play too.

Jason: Daria had some. (*Points to the little glob he gave her.*)

Kris: Let's let Daria finish.

Daria: I needed more to play, so I took it.

Kris: Let's see, is this right? Jason, you were making a big nest with the playdough. Daria came and didn't have any. Jason gave Daria some. Daria, you didn't have enough, so you took more so you could play too?

Both children nod, which assures Kris that they both feel like they have been heard and are ready to move forward.

4. **Solves** the problem with the children—not for them.

   Kris: So how can we fix this so you can both play?

   Daria: He can share more.

   Jason: But not too much.

Kris: (*Sets the playdough in front of Jason, who gives Daria a bit more. Daria and Kris both look at Jason. He grimaces but hands over enough to satisfy the other two.*)

Kris: Thank you, Jason. Can you still make a dinosaur nest or maybe just an eagle nest?

Jason: A littler dinosaur nest.

Kris: Daria, Jason was on the floor, and he was upset. He has given you more playdough. Seems like you need to do something here to make things better. (*Instead of forcing Daria to apologize, Kris guides the child to think about what would make Jason feel better.*)

Daria: Thank you, Jason. Sorry. Can I make you some eggs?

Jason: Yeah, a whole bunch.

5. **Follows up** with one or both children by having a *guidance talk*. Sitting next to Daria, Kris thanks her for helping to solve the problem and talks with her about what to do next time so no one is hurt. They agree that if a classmate won't share, Daria will ask a teacher for help.

Although guidance may seem time consuming, a scene like this can play out in just five minutes. If you truly do not have time to engage in all five steps at that moment, do steps 1 and 2 right away and tell the children when you will get together to finish the mediation. Don't forget! If the problem is no longer a big deal to both children when you get together, skip to step 5 for a guidance talk. Help each child learn how to get along better next time.

Seeing the Value of Guidance

Why is guidance well worth the time it takes? Here are four reasons.

First, the teacher does not make one child seem like a perpetrator and the other seem like a victim. Adults can actually start bully–victim patterns if they consistently comfort the "helpless" victim and punish the "guilty" perpetrator. Kris handled this situation so both children felt they were worthy individuals who belonged in the class and were capable of solving their problems.

Second, Kris worked *with* Daria. Children who have the boldness to take things from others most often also have the individual strength to become leaders who can work cooperatively with others (like Jeremiah), if we support them in developing their emotional and social skills. This change requires belief in the child's agency and firm, friendly, and consistent guidance (with an emphasis on the friendly).

Third, every use of guidance provides powerful lessons in language arts and social studies. Children who learn to put strong emotions into nonhurtful words gain vocabulary and communication skills that serve them well for their entire lives. Children who learn the social studies lessons of overcoming differences and solving problems together are gaining democratic life skills.

Finally, every time members of an encouraging classroom see guidance at work, children and adults together learn the vital lesson that everyone is a worthy individual, belongs in the group, and can participate in solving problems. For all of us, this is important learning for making our democracy "more perfect."

Conclusion

Guidance should not be considered a weak alternative to traditional discipline—it's about being a good coach who doesn't give up on any member of the team. Your efforts at guidance don't have to be perfect, but if you persist and reflect, you will get good results. Like Beth and Kris, we learn even as we teach. Do these things, and you will feel positively about yourself as a teacher—and that will help provide the inner calm you need to guide children toward healthy emotional and social skills.

DAN GARTRELL, EdD, is an emeritus professor of early childhood education and a former Head Start teacher. The ideas here come from *Guidance with Every Child: Teaching Young Children to Manage Conflict* (2017) and *A Guidance Guide for Early Childhood Leaders* (2020).

CHAPTER 5

Preventing Exclusionary Discipline Practices in Early Childhood

Sarah C. Wymer, Amanda P. Williford, and Ann S. Lhospital

When most people hear the words *suspension* and *expulsion*, they do not think about children ages 5 and under. However, young children in state-funded preschool settings are expelled at three times the rate of K–12 students, and children in private and community programs are expelled at even higher rates (Gilliam 2005; Gilliam & Shahar 2006); US Department of Education 2016). Both suspension and expulsion are forms of exclusionary discipline practices, or practices that remove a child from the learning opportunities available in the classroom (Noltemeyer & Mcloughlin 2010).

What makes the use of exclusionary discipline even more problematic is that children of color are much more likely to experience exclusionary discipline than White children. In preschool, Black children are twice as likely to be expelled as White children, and 42 percent of suspended preschoolers are Black, even though only 18 percent of all preschoolers are Black (USDHHS & ED 2014). Research shows that these disproportionalities are not because Black children display worse behavior than their White peers (Bradshaw et al. 2010; Skiba et al. 2011); the different rates of discipline are not caused by different rates of behavior problems but are likely driven by educators' implicit bias against Black children.

Because of the short- and long-term negative consequences of suspending and expelling young children, particularly children of color, many national organizations—including NAEYC—and federal agencies such as the Department of Education and the Department of Health and Human Services have called for an end to suspensions and expulsions in early childhood. While policies to minimize the use of suspensions and expulsions in early childhood are an important step, eliminating those disciplinary strategies as an option does not necessarily help teachers support children's positive behavior and engagement in classroom activities. In fact, even if suspensions and expulsions are eliminated, children may still be excluded in more subtle ways.

> Ms. Lawson hears yelling across the pre-K classroom during center time. She looks up and sees two children, Caleb and Michael, struggling over a toy. She immediately knows who must have started this: Caleb. Caleb is often out of sync with the rest of the class during transitions, fights with his peers, and refuses to follow instructions.
>
> Ms. Lawson feels as though she is constantly calling out Caleb's name, needing to redirect or reprimand him repeatedly. This keeps her from providing instruction to or having meaningful interactions with the rest of the class, and it does not seem to be helping Caleb behave better. She has regularly voiced her concerns to the director but has received no help or support.
>
> She calls over, "Caleb, give Michael back the toy." Caleb scowls and pushes Michael. Ms. Lawson hurries over, yelling, "No, Caleb!" She grabs his hand and walks with him to the classroom of younger students next door. She knows Caleb will entertain himself with the toys there and she can focus on the other children back in her classroom.

"Soft" exclusionary strategies are not official suspensions or expulsions but still result in children being excluded from learning opportunities. This could include sending a child to a different classroom (as Ms. Lawson did with Caleb), putting a child in time-out, or assigning a child to "silent lunch." Even more subtle strategies, like moving a child away from the rest of the class during story time, where the child can still hear the teacher but not see the book, reduce the child's ability to participate and learn from experiences in the classroom. In Caleb's case, he receives little grade-level instruction and few opportunities to engage with peers while he is in the other classroom with younger children.

Repeatedly removing a child from learning activities can also perpetuate cycles of negative teacher–child interactions, damaging the relationship. This is concerning because positive teacher–child relationships play a critical role in children's learning experiences (DeHaney, Thompson Payton, & Washington 2019). Being excluded can make a child feel that the teacher does not like them. A child who struggles to regulate their behavior is often repeatedly in this situation, setting a negative tone in the teacher–child relationship. Lacking self-regulation skills and being stuck in a negative cycle with the teacher, the child continues to behave in the same way (or even worse), resulting in escalating exclusion and frustration for everyone.

> Caleb has had another rough day at school, hitting his peers and taking their toys. Ms. Lawson is not sure how to get his behavior under control and doesn't think he is getting anything out of being in the classroom when he is like this. She calls his mom to see if she can pick him up. As he waits for his mom in the office, Caleb feels upset thinking about how he is going to miss outside time with his friends. His mom is clearly frustrated when she picks him up, which makes him feel even worse.

> Caleb's mom doesn't know how she is going to manage her work schedule with having to pick up Caleb so often; she isn't sure how much longer this can work. She spends the drive home lecturing Caleb about how he needs to be good at school and respect Ms. Lawson.

> This is the message, as Caleb interprets it: He gets sent home because he's bad and because Ms. Lawson doesn't want him around.

Over time, the situation can become unsustainable for families like Caleb's, who often have to leave work to pick up their children and find alternative child care arrangements. Eventually, the children may be moved to new settings where they have a good chance of experiencing exactly the same issues because educators have not spent time building a trusting relationship with the children and helping them learn self-regulation skills. Instead of being set up for success and supported by their educators, the children have a more negative view of school, teachers, and themselves than if they had never attended school at all—all before entering kindergarten.

More Inclusive Practices

Teachers are the most essential element in creating successful educational experiences for children in the classroom and minimizing the negative impacts of implicit bias and exclusionary discipline in schools. The harm done by using exclusionary strategies is exactly the opposite of what most teachers intend, so what steps can teachers take to support children to successfully interact with teachers and other children and fully engage in classroom activities? First, teachers need to look inward.

Four Steps for Addressing Implicit Biases

While everyone has implicit biases, those biases do not have to be permanent. Research has shown that unconscious biases can be changed and steps can be taken to reduce their impact on our behavior (Dasgupta 2013).

1. **Understand implicit bias:** Noticing differences between people is completely normal; human cognition involves quick categorizing. From a young age, we are exposed to direct and indirect messages about those differences; being saturated with negative messages about people of color contributes to holding and acting on unconscious biases, even if they conflict with conscious beliefs. Understanding our implicit biases and that they do not necessarily reflect our conscious beliefs is an important first step toward being able to look at and challenge those biases.

2. **Increase self-awareness:** Recognizing bias in ourselves helps us understand how bias impacts interactions in educational settings and how our interpretations of children's behavior is a function of racial, linguistic, or ethnic match (Bates & Glick 2013). This can be accomplished by learning about what biases most people hold, reflecting on the messages we received growing up about different groups of people, and learning strategies to counter and reduce these biases. The more we become aware of a bias, the less likely it is to unconsciously influence our decision making.

3. **Discuss and reflect:** Conversations about bias help us understand ourselves and our own biases, and they also help others recognize and understand their own biases. Initially, people often find it very uncomfortable to talk about biases and how they impact interactions in educational settings. Part of the work in exploring biases is learning to become comfortable with being uncomfortable in order to make progress. It is important when exploring these issues to set up a safe space in which people do not feel judged or attacked when being open and vulnerable.

4. **Use research-based strategies that minimize bias:** One way to minimize bias is to collect meaningful data on children's behavior, such as from observations and rating scales from multiple adults across different settings, and make decisions based on those data rather than on impressions. Data can be used to monitor progress, to determine when a child needs additional support, and to track whether there are disparities in how interventions and consequences are being administered.

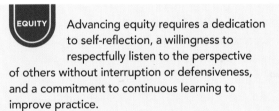

EQUITY Advancing equity requires a dedication to self-reflection, a willingness to respectfully listen to the perspective of others without interruption or defensiveness, and a commitment to continuous learning to improve practice.

Key Positive Behavioral Interventions

Although an in-depth discussion of facilitating positive behavior is beyond the scope of this chapter, the important components include setting up children to be successful, acknowledging and rewarding success, and teaching new skills. Here are some strategies that can help reduce discipline disparities:

› **Focus on relationships.** Reexamine the way you work with young children and families, establishing positive, strengths-based relationships (DeHaney, Thompson Payton, & Washington

2019). Discovering the unique skills children and families bring to your program helps you reduce bias in classroom interactions. To prevent negative interaction cycles and provide a warm, supportive relationship to children who need the most help, focus on building a more positive relationship with children who are struggling most. One research-backed strategy is Banking Time (Pianta, Hamre, & Williford 2011), an intervention designed to support teachers in developing close, positive relationships with particular children. A few times a week, the teacher and individual children spend one-on-one time together during brief (10–15 minute), student-led sessions called Banking Time. During each session, the teacher interacts with the child in a specific way (e.g., asking limited questions, labeling the child's emotions) that helps both the teacher and the child change how they perceive each other. Banking Time has been shown to decrease preschoolers' disruptive behaviors over the school year (Williford et al. 2017).

> **Understand the *why* of behavior.** Seek to understand what a child is trying to communicate through their behavior. Is the behavior related to instruction that is beyond the child's current abilities; will scaffolding help? Is there something about the learning environment that is not meeting the child's need? Have you provided engaging play-based activities that allow for interaction and movement? Are the activities connected to children's interests, cultures, and home languages? Reflect on your own behaviors and expectations and consider the changes you can make to help the child develop positive self-regulation skills. For example, you might develop open-ended activities that require children to work together and solve problems to support the learning of prosocial behaviors. Taking the time to consider possible actions reduces the chance that implicit biases will influence an in-the-moment decision.

> **Implement restorative practices.** Instead of using punishment, teachers can put in place *restorative practices*, or practices that focus on repairing the harm caused by a behavior. For example, bring back to the block area a child who knocked over another child's block construction and have that child help the harmed child clean up. The solution is logical and focuses on fixing any harm that was done rather than on punishing the child.

> **Set challenging but achievable goals.** Provide supports as needed and communicate your authentic confidence in each child's ability to achieve these goals (NAEYC 2019a). Be sure to establish behavioral systems that acknowledge positive behaviors rather than draw attention to negative ones. You can also help children develop responsibility and self-regulation by modeling and teaching calming strategies.

 Differentiating support in a strengths-based way is the most equitable approach to meet each child's needs.

Conclusion

Ms. Lawson knows that she often gets frustrated with Caleb and has started thinking of him as aggressive, and she is working on changing her relationship with him. She knows from Caleb's mom that Caleb has much older brothers and doesn't usually have to share his toys. Ms. Lawson decides to test the idea that maybe Caleb just needs some help in learning how to ask for toys more appropriately. The next day, Ms. Lawson takes Caleb aside to play a new game. She has collected some of his favorite toys and has Caleb practice asking her to play. Ms. Lawson gives Caleb enthusiastic praise when he asks. She then recruits another child to play with them, and they take turns practicing asking each other to play together.

Later in the day, Ms. Lawson notices that Caleb appears frustrated while watching a peer play with a toy he likes. She calls Caleb over and whispers in his ear a reminder about how to ask to play with a friend. Caleb goes back to his peer and asks if he can play; the child says yes, and Caleb sits down. Ms. Lawson smiles at Caleb and later tells him how proud she is of the way he asked politely and played so well with his friend.

Addressing our implicit biases and managing children's difficult behavior in the classroom are both challenging tasks. However, the strategies discussed here are both effective and essential for preventing the harm that exclusionary discipline techniques do to all children—and to children of color in particular. [For more on implicit bias, see "Beginning (or Continuing) the Journey to a More Equitable Classroom" on page 141 and "Incorporating Anti-Racist Approaches for Asian American Children" on page 145.] While the strategies may require new ways of thinking about and doing things, finding ways to maintain a strong relationship while keeping a child engaged in learning opportunities makes the difference between the child entering elementary school already believing that they don't belong in the classroom and a child who thrives in an equitable learning community.

SARAH C. WYMER, PhD, is a clinical psychologist in the Sheila C. Johnson Center at the University of Virginia, in Charlottesville, Virginia. Sarah provides assessment and intervention services to children and their families.

AMANDA P. WILLIFORD, PhD, is professor in the School of Education and Human Development at the University of Virginia and associate director for early childhood education at the Center for Advanced Study of Teaching and Learning, in Charlottesville, Virginia. She focuses on creating and evaluating early interventions, understanding classroom processes critical for children's school success, and applying research to practice.

ANN S. LHOSPITAL, PhD, is a senior research scientist at the University of Virginia, where she helped develop the mental health consultation model, LOOK and supports quality enhancements, including social and emotional practices, in preschool programs across Virginia.

PART 2

Engaging in Reciprocal Partnerships with Families and Fostering Community Connections

RECOMMENDATIONS FROM THE DAP POSITION STATEMENT

Developmentally appropriate practice requires deep knowledge about each child, including the context within which each child is living. Educators acquire much of this knowledge through respectful, reciprocal relationships with children's families. Across all ages, families' expertise about their own children is sought out and valued.

Educators who engage in developmentally appropriate practice take responsibility for forming and maintaining strong relationships with families and communities. They recognize that the traditional models of "parent involvement" or "parent education" are one-sided approaches that fail to give educators the knowledge or insights they need to provide learning experiences that are fully responsive to each child's needs and experiences. Instead, educators build reciprocal partnerships with families. Teachers can be creative and consult with families to find opportunities that work for them based on their preferences and schedules, as this teacher did:

> Ding, a family child care educator, knows that the family of a child in her class owns a food truck and is not available to come to the program for read-alouds because of their work schedule. After discussing with the family, she invites them to park the truck outside her program one morning to share food items with the children and show them steps the family takes in preparing and selling food. Ding also plans vocabulary activities based on food prices and menus from each child's culture. She chooses related books in Spanish, English, and Vietnamese—the home languages spoken by the children in her program—and prepares materials for the children to use in creating a food truck in the dramatic play area. She also invites families to provide items from home that might become part of their food truck theme. (Adapted from "Promoting Linguistic Diversity and Equity: Teaching in Multilingual Learning Spaces," page 44)

Ding embraces each and every child's culture, linguistic diversity, and family dynamics by using proactive and inclusive strategies that rely on the strength of family–teacher partnerships. Ding regularly invites families to be participants in their children's learning through shared experiences like the food truck and builds on these experiences by incorporating them into curricula and learning activities. Educators who actively engage with families and seek to understand families' cultural and linguistic practices are able to build on children's knowledge and experiences to promote their learning.

Effective educators establish respectful, reciprocal relationships with and among families. When young children enter your preschool setting, they do not enter alone. They bring with them their family and community practices and the many experiences they have learned from and with others. As their child's first teachers, families have much knowledge to offer you about their child. What are their likes and dislikes? What language(s) do they speak at home and with whom? Effective educators value family's knowledge of their child and seek to discover as much as they can about the family's funds of knowledge, including their cultural and linguistic wealth. They then use this information to develop learning experiences and inform their curriculum planning. It is only when educators recognize and build on the strengths of children and their families that they ensure that children receive equitable education.

Part of developing respectful and reciprocal relationships with families involves the simple act of welcoming family members into your setting and creating multiple opportunities for them to participate in their child's development and learning. These opportunities include discussing and jointly setting learning goals, sharing children's developmental progress, and making decisions about children's education. They also include invitations to contribute to or spend time in the classroom if schedules allow. Family members might be interested in reading their child's favorite book to the class or as a recording, sharing artifacts and pictures from home, or demonstrating a skill in cooking or gardening. Collaborating with families involves frequent two-way communication (employing a variety of communication methods) and acknowledgment of families' preferences and concerns for their child's education.

The best way to establish reciprocal partnerships with families is to listen to family's questions and concerns, talk with families when they drop off or pick up their child, and engage families in the learning process. Families want to participate; they just might not know how, or what's appropriate, or what opportunities might exist outside of the school day.

Learning about the community in which you work can help you identify resources to bring into your curriculum. For example, is there a nature center nearby that can bring insects for the children to observe? What resources are available for families? How can you contribute to the development of the community?

Finally, reflect on your own beliefs, values, and biases about the children and families you work with. How might these be affecting your interactions with families? How might they be influencing your teaching practices?

Part 2 reveals how educators develop respectful and reciprocal relationships with families and communities through educational activities that build on families' funds of knowledge, including children's linguistic and cultural wealth. Through these chapters we see educators who are intentional in reaching out to families and purposeful in creating environments that foster children's sense of belonging, purpose, and agency. We also see how educators acknowledge family's choices and goals for their children as they create multiple opportunities for family participation.

READ AND REFLECT

As you read the chapters in this section, consider and evaluate your own classroom practices using these reflection questions.

"5 Rs for Promoting Positive Family Engagement" offers strategies for nurturing reciprocal relationships by highlighting what families are most looking for from their child's teacher. **Consider:** How have you included families in making decisions about their child's learning? How have families responded to these invitations to participate as partners?

"Many Languages, One Community: Engaging All Families" reveals how staff members at one center ensure that families have a strong presence at the center and feel that they and their children belong to the learning community. **Consider:** How do you learn about families' customs, languages, and values? How do you integrate this information into your learning environment?

"Integrating Families' Funds of Knowledge into Daily Teaching Practices" illustrates how families' artifacts and photographs allow teachers to integrate the children's lives into daily classroom activities that are culturally relevant and sustaining. **Consider:** What resources are found within your children's communities? How can you connect these resources to your curriculum?

"Building Relationships: The Key to Engaging Fathers" reminds us that educators can provide intentional and responsive supports to fathers and their children by encouraging fathers in developing their own ideas of what a positive father–child relationship looks like. **Consider:** How might you engage fathers and other men important in the children's lives in discussions about children's learning? What activities or tasks can you create for fathers to do at school events?

"Learning with Families About the Contexts of Young Bilingual Children with Disabilities" discusses the importance of learning to know and respect families' preferences and concerns about their child in order to plan for children's unique needs. **Consider:** How would you respond if a family's desire appears to conflict with your professional knowledge or presents an ethical dilemma?

"Promoting Linguistic Diversity and Equity: Teaching in Multilingual Learning Spaces" offers practical strategies for enhancing family engagement and responsive environmental supports that cultivate agency and confidence for young dual language learners. **Consider:** How you have contributed to the ongoing development of your learning community? What are your next steps?

CHAPTER 6

5 Rs for Promoting Positive Family Engagement

Bweikia Foster Steen

Developing positive partnerships with the families of the children you teach is one of your most important tasks as a teacher. It can also be one of the most intimidating! As our country's demographics continue to change, it is critical that early childhood educators create learning environments that welcome all families and integrate their cultures and languages into the school curriculum. In this chapter I offer five Rs—respect, reassurance and responsiveness, relationship, reciprocity, and reflection—to help you build trust and promote positive family partnerships in your preschool classroom.

Families Want Respect

Showing families respect is more than being polite—it is esteeming or honoring families. Family members want to feel respected as their child's first and most important teacher; they also want to see that you respect their family values, language(s), culture, and home experiences.

Here are strategies you can utilize to develop respect:

> **Listen to and learn from families.** First and foremost, allow enough time to truly listen to families. *Telling* families about their child is a one-way form of communication. Two-way forms of communication give families opportunities to collaborate with you and to actually talk about their concerns, wants, goals, and dreams. Listening to families confirms to them that you value their thoughts, suggestions, and opinions. Learn from and about families' funds of knowledge (for example, knowledge gained from their cultures, life experiences, and professions) and then consider ways to integrate this knowledge for children's learning (such as inviting a family member who is a plumber to describe how they discover the cause of a leak).

> **Maintain flexible and open communication with families through apps and other means.** Use an app (like Seesaw or Bloomz.com) or design a private, secure webpage that includes the following: the classroom newsletter, weekly plans, photos of the children, resources and upcoming events section, a forum for asking questions, and an activity for families to complete with their child. Activities should be meaningful and doable, such as an "all about me" questionnaire (which you might complete first to help introduce yourself to children and families). You can also share photos and videos. Include the same items on a family bulletin board inside or near your classroom.

> **Foster classroom community with a Family of the Week backpack.** To foster cross-cultural learning and deeper relationships in an ongoing way, ask family members to complete an "all about my family" activity that you package in a backpack. Ask families to include items that are important to them in the backpack and to unpack it in class as they share information about each item and answer children's questions. If family members are not able to join in person, don't worry. They can join virtually using video conferencing or share a recorded video of themselves unpacking the backpack and explaining the items they pull out. If families are unable to participate directly, the child can share the backpack while showing pictures of their family.

> **Suggest that families include items that represent their culture, a favorite family memory, and a family interest or hobby.** Use the information and experiences shared to connect with the broader curriculum so that families' funds of knowledge are integrated into learning in meaningful and sustained ways. For example, find children's literature that mirrors cultures, languages, or experiences shared. (Check out weneeddiversebooks .org or tfcbooks.org/best-recommended/booklist to find children's books that celebrate diversity.)

Families Want Reassurance and Responsiveness

Family members need to be reassured that you care about meeting their child where they are and that you are knowledgeable about their child as an individual and as a part of social and cultural communities. They want to be reassured that their child will not be singled out, labeled, forgotten, or harmed—but will be kept safe and be engaged in activities that are suited to the child's unique strengths, interests, preferences, and needs. They also want to feel that you are responsive and that they can trust you to address their concerns and questions. For educators to be responsive, they must embrace flexibility. Educators who are flexible in their understanding, their expectations, and their responses to the families they serve will build that trust.

Here are strategies for offering reassurance:

> **Share photos and videos with families.**
> Keep a device nearby to take photos and video recordings (and keep in mind which families have agreed to have their children photographed and what types of sharing they are permitting). Families feel included and reassured when they know what their child does during the day, who they play with, the activities they enjoy, and how they are progressing, and photos and videos are a great way to share these happenings. Gather documentation for every child on a regular basis to share with their families.

> **Provide daily or midweek talking points.**
> Talking points can be just a few sentences to let families know topics, concepts, or vocabulary words that their children are learning and how to expand on those things at home.

> **Pick up the phone.** Responding to family members is the most important and easiest way to develop a trusting relationship with families and to reassure them that you are on their team. Make an effort to respond to phone calls, emails, and other messages within 24 hours. Returning these in a timely manner reassures families by showing them that their questions, thoughts, and concerns are important to you.

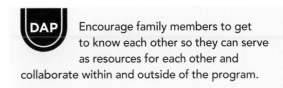

DAP Encourage family members to get to know each other so they can serve as resources for each other and collaborate within and outside of the program.

Families Want a Relationship

Creating and maintaining partnerships with families is an essential component of developmentally appropriate practice and for good reason: families have expertise about their children, and they play a critical role in their children's growth and learning. When families do not feel that they are part of the classroom community, they might distance themselves from the school or program. This might impact their willingness to interact with you and to volunteer in classroom activities.

Here are strategies for building relationships:

> **Say "Hello!"** It is amazing how far a simple, heartfelt greeting will go toward building a positive relationship. Learn how to say hello and other greetings in the family's home language. Using their home language validates their culture and bilingual identity. Just by acknowledging a family member's presence, you are being welcoming. Short, inviting conversations can lead to positive relationships and family engagement.

> **Invite family members into your classroom community.** Some families may not know whether they are allowed to be involved in their child's classroom and may not be clear about how to support their child's learning at home. Inviting families to participate in the program provides a great opportunity to engage families with your program's community and to share activities for extended learning. Be sure to support families' decisions as to how they wish to be involved. Invite families to share their home literacy practices. You can also ask families to serve as a mystery reader or a mystery guest speaker (virtually or in person). Ask children to guess the mystery reader or speaker by providing clues. For at-home learning, consider providing a weekly calendar (such as the one supplied at RIF.org) of culturally relevant activities families can do at home with their children.

> **Make it easy for families to ask questions.**
Offer opportunities at the program and online
for families to communicate their questions,
concerns, comments, or suggestions. You could
create forum space on your classroom webpage,
in your newsletter, or on your family bulletin
board. You could also have a comment box
in your classroom for families to share more
private communications.

Families Want Reciprocity

Reciprocity often involves a shift in thinking about
engagement and communication because it relies
on *interdependence*, or depending on each other to
accomplish something. One member of a relationship
must coordinate their thinking and actions with others
to reach shared understanding and decision making.
Such coordination involves being flexible with our
approaches and expectations. When we do so, we
can foster a supportive and trusting relationship with
families that will lead to positive outcomes for children.

Here are strategies for practicing reciprocity:

> **Involve families by dialoguing and including
them in making decisions.** Inquire about a
family's goals and expectations for their child, their
child's teacher, and their child's school. Telling
families about their child is a one-way form of
communication. Two-way forms of communication
give families opportunities to collaborate with you
and to actually talk about their concerns, wants,
goals, and dreams. In addition, keep families
informed about upcoming plans or changes,
with sufficient time to consider their options and
preferences, to ask questions, and to communicate
with you. As stated in NAEYC's position statement
on advancing equity, educators should "uphold every
family's right to make decisions for and with their
children" (2019, 8).

> **Consider culture, language, and literacy
when communicating with families.** This
means knowing about the families and ensuring that
accommodations are made so that every family can
access and respond to the information you share.
Translate documents into families' home languages

and use interpreters to help strengthen the two-way engagement and communication between you and families.

> **Ask questions of your families.** True reciprocity requires you to ask families questions so that you get to know them better. Ask families about their cultural and linguistic expertise. This way you can invite them to share their knowledge and experience with the classroom. For example, families can share songs, rhymes, or cultural sayings that you can integrate into your daily routines.

Families Want Teachers to Reflect

True reflection is ongoing and an essential part of assessment and teaching. Reflecting helps teachers engage children and families intentionally instead of falling into routines. Reflection also supports your own professional learning. You may find it most useful to reflect daily or weekly (such as taking an extra 10 minutes before you write your weekly update for families). As long as you find time to reflect while your memories are still fresh, you'll have new insights that will positively impact your instruction and your interactions with each child and their family.

Here are strategies for promoting reflection:

> **Ask yourself:** How well do I know each of the children and their families, and how can I learn more about them? What strategies do I use to ensure that families know they are an important part of the learning community?

> **Ask family members:** How would you like to be involved in the classroom? Is there a book you would like to read to the class, a cultural tradition you would like to share, or an activity related to your job or a hobby (like bird watching) you would like to lead? What do you think your child needs to have an even more enjoyable and educational experience in the classroom? Learning about the backgrounds of the children at your school or center helps you understand who they are and where they come from (Alanís, Arreguín, & Salinas-González 2021).

> **Ask your colleagues:** How do you engage families? Is there something we should do together—like host a family science and art night—to get to know family members better and show ways to extend learning at home? Consider how your community serves as a resource for implementing the curriculum. This is also good time to discuss how you can connect families to community resources for a range of services based on their self-identified needs.

Conclusion

At its best, early childhood is a time when teachers, children, and families open themselves to each other, inviting joyful play, collaborative inquiry, thoughtful observation, and deep caring. Together, families and early childhood educators nurture children's social, emotional, and intellectual development. When you actively help families feel welcomed and respected, you develop partnerships that can lead to positive outcomes for children (Martinez-Hickman & Amaro-Jiménez 2018).

BWEIKIA FOSTER STEEN, EdD, is associate professor of education at George Mason University in Fairfax, Virginia, where she also serves as the early childhood internship coordinator. Her research focuses on exploring developmentally appropriate practices that promote social, emotional, and academic success among diverse children during the early years.

CHAPTER 7

Many Languages, One Community
Engaging All Families

Lorraine Cooke

Having served as the executive director of Egenolf Early Childhood Center (ECC), a NAYEC-accredited preschool, for more than 25 years, I know that forming meaningful relationships with families is one of the most important things my staff and I do. It's so important that Egenolf ECC has dedicated staff whose specific role is to develop positive relationships with each and every family. In this chapter, I share how we welcome families and bring them into our school community.

> Carolina recently enrolled Liam in the center and is anxiously awaiting his first day of preschool. Alicia, a family worker, meets with Liam's mother at the preschool to conduct the intake process.
>
> "Good morning, Carolina," Alicia says to Liam's mother.
>
> "Buenos," Carolina says.
>
> "It is so nice to meet you. My name is Alicia. I'm your family worker."
>
> "Igualmente. Mi nombre es Carolina."
>
> Understanding that Carolina is more comfortable speaking in her native language, Alicia continues the conversation in Spanish.

Alicia is fluent in Spanish, English, and Portuguese. This is a huge advantage since most of the families living in our community speak one or more of these languages. In order to gain families' confidence and trust, Alicia welcomes as many of them as possible in their home languages. The families feel accepted as members of our preschool community, and their fears about their children's care and education diminish.

Our center's intake process is a critical first step in how we establish trusting relationships with families. Alicia takes time to ensure that families understand our policies and procedures, and that families acknowledge

receipt and understanding of the policies with their signatures.

Alicia also devotes lots of time to discovering families' preferences for their children.

> Alicia continues with the intake process, asking a variety of questions to get to know Carolina and Liam.
>
> "¿Carolina, cuáles son tus deseos para Liam, durante el año preescolar?" (Carolina, what are your wishes for Liam while in preschool?)
>
> "¿Liam es tímido o sociable?" (Is Liam timid or sociable?)
>
> "¿Ha estado él en cuidado de grupo antes de este programa?" (Has he been in group care prior to this program?)
>
> "¿Le lees libros a Liam? ¿En que lengua?" (Do you read books to Liam? In what language?)
>
> "¿Cuál es la comida favorita de Liam?" (What is Liam's favorite food?)
>
> As Carolina answers these and several other questions, her aspiration for Liam to learn English emerges. She also shares her profound fear that he will either lose his home language or become confused and encounter difficulty because he will be learning two languages.
>
> Alicia reassures Carolina that families often express this concern. She explains that all of the center's teachers are experienced in working with young children who are learning more than one language and in supporting the development of two or more languages.
>
> Alicia takes Carolina to Liam's assigned classroom, and Carolina is overcome with joy. The classroom dances with pictures of children from all around the world. Labels appear everywhere in English and Spanish, and in other home languages of the children in the classroom. The classroom library

also has books in many languages. Carolina is excited to learn that this is a lending library, so she can take books home to read to Liam. Seeing many books in Spanish, Carolina realizes that this center really does value her home language.

Continuing their conversation in Spanish, Alicia lets Carolina know that Ms. Julie will be Liam's teacher and Ms. Camilla, who speaks English and Spanish, will be his teacher's assistant. While sharing tips to ease Liam's transition into preschool, Alicia suggests that Carolina provide a family photo for Liam to keep at school. Feeling confident that she is making the right choice for Liam, Carolina gives Alicia a hug at the end of the intake meeting.

On the first day of preschool, Carolina brings Liam to the classroom. She is warmly greeted by Ms. Julie and Ms. Camilla. Carolina is reserved and noticeably worried about leaving Liam, but Ms. Camilla reassures her, in Spanish, that Alicia has shared lots of information about Liam and that he will be fine. Carolina hands the photo of her family to Ms. Julie and is happy to see Ms. Camilla take Liam over to the block center: during the intake conversation, Carolina had shared that building huge towers is one of Liam's favorite activities.

The next week, the center stays open in the evening for a family night. Carolina is apprehensive when she receives the invitation because of her limited English skills, but her reluctance vanishes when she learns that the meeting will be simultaneously translated.

> **EQUITY** Taking the initiative to hire interpreters for school or program events sends a powerful message to families and elevates the need for bilingual individuals.

During the meeting, Carolina enjoys getting to know the other families and learns a lot about the program as she and many other parents ask questions. Since Carolina doesn't have any evening child care options, she's grateful that families are invited to bring their children. And since she sees that Liam is having a great time in the dramatic play center, she finds it easy to focus on the details Ms. Julie offers about the curriculum and how families can extend learning at home.

Ms. Julie also asks families to bring learning from home into the preschool. She invites each family to schedule a visit to the classroom to share their cultures with the children. Ms. Julie suggests doing an art activity, sharing a song, reading a story,

or engaging in another activity of their choice that enables the children to learn more about the family's cultural heritage.

Carolina eagerly signs up to do a craft project that her mother taught her when she was a young girl in Guatemala. She plans to show the children a doll she made out of a wooden clothespin when she was a child, share a story about that doll, and then distribute wooden clothespins to all the children so they can make their own dolls using paint, fabric, markers, yarn, feathers, and string. She is delighted and honored that her preschool program is so welcoming and accepting of her, her son, and her culture.

At the end of the meeting, Ms. Camilla gives each family a cardboard frame of a house. She asks them to decorate the house representing their home, family, and culture for the classroom's Family Wall. Carolina is excited and starts planning her artwork with Liam on their way home.

At Egenolf ECC, I have realized that being intentional about hiring staff members who speak the same languages as the children makes a huge statement to families. If there are many languages in your community, your program may be challenged to find staff members who speak each and every child's home language. I've found that families are delighted to provide key words and phrases to ease their child's transition. Occasionally, with a family's permission, I've also reached out to friends or families who previously had children enrolled to help with communication. And in the classroom, a picture-based schedule showing the sequence of activities helps all children know what to expect and to prepare for the next activity.

In my years of experience at Egenolf ECC, I have realized the importance of inviting families into the classroom to celebrate their cultures and languages with the children—barriers that impede family–school partnerships break down, and children thrive.

LORRAINE COOKE is executive director of Egenolf Early Childhood Center in Elizabeth, New Jersey, a NAEYC-accredited program since 1994.

CHAPTER 8

Integrating Families' Funds of Knowledge into Daily Teaching Practices

Iliana Alanís and Irasema Salinas-González

The children in Ms. Silva's inner-city preschool are excited about going on a neighborhood walk to learn about their many local community helpers. They visit the local shoe repair shop where 4-year-old Theresa's grandfather works. The children are interested in the types of shoes that he repairs as well as how much it costs and how long it takes to repair shoes. One child indicates that she's going to ask her mother to bring her favorite pair of sandals that "don't work anymore" because they don't have a strap. On the way back to their preschool, they stop by the local panadería (bakery) and meet 4-year-old Mauricio's tío José. The children's eyes widen as they smell all the sweet scents found inside. José engages them in the math and science of baking, and the children formulate all types of comments and questions. Gerardo says that sugar feels like salt, while Maya asks why sugar is sweet. At the end of their visit, José gives Ms. Silva a box of conchas (a type of sweet bread) that the class will share when they get back to their classroom.

Children learn and play in the context of meaningful activities within families and communities, who are children's primary sources for learning about their world (NAEYC 2020). Effective teachers like Ms. Silva view children's home and community experiences as resources that contribute to children's funds of knowledge (González, Moll, & Amanti 2005). When you understand a child's funds of knowledge—the skills and assets they bring to the classroom—you are in a better position to create learning environments that reflect children's homes and communities. You are also in a better position to create culturally responsive activities that support children's cultural and linguistic identities (Castro, Espinosa, & Páez 2011). We believe that educators must understand and respect children's cultural capital so they can collaborate with families to create learning environments that leverage children's unique skills, strengths, and experiences (Yosso 2005a).

In this chapter, we share examples of developmentally, culturally, and linguistically appropriate practices that include families' funds of knowledge through the use of family artifacts and photographs (Alanís, Arreguín, & Salinas-González 2021). These ideas are presented through multiple vignettes that are based on our observations of numerous teachers in dual language programs and our own experiences as bilingual teachers. Although we focus on dual language classrooms, the strategies illustrated here can be used by any early childhood teacher to facilitate young children's overall development.

The Use of Family Artifacts

Family artifacts include objects found within families' homes such as kitchen items, religious items, and clothing. Anything that is unique to the family can be considered a family artifact and can be integrated into your curriculum. In this section, we discuss three uses for family artifacts: (1) prop boxes for dramatic play; (2) story boxes; and (3) activities that support children's learning of concepts and skills, such as sorting.

Prop Boxes

Prop boxes are a collection of items that relate to a theme. These prop boxes are placed in dramatic play centers to stimulate imagination and creativity as children create roles and scripts for their role play. Culturally relevant prop boxes reflect children's daily experiences and practices and facilitate children's language development (Salinas-González, Arreguín-Anderson, & Alanís 2019). They can also stimulate symbolic play. After the class visited Theresa's grandfather's shoe repair shop and Mauricio's uncle's bakery, Ms. Silva asked families to donate or lend items for their prop boxes. She placed them in the dramatic play center during the class's studies about their community and community helpers. Other themes that emerged from their whole group discussions included the carnicería (meat market), gas station, car wash, frozen food factory, and the lavandería (laundromat). An environment that promotes learning through familiar props and objects establishes an informal, nonthreatening space where children are more likely to take risks with their language; it also encourages them to interact and play with other children. For example, in our research we found that young dual language learners creatively used language with non-Spanish speakers to invent and imagine characters, scenarios, and dialogues in dramatic play centers (Arreguín-Anderson, Salinas-González, & Alanís 2018). When creating prop boxes for your classroom, think of the children in your community and what themes might reflect their daily experiences and practices.

Educators learn about the community in which they work, and they use the community as a resource across all aspects of program delivery.

Story Boxes

Children are eager to share artifacts from home and their experiences and knowledge about them. In Mrs. Miller's bilingual preschool, a clear home–school partnership activity took place every week. Mrs. Miller created a covered shoebox labeled "Story Box—Caja de Cuentos." She created a routine where children took turns taking the story box home on Friday and returning it on Monday, filled with family artifacts that suggested a family story. On one particular morning, children were engaged in a conversation about Adrian's story and the items he had placed in the story box: a molcajete (mortar and pestle), a wooden spoon, and a collection of envelopes with spices for cooking.

Children excitedly discussed their personal experiences with these items, including seeing a molcajete at Grandma's house and familiar foods made with the spices. Oral storytelling is a critical way that families share generational and cultural knowledge and support children to become knowledge holders (Delgado-Bernal 2001) who learn from the experiences of others (Curenton 2006). Storytelling creates opportunities to hear rich language, repetition, and rhyming, important elements for developing expressive and receptive language skills. Children who participate frequently in storytelling are more likely to have strong expressive and receptive language skills (Gardner-Neblett, Pungello, & Iruka 2012). When you think of your school day, when might you engage children in storytelling?

Activities that Support Children's Concept and Skill Development

Children are familiar with the uses of items found in their homes. When such items are used for learning activities in the classroom, such as sorting, children eagerly and successfully engage in the activities, and families experience a sense of pride in sharing items that relate to their family and contribute to children's learning.

On a recent visit to Mrs. Lara's preschool Spanish–English dual language classroom, for example, we observed as she engaged in a read-aloud with *Pete the Cat: I Love My White Shoes* by Eric Litwin. Mrs. Lara asked her children to look closely at their shoes. She asked them if they had laces or Velcro, what type they were, and what color they were. The children excitedly responded with comments like "Mine have laces," "Mine are boots!" and "Yo tengo Velcro" (I have Velcro). Mrs. Lara then collected the shoes children were wearing and asked the children to help her sort them by color. She asked them to think of other ways to sort the shoes. With this simple activity, she introduced them to the concepts of pairs, doubles, and patterns. Mrs. Lara extended this sorting activity by asking families to send items from home that children could sort in the math center, such as socks, buttons, clothespins, or other objects.

Using Family Photographs

Resources from home can lead to many opportunities for language, social and emotional, and conceptual development. In this section, we discuss three uses for family photographs: (1) developing personal narratives, (2) creating games, and (3) making puzzles.

Developing Personal Narratives

Mrs. Benavides, a teacher in a preschool Spanish–English dual language program in South Texas, asked families to send a variety of personal photos to prompt ideas for narrative writing for each child. Mrs. Benavides encouraged the children to talk about their family pictures and then write about them at the writing center. She asked children to share their written stories with peers during their writing center time and had children sit in the class author's chair to read their stories to their classmates.

To facilitate children's writing, she developed a word wall at the writing center with pictures of family members, friends, and pets that related to the family pictures. Through their writing, children shared their cultural, linguistic, and literacy strengths (see Alanís, Arreguín, & Salinas-González 2021 for further description of this activity). Such experiences empower and motivate children to write because they are writing about what they are deeply connected to—their funds of knowledge.

 Educators welcome family members in the setting and create multiple opportunities for family participation.

Creating Games

Mrs. Dion, a teacher in a preschool Spanish–English dual language program in Central Texas, used photos of items from family pantries, such as cereal, pasta, and hot chocolate, to create a game of concentration. We observed children as they excitedly set up the photographs to play the game. Each turn led to multiple opportunities for language development as children discussed the pictures and what they remembered about the picture placement. Such play-based activities that nurture language development also support children's social and emotional, cognitive, and physical growth and cultural identities. Consider asking families to contribute photographs that you can use to make games for your learning centers.

Making Puzzles

When visiting Mr. López's prekindergarten dual language classroom in South Texas, we were particularly drawn to a photo of Yamilet's dad working in a pumpkin field as a migrant field worker. Mr. López had enlarged the photo, laminated it, and cut it into several pieces to create a simple puzzle (Alanís, Arreguín, & Salinas-González 2021).

Putting the puzzle together created a space for children to ask questions about field work and the work of Yamilet's dad in particular; it also created endless opportunities for language development as children discussed the various aspects of planting and harvesting pumpkins. In addition, the activity created a learning environment that valued Yamilet's cultural identity and funds of knowledge.

Family artifacts and photographs are just two examples of how educators can facilitate children's learning and development—and families' engagement—by integrating families' rich cultural knowledge and experiences in the classroom in meaningful ways. There are several steps you can take to better understand children's funds of knowledge. Here we name a few to get you started:

> Use home visits, family nights, and family meetings to engage in meaningful dialogue with families to discover their funds of knowledge and ensure that learning experiences in the program are relevant and respectful.

> Listen to children's daily conversations when they play with their peers. Preschoolers eagerly talk about what they see and do at home and in their communities. These conversations reveal a lot about what children know and can do.

> Read the writings and study the drawings in children's journals; they reveal a great deal about families' funds of knowledge as well as children's writing approximations.

> Actively find ways for families to participate in children's learning as curriculum codesigners by inviting them into your classroom to share their expertise.

Conclusion

It is important to understand all the influences on a child's development—family, home language, individual developmental and learning characteristics—so you can create learning experiences that both affirm children's identities and knowledge and expand their horizons (NAEYC 2020; NASEM [National Academies of Sciences, Engineering, and Medicine] 2017). It is just as important to form reciprocal relationships with families to learn about their strengths and to value the rich environments families and communities provide for children's development. This knowledge leads to the integration of culturally and linguistically responsive strategies for children's education and care (for more strategies, see Alanís, Arreguín, & Salinas-González 2021). This strengths-based approach to learning and development facilitates positive family–educator partnerships and meaningful family engagement. It is only when educators recognize the strengths of children and their families that they bring an equity lens to the early care setting, thereby ensuring that all children thrive and realize their full potential (Allen et al. 2021).

ILIANA ALANÍS, PhD, is a professor of early childhood/elementary education at the University of Texas–San Antonio. A native of the Rio Grande Valley, she has been working with and learning from dual language teachers for more than 20 years.

IRASEMA SALINAS-GONZÁLEZ, EdD, has been a bilingual–early childhood education professional for more than 30 years as a teacher of children in preschool and kindergarten, college students, and in-service teachers.

Building Relationships
The Key to Engaging Fathers

Lindsey L. Wilson and Holly S. Schindler

Larry, a father of 3-year-old Jacob, proudly shares his feeling that his child's home visitor cares about his entire family—and that this caring increased his participation in Jacob's early childhood program. It's a sentiment we hear often as we interview fathers about how to build engagement.

Disclosing his hesitation during Jacob's enrollment, Larry emphasizes the importance of his relationship with his child and the early education provider. Larry sees his connection to Jacob as the foundation of other essential building blocks in Jacob's development. He also notes how important it has been for the home visitor to build a strong rapport with both Jacob and him. Larry especially appreciates that the home visitor has addressed Larry by his first name, provided information about Jacob's development while supporting Larry in deciding what is best for his family, and showed interest in Larry's work and hobbies.

Positive father involvement can promote the healthy development of young children that goes above and beyond the benefits of mother–child interactions (Cabrera, Volling, & Barr 2018; Levtov et al. 2015). This may be due at least in part to the sometimes unique ways fathers communicate, engage in physical play, and scaffold their children's cognitive skills, such as problem solving (Levtov et al. 2015; Posey-Maddox 2017). Fathers' involvement with their children demonstrates positive effects on the children's development and positive outcomes in children's self-esteem, academic achievement, physical and emotional sense of security, and long-term generational impact (Jessee & Adamsons 2018; Levtov et al. 2015). Early childhood educators can offer more support for the fathers of children in their programs by better understanding the ways fathers think about their parenting.

This chapter offers a diverse set of questions and strategies for staff to consider and employ in their current practices. Educators can use these as a part of their reflection, writing down initial responses as they read through the suggested questions and then identifying a focus area to implement a recommended strategy as a next step. Suggested strategies can be used in a variety of early childhood settings, including programs that offer home visits, center-based care, or a combination.

The Power of Positive Relationships

The more positive relationships fathers have—with their own parents, their children, and their children's teachers—the greater fathers' involvement with their children. Based on interviews we conducted (Schindler, Fisher, & Shonkoff 2017) with a diverse group of fathers in lower-income, less flexible careers, such as those in the restaurant and construction industries, we developed three principles early childhood programs can use to encourage fathers' engagement in their children's education.

Principle 1: Fathers' Relationships with Their Parents Are Influential

Eighty percent of the fathers we interviewed mentioned their own parents as being influential in their fathering roles, with some noting positive interactions with their dads as particularly important. For example, a 33-year-old father of two who works full-time reported that his positive childhood relationship with his father served as a model for his interactions with his toddler: "My dad has always been good . . . he would come home and would play with us, even though he was tired. And I say that if you give time to your child—that is what will be the most valuable to them. Although one gets tired, one must have strength."

For some fathers, their childhood relationships with their mothers also played a significant role in their parenting choices. A 39-year-old, stay-at-home father of three reflected, "I grew up in a good home. My mom had her challenges . . . like every mom does. But she wanted her kids' [childhood] to be better than hers, so she instilled a lot of those values in us."

Questions for program staff to explore:

> In what ways does the program encourage fathers to explore their family histories and upbringings?

> In what ways does the program actively welcome the participation of the extended family in activities?

Strategies to employ:

> Encourage families to explore family traditions, including the traditions they want to continue and those they would like to replace or update.

> Ask fathers how they hope their children will describe them in 10 years.

> Assist fathers in exploring their childhood relationships with their parents and how those histories may be influencing their parenting styles.

Supporting fathers in exploring their childhood relationships can be challenging; nonintrusive ways of employing the recommended strategies include providing reflective questions or activities. For instance, a teacher could ask a father, "Growing up, what is one of your favorite memories with your parents?" This could also be captured during a family week where teachers suggest topics for families to explore at home. Teachers might also share information about various parenting styles with fathers and encourage them to reflect on which they most identify with and why.

 DAP Learning about a family's background and experiences helps you integrate relevant activities into your curriculum. This knowledge facilitates integration of culturally and linguistically responsive strategies for children's education and care.

Principle 2: Fathers Place a High Value on Building Positive Relationships with Their Children

When asked which potential benefit of early childhood education programs was most important to them, fathers overwhelmingly chose support in strengthening positive relationships with their children. For example, one father described building a positive relationship with his children as "the most important thing of all." Another father stated that the most important thing is for "the dad to have . . . a close relationship [with his child] . . . for the educational side and for brain development, and all of that comes from a good relationship with the parent." Supporting fathers in developing a positive relationship with their child based on the perspective of the father is vital. Educators take on a supporting role that is free of their own opinion and centered in the father's viewpoint.

Questions for program staff to explore:

> How do fathers define positive relationships?

> How do staff members engage in discussions with fathers about the relationships they have with their children?

> What steps do staff take to encourage father–child relationships?

Strategies to employ:

> Engage in frequent conversations with fathers about the types of relationships they have or want to have with their children. If possible, these discussions should be in the father's home language.

> Strive to understand and support fathers in developing their own ideas of what a positive father–child relationship looks like. In other words, how do fathers describe the connection they want with their children?

> Explore stereotypes or misconceptions that may be interfering with fathers building the relationships they want with their children.

> Consider providing a workshop for fathers, specifically driven by topics fathers feel are important or that may encourage the types of connections they are looking to build with their children.

Principle 3: Supportive Relationships with Early Childhood Staff Encourage Fathers to Participate

Positive relationships between early childhood staff and fathers can promote fathers' participation in program activities. Fathers in our study highlighted the support home visitors offered them by answering their questions, providing resources, assisting them with their child's development, serving as role models, and dedicating time just for them as fathers. When these supportive relationships with staff were established, some fathers even reported changing their work schedules to participate in home visits and other program activities.

Questions for program staff to explore:

> How are staff interactions with fathers similar to or different from staff interactions with mothers?

> What opportunities are provided for fathers to connect with program staff?

> Do fathers see themselves or other men represented in the early childhood staff or in the classroom? If not, what changes can we make?

> Are programs focused on the well-being of the family as a whole?

Strategies to employ:

> Make it a point to invite fathers into the classroom, and communicate directly with them. Greet them by name and use the word *fathers* to let them know they are included (also use terms such as *caregivers* to be sure all of the important adults in children's lives are welcomed and respected).

> Have activities or tasks for fathers to do when inviting them to events; many fathers like to know that there will be something concrete for them to do when they arrive.

> Make sure all program materials and policies are inclusive (for example, leaving space for all primary caregivers to sign documents).

> Ask fathers (and all other primary caregivers) about their experiences when discussing their children's development.

> Ask fathers about topics beyond their children's development (hobbies, work, summer plans). Listen to what fathers in the program have to say about their children, their own lives, and other experiences.

Conclusion

Fathers find positive relationships meaningful, especially when those relationships involve their children. Building positive relationships with fathers can increase their participation in early childhood programs and strengthen their relationships with children. Despite the critical role of the father–child relationship, research continues to demonstrate that men face unique challenges regarding involvement as a result of interpersonal, organizational, and societal factors (Bateson et al. 2017). For instance, biases around fatherhood are still deeply ingrained and depicted in the United States. A successful father is often described as one who can financially provide and physically protect; such stereotypes limit the ways that early childhood educators and other stakeholders engage fathers (Wilson & Thompson 2021). In addition, organizational policies both in the public and private sectors contribute to unequal participation in unpaid care work (Levtov et al. 2015). While fathers do experience unique barriers, it doesn't mean they don't want to be involved or won't attempt to make adjustments—especially if they have a connection to the program and to the staff.

LINDSEY L. WILSON, PhD, is an educator, trainer, published author, and speaker on the topics of equity and early childhood education in Dallas, Texas.

HOLLY S. SCHINDLER is an associate professor in the areas of early childhood and family studies, learning sciences, and human development at the University of Washington in Seattle.

CHAPTER 10

Learning with Families About the Contexts of Young Bilingual Children with Disabilities

Cristina Gillanders and Sylvia Y. Sánchez

"¿Ahora qué? Gabriela has a disability," Isabel thinks as she leaves the pediatrician's office. She took her 4-year-old daughter Gabriela for a visit after her early childhood teacher recommended getting a screening. According to the pediatrician, Gabriela will not develop at the same rate as the other children. "Now I understand why she took so long to sit and talk. Did I do something wrong during my pregnancy? Was I too stressed? Did I eat something that made her sick? Is this a test that God has given me?" Isabel asks herself. Then she begins wondering about the future: "How can I raise my daughter when I don't know anything about children with disabilities? What can I do to help her learn like other children? Should I speak to her in Spanish? Will she be able to learn both languages or will it be too much for her? Am I capable of raising her without my family living near us? Will she be able to go to school? What will happen when I am no longer able to take care of her?"

These are questions that many parents of children with disabilities ask themselves, and they often turn to early childhood educators for guidance in understanding how best to support their children's growth and development. To help Isabel navigate her many questions and concerns about Gabriela's disability and bilingualism, Gabriela's teachers can build a positive partnership and reciprocal relationship with her and her family. This involves humbly learning *with* the family about Gabriela's strengths and preferences, the family's beliefs about disability and bilingualism, goals and dreams the family has for their daughter, their cultural community and support system, and the family's everyday practices and routines (Gillanders & Sánchez 2021). Examining their own beliefs and potential biases about a child with a disability and who is bilingual is also critical to the teachers' ability to meet Gabriela's and the family's needs.

> ## Authors' Note
>
> While NAEYC's publication style is to use *dual language learners* to refer to young children who are learning English simultaneously with their home language, in this chapter we use the term *bilingual* to describe these children.

Through this relationship-building and learning process, the teachers can create a space for Isabel to share her fears and anxieties. Working together, and with the specialists who will also be a part of Gabriela's educational team, the teachers and family can seek to understand the implications of Gabriela's disability and her bilingualism and to establish achievable goals for Gabriela.

All children develop and learn within the social and cultural contexts of their families and communities (including their early childhood programs). Forging positive, reciprocal relationships with families provides educators invaluable knowledge and resources for understanding these contexts. In this chapter we explore some considerations around these contexts that can guide teachers in their work with bilingual children who have a disability.

Exploring Perceptions of Bilingualism and Disability

Typically developing children from linguistically diverse backgrounds are often judged by their ability to use English rather than by their capacity to use both languages. Frequently, instead of viewing a child's home language(s) as an asset and using it as a springboard for building their English skills, educators focus on helping the child learn English as quickly as possible.

Similarly, the general public and many educators view a child with a disability as "different and inferior" (Artiles 2013, 334). The focus is on what the child *cannot* do in certain settings rather than on what the child *can* do. Often, the goal in education is to "fix" the disability by focusing on and correcting whatever is viewed as problematic in the child's functioning in the physical, emotional, or other developmental domains (Dalkilic 2019). In this medical model, the child is identified mainly by their disability rather than by being a child.

 DAP Each child is an individual reflecting their unique experiences, including language skills, interests, and strengths.

These views of bilingualism and disability disregard that the child—like any other child—lives in a complex set of social and cultural contexts. Bilingual children with disabilities are in a double bind (Artiles 2013). They may be excluded in various ways from fully participating in classroom activities because they are members of linguistically, ethnically, and racially minoritized groups as well as because of their unique developmental needs related to their disability. Seen through the lens of the two characteristics—language and ability—these children's strengths are often overlooked.

What might be overlooked in one context, however, might be recognized and valued in another. Specific settings require specific capabilities to function in those settings. It all depends on the particular context. For example, a bilingual child with a disability may have developed strengths within their cultural community and be viewed as strong and capable by their family and community. However, in an early childhood setting, teachers might see that child as lacking the capabilities to participate in certain experiences in the classroom, such as playing outside with other children, listening quietly when the teacher is reading aloud, and learning to identify letters (because of the particular disability and/or because the child's stronger language is their home language). The teachers may overlook or disregard the child's strengths by not considering the language and cultural practices of the child's family and community

and how the child's family and community view the child's disability.

To use a strengths-based view of bilingual children with disabilities, teachers can seek to learn about three aspects of context: families' everyday lives, their ideas about their child's bilingualism, and their perceptions of their child's disability.

Understanding Families' Everyday Lives

A child's unique and personal context is formed by their family's cultural practices and community activities, the family's values and beliefs, the child's home environment, and the language(s) used in everyday life. As early educators build a positive, authentic relationship with families of bilingual children with disabilities, learning about the families' everyday routines provides insights into creating learning experiences that fit with their values and practices (McWilliam 2012) and that will promote the child's knowledge and skills.

For example, during a visit to Gabriela's home, the teachers notice that music is continually played and that Gabriela often dances to the music. Recognizing that Gabriela is developing her motor control, balance, and awareness of space and directionality as she joyfully dances, the teachers decide to incorporate some of this music into the classroom to benefit Gabriela and the other children. With Isabel's help, the teachers select one of the songs they heard in her home and create a chart of the lyrics to do shared reading with the children. The song is in Spanish, so this experience is also a significant way to use Gabriela's home language in the classroom and allow her to teach this song to her peers.

Understanding Families' Ideas About Bilingualism

Bilingual families have different views about home languages and bilingualism. Some believe that bilingualism is an asset and are intentional in exposing their children to situations that strengthen their use of their home language. Their motivation to support bilingualism varies. Parents may want their children to communicate with family members in other parts of

the world, develop pride in their cultural and bilingual identity, or have better career opportunities by being fluent in more than one language. Some parents, like Isabel, also have these desires but are concerned that learning two languages may hinder their child's development and learning in the short term, especially if their child also has a disability.

As teachers explore families' ideas about supporting children's use of both the home language and English, they also need to examine their own understanding and beliefs about home language, bilingualism, and second language acquisition in young children. Challenges emerge when educators who do not speak the families' home language believe that parents should speak in English to take full advantage of the intervention or services provided for their child. Some educators believe that using two languages might undermine the child's English language development. However, multiple studies have found no indication that bilingualism is detrimental to children with autism spectrum disorder, language impairment, or Down syndrome (Bedore & Peña 2008; Bird, Genesee, & Verhoeven 2016; Hambly & Fombonne 2012). Rather, using two languages provides a child with more resources at their disposal to communicate.

Recall that after learning Gabriela's diagnosis, Isabel had many questions about how to support her daughter's development. She wanted to make sure that Gabriela could communicate with her abuelitos (grandparents) when they talked on the phone. Also, she felt much more comfortable using Spanish to communicate with and support Gabriela because that is the language she had used with Gabriela since she was born. At the same time, Isabel feared that learning two languages would be an additional burden for Gabriela. But when Gabriela's teachers shared with her the benefits of bilingualism, it helped to ease Isabel's fears. Isabel was relieved and pleased to know that Gabriela would benefit from continuing to speak Spanish.

Understanding Families' View of Their Child's Disability

Families' interpretations of their child's disability might vary due to cultural views of disability, their experiences with individuals with disabilities, or information they have received about a particular disability. For example, some parents might believe that the child's disability is a test from God to overcome (Skinner et al. 2001) or that the disability is an illness that will not be fixed with any intervention (Ijalba 2016). Other parents might react negatively to certain behaviors and characteristics of their child, attributing them to the child's willfulness rather than a characteristic of the disability. Such interpretations might influence not only parents' views of a disability but also their willingness to seek a professional evaluation and work in partnership with early educators.

Let's return to Gabriela's story. Her teachers can listen to Isabel's ideas about disability to gain a better understanding of her childrearing decisions. As they share information about Gabriela's disability with Isabel, they can remind her that each child is different. Children who have the same disability might express it differently, depending on the child's experiences, individuality, and social and cultural contexts. As is often said, "If you've met one person with autism, you've met one person with autism."

Conclusion

Understanding key aspects of a child and family's sociocultural contexts allows teachers to effectively teach the bilingual child with disabilities and support the family in culturally sustaining ways. Bilingual children with disabilities are first and foremost children and should not be defined by their disability *or* their bilingualism. Each child is an individual with specific interests and characteristics that interact with their family and cultural contexts. Respectful partnerships with families are essential to understand the child's interests, strengths, and development. Gabriela's teachers can get to know what interests her and include it in their teaching and curriculum. They can also observe her interactions with other children and adjust the environment, materials, and level of support to ensure that Gabriela is included and participates meaningfully in play and learning experiences.

As a child grows and interacts with larger communities, systems, and environments, the child continues their development in unique ways as an individual and in ways that are appropriate for and supported by their cultural community. This is a complex, lifelong process. Teachers can facilitate this process by learning with families and connecting each child's strengths, interests, preferences, and skills—as shared by the family and the cultural community and learned through their own observations of the child—to create culturally responsive and sustaining learning experiences.

CRISTINA GILLANDERS, PhD, works as an associate professor in early childhood education at the University of Colorado, Denver.

SYLVIA Y. SÁNCHEZ, EdD, is an associate professor emerita in early childhood education and multicultural education at George Mason University in Fairfax, Virginia.

CHAPTER 11

Promoting Linguistic Diversity and Equity
Teaching in Multilingual Learning Spaces

Carola Oliva-Olson, Linda M. Espinosa, Whit Hayslip, and Elizabeth S. Magruder

Matthew, a monolingual English speaker, and two assistants who speak Spanish and Tagalog teach in a preschool classroom with children who speak a variety of languages, including Spanish, African American Vernacular English (AAVE), Vietnamese, and American Sign Language. The classroom buzzes with new songs and phrases in English and sometimes words of comfort in each language. Carefully placed pictures and labels help children see and interact with key words and items from all their cultures. In one corner of the classroom, Matthew welcomes a new parent and arranges a family language and cultural background interview.

Are you one of the many teachers today with children in their classrooms who speak a number of different languages and are just beginning to learn English? Teaching in a classroom like this is a challenge! How in the world do you go about it?

You need concrete strategies you can use to support children's language development in both English and their home languages. Of course, it's ideal when teachers speak the children's languages. But in superdiverse classrooms, that's unlikely to be the case.

Here, we offer two family-focused strategies from an approach we call *personalized oral language learning* (POLL). Teachers who have tried these strategies find them especially useful for supporting the learning and development of children in classrooms with a range of languages.

Personalized Oral Language Learning

As centers and schools serve more and more culturally and linguistically diverse children—and as we recognize the many benefits of children retaining their home languages and cultures—teachers often ask us, "What specific strategies should I use to support my dual language learners?" POLL answers this question with three types of assistance: (1) family engagement, (2) environmental supports, and (3) conversation and interaction. These strategies affirm children's use of their home dialects and language and support the development of English. In this chapter, we address the first two family-focused strategies.

Family Engagement

Start by gathering information about each child's experience in the home language and in English. This is a critical step. We highly recommend that you meet with families in a personal, face-to-face interview to collect this information—along with information about the family's background and their shared interests and activities. (For a sample interview form about family languages and interests, see page 46.) A personal meeting is much more effective than sending home a questionnaire or having an informal conversation. This is not the only time for the teaching team to meet with families, but it's the beginning of a relationship and dialogue focused on the importance of both home language and English language development.

Two Classroom Language Models

In schools across the United States, many teachers who try to help children become multilingual use one of these two language models. Both work well with our POLL strategies. This chapter elaborates on the second one.

The Fifty-Fifty Dual Language Model

Teachers make sure children experience (hear, speak, see in print, etc.) both English and their home language in all content areas (literacy, math, outdoor play, etc.). With careful planning, teachers ensure that children experience equal exposure to both languages and are provided with plenty of opportunities and support for producing language. While teachers provide a clear structure for language separation, both codeswitching and the use of home language to enhance learning and social and emotional development are supported and encouraged.

This is a great model for supporting emergent multilingual children, but it is most feasible when all or most of the children speak the same home language (e.g., Spanish). Two different home languages should be supported in this model through careful allocation of time, addressing teacher breaks, number of hours for children attending each day, and other instructional resources.

The English Language Development with Home Language Support Model

Teachers most often use this model when they are not proficient in the children's home languages or when there are a wide variety of languages without a large group representing one that the teacher is proficient in. This model gives educators a clear and consistent plan for when and how to use English and when and how to use the children's languages. Children learn mainly in English during instructional time but benefit from home language and multicultural supports that teachers intentionally interweave throughout the daily routine.

Through this type of teacher–family collaboration, you can plan together how to weave linguistic and cultural information into activities at school and at home. For example, families can have conversations with their children in their home languages on the topics/themes and new words shared by the teachers each week. Building on the initial conversation, ongoing communication also provides perfect opportunities for you to invite parents and other family members to volunteer in the classroom or in other ways and offer their knowledge of classroom topics/themes.

As the school year progresses, be sure to keep families involved in the classroom's storybooks, themes, and learning concepts. Communicate with them in the languages they are most comfortable speaking (you may need to use an interpreter). Try reaching out in different ways, such as frequently sending home two-way journals for families to read, write in, and return; sending audios and recorded videos, having regular small-group coffee chats with parents before the school day; emailing, texting, and holding frequent casual conversations at pickup and drop-off; and scheduling one-on-one conversations. Your reminders will reinforce families' awareness of the importance and benefits of using their home language in everyday activities, having rich conversations with their children, reading, telling stories, and playing.

 DAP Effective educators employ a variety of communication methods that meet families' needs.

The home languages of the children in Ding's family child care program include Spanish, English, and Vietnamese. Ding's home language is Vietnamese, and she speaks English fluently.

Ding knows that one child's family owns a food truck. She has invited the family to park the truck outside her home one morning to share food items with the children and show them steps the family takes in preparing and selling food. Ding also plans vocabulary activities based on food prices and menus from each child's culture. She chooses related books in all three languages and prepares materials for the children to use in creating a food truck in the dramatic play area. She also invites families to provide items from home that might become part of their food truck theme.

Family Languages and Interests Interview

Child's Name: _____ **Date:** _____
 (first, middle, last)

Child's Date of Birth: _____ / _____ / _____
 (month) (day) (year)

1. Who are the members of your family that your child interacts with regularly? _____

2. Are there other people (not family members) who live with you and your child? If yes, what varieties of language(s) do they most often speak to your child? _____

3. Who is the primary caregiver of your child? _____

4. What varieties of language(s) does the primary caregiver speak most often with your child? _____

5. What varieties of language(s) did your child learn when they first began to talk? _____

6. Can you tell me what varieties of language(s) each of the following people in your household speak to your child?

	Only English	Mostly English, plus another language (identify)	Mostly another language (identify), some Engish	Only another language (identify)
You/parent				
Parent				
Extended family members				
Primary caregiver other than parents				
Others, such as siblings and cousins				

7. Are there activities in the community where your child interacts with others who speak your home language? _____

8. What special talents or interests does your child have? _____

9. What kinds of stories does your child enjoy? _____

10. Who does your child play with most often, and what language do they speak? _____

11. What are your hopes and dreams for your child? _____

12. Do you have any concerns about your child learning English and your family/community language? _____

13. What are your expectations for your child for the coming year? _____

14. Do you have any hobbies or interests that you would like to share with your child's class? _____

15. Would you be interested in volunteering in your child's class? _____

> Note: We use the term "varieties of languages" to refer to all languages, including dialects, American Sign Language, African American Vernacular English, and Indigenous languages, for preservation, revitalization, and maintenance.

Environmental Supports

A teacher placed a large poster outside the classroom that said, "Your Language is Welcome Here," and both children and families were delighted. When you create a warm, nurturing environment, one that welcomes children and families, you send the message that you value and respect them, their language, and their culture. When your classroom includes the home languages and cultural backgrounds of all the children and families, they see and feel that they are natural and important parts of classroom activities. You'll soon notice positive results: young dual language learners will develop confidence, communicate their thoughts and feelings more readily, concentrate better, and learn more.

Create language-rich environments that focus on the diversity and complexity of language found within children's communities. Transform your classroom into a rich setting with areas for children to talk and play, and with spaces for both quiet and active learning and small group interactions.

Here are some supports to use:

> Use labels to describe materials and title projects in each of the home languages of the children, with one color for each language used consistently throughout the classroom for schedules and topic displays. (Use an online translation tool, like Google Translate, and ask families to help with specific words.) Given the regional nature of language, it is okay to have multiple words for the same object. These multiple labels increase children's linguistic repertoire and build on children's linguistic knowledge. Instead of making assumptions, ask families how they would like to address specific dialects, ASL, and AAVE.

> Place environmental print in all the children's home languages—everyday objects like magazines, food packaging, commercial products, etc.—throughout play areas and the classroom. Use these for playful interactive classroom activities that require children to engage with peers to enhance their language development.

> Display family photos, books, artifacts, and posters and other visuals from all the children's cultural backgrounds throughout the classroom at child's-eye level and in learning centers. Families are often eager to help supply the classroom with items from their home that represent family and cultural traditions, such as examples of artwork, empty food boxes, pictures, etc. Integrating these objects and artifacts enables other members of the learning community to recognize the unique contributions of families' home cultures and languages. Children learn best when the concepts, language, and skills they encounter are related to things they know and care about. Use these items to design learning activities that affirm the life and cultural experiences of each child.

Work with librarians to select books in the children's languages that relate to curricular themes, and adapt puzzles to include writing in all the children's languages. Ask families to share songs, rhymes, and dichos (playful sayings) in all the languages of the children; they can also help stock the dramatic play area and art center with clothing and cultural artifacts from each child's background.

EQUITY Integrating objects and artifacts from children's homes into the classroom enables other members of the learning community to recognize the unique contributions of families' home cultures and languages.

Conclusion

Without a doubt, fostering young dual language learners' development of English and also of their home languages is a major challenge. But if you use the personalized oral language learning strategies outlined in this chapter, you can partner with families and create a responsive environment that supports children's cultural and linguistic identities and their learning.

Note: See the February/March 2019 issue of *Teaching Young Children* for the third POLL strategy. All three strategies foster conversations and interactions with children who are dual language learners. The two strategies addressed in this chapter focus particularly on families.

CAROLA OLIVA-OLSON, PhD, executive director of language justice and multilingual education at the Institute for Racial Equity and Excellence, has 30 years of experience, in multilingualism, diversity, equity, early childhood education, higher education, and professional development. She leads the Language Justice Initiative, focused on building an early education workforce and educational community that centers on racial and linguistic equity for every child to thrive in school and in life.

LINDA M. ESPINOSA, an emeritus professor of early childhood education at the University of Missouri, Columbia, was a coprincipal investigator for the Center for Early Care and Education Research–Dual Language Learners at the Frank Porter Graham Child Development Institute, the University of North Carolina at Chapel Hill.

WHIT HAYSLIP serves as a consultant to the California state-funded Language Learning Project and to the David and Lucile Packard Foundation Starting Smart and Strong Initiative. Prior to his work as a consultant, Whit was assistant superintendent for early childhood education in the Los Angeles Unified School District.

ELIZABETH S. MAGRUDER, a senior program director at WestEd, has more than 25 years of experience in California's education system from early education to higher education, serving as a provider, teacher, coach, mentor, supervisor, and administrator. Ms. Magruder leads multiyear projects that support state, regional, and local needs and capacity building efforts.

Observing, Documenting, and Assessing Children's Development and Learning

RECOMMENDATIONS FROM THE DAP POSITION STATEMENT

Formative assessment (measuring progress toward goals) and summative assessment (measuring achievement at the end of a defined period or experience) are important. Both need to be conducted in ways that are developmentally, culturally, and linguistically responsive to authentically assess children's learning. This means that not only must the methods of assessment, both formal and informal, be developmentally, culturally, and linguistically sensitive, but also the assessor must be aware of and work against the possibility of implicit and explicit bias, for example through training, reflection, and regular reviews of collected data.

Mrs. Schmidt created a sink-or-float discovery center in the science area of her classroom using a water table along with a variety of materials for exploration. The children became intrigued with exploring how the different materials responded to being placed in the water. As she observed the children's play, she supported them in their discoveries by asking open-ended questions like "What do you think will happen to the crayon when we put it in the water?" and "Why do you think that?" Together, the children and Mrs. Schmidt created a chart noting which materials floated and which sank.

Throughout this experience, Mrs. Schmidt was carefully observing, making notes, and gathering children's writing and drawing samples to informally assess children's understanding of the topic. She was also able to observe and assess children's peer interactions. (From "Practical Approaches to Informal Assessment of STEAM Experiences," page 52)

This excerpt highlights how educators can integrate intentional assessment strategies to determine how children are learning and what they are understanding. Play and exploration provide numerous opportunities to observe and interact with children as you ask questions to assess what children already know and then determine how you might build on their learning.

Assessment involves collecting and documenting information about children's learning and development to monitor children's progress toward learning goals, make curriculum decisions, and improve teaching practices (NRC 2008). Developmentally appropriate assessment involves three steps (Heritage 2010):

1. **Gathering information about children.** To understand children's learning and progress toward developmental and educational goals, educators observe children throughout the day and use valid assessment tools to collect information.

2. **Documenting the information.** Educators record what they learn about children by writing down their observations (for example, through anecdotal notes), taking pictures or videos of children's accomplishments, recording children's answers/responses to specific tasks on forms, filling out checklists, or other authentic means.

3. **Reflecting on what is learned about the children.** Educators look at the information they've documented, think about what it means about the child, and make decisions about learning experiences and interactions that would best support the child's development. Reflection can take place individually, with colleagues and family members, and depending on the situation, with the child.

Educators use both informal and formal assessment tools to document a child's learning progressions in a way that captures how the child is using skills and applying knowledge while engaging with materials and peers in a play-based setting. In this way, assessment is focused on the complex process of learning rather than on isolated skills. Effective educators use this information to plan learning experiences that build on children's developmental and linguistic skills.

Developmentally appropriate practice requires educators to be intentional about helping children meet learning goals with assessment tools that are culturally and linguistically responsive to children's developmental levels. As such, assessment should be ongoing and a regular part of the school day. This requires you to plan for assessment within the context of meaningful and playful activities that are focused on specific areas of children's learning.

When you are intentional, reflective, and purposeful, your methods of assessment are responsive to children's accomplishments, languages, and experiences. Part of intentionality is having a system in place to collect assessment information. This not only makes it easier for you to document children's learning progressions but also leads to relevant information for planning and implementing curriculum and learning activities. Involve children in this documentation process. Use documentation panels, portfolios, or other representations of learning that will help children reflect on their own learning.

You can also use assessment to evaluate and improve your effectiveness as a teacher. For example, daily reflection leads you to question whether or not you are using reliable and valid assessment tools. Are your assessments allowing children to demonstrate their competencies in multiple ways? Are the tools you are using appropriate for children with delays or disabilities and dual language learners who are in the process of acquiring English skills? If not, what other ways can children show you what they know and what they can do? For example, observing and listening to children play with peers and allowing them to draw representations of their understanding are methods of assessment that are authentic and integrated with teaching and learning.

Last, essential to the assessment process is collaborating with families as partners. This collaboration allows for a more complete picture of a child's learning in numerous settings (home, community, neighborhood). As children enter preschool, asking families about children's responsibilities at home, languages used, and activities they enjoy provides valuable insight into children's prior experiences, strengths, and cultural practices. Reciprocal conversations with families are particularly crucial when working with dual language learners and with children who have delays or disabilities. The information you gain will assist with initial screening, ongoing assessment, and decisions about placement or specific services.

Part 3 shows examples of systematic and purposeful assessment that is strengths based, authentic, and sensitive to children's developmental levels. The educators featured assess children across a range of content areas

using varied forms of documentation that are culturally and linguistically responsive to the children's learning. They make assessment a natural part of their daily routines and include families as partners in the process.

READ AND REFLECT

As you read the chapters in this section, consider and evaluate your own classroom practices using these reflection questions.

"Practical Approaches to Informal Assessment of STEAM Experiences" looks at developing informal assessment strategies, including asking open-ended questions, during an activity in which children use their curiosity and natural inclination for inquiry. **Consider:** How can the methods used in this chapter enhance your understanding of children's STEAM content knowledge?

"Anecdotal Records: Practical Strategies for Taking Meaningful Notes" describes simple but effective ways to document intentional observation that provides information for planning responsive instruction. **Consider:** What processes have you developed to ensure that you can reflect on your observations of children's experiences and learning?

"Developmental Moments: Teacher Decision Making to Support Young Writers" presents three questions to guide educators as they determine children's writing progression. Authors remind teachers to focus their analysis on what children know, not what they don't yet know. **Consider:** What are your beliefs about children's writing abilities? What has influenced these beliefs? How do these beliefs influence your choice of learning activities?

"Authentic and Meaningful Developmental Screening in Early Childhood" explains what developmental screening is, who is involved in screenings, when and why they are used, and ways to support families through the screening process. **Consider:** How might you have supportive conversations with a family before, during, and after their child participates in a developmental screening?

"Learning Stories: A Framework for Authentic Assessment and Critical Pedagogy" illustrates the power of a narrative-based approach to assessing dual language learners in which educators document children's strengths and families' goals for their children. **Consider:** What steps have you taken to ensure you are focusing on what children can do in a given context rather than on what children are *not* doing? What can you do to create fair and equitable approaches to assessment in your early childhood context?

Practical Approaches to Informal Assessment of STEAM Experiences

Angela Eckhoff and Sandra M. Linder

Informal assessment, such as observing and reflecting on children's play, is a critical part of high-quality early STEAM (science, technology, engineering, art, and mathematics) experiences. Young children's play provides educators with numerous daily opportunities to assess children's learning. Informal assessments for STEAM experiences include teacher observations, samples of children's drawing and writing, and photographs or videos of children's interactions during learning experiences.

With informal assessment, you can observe and interact with the children and take notes to use for later planning without the children knowing they are being assessed. If you join children during their play and ask open-ended, person-oriented and process-oriented questions (see the sidebar), you can gain information about what each child understands and is coming to understand. With the information gained through informal assessments, you can plan appropriate activities, read-alouds, materials, and centers to effectively teach each child.

Person-Oriented and Process-Oriented Questions

Person-oriented questions encourage children to make connections between what they already know and what they are exploring, such as

> What do you think is happening to the ice when we put it outside?

> What do you think will happen next in the story?

> What do you think we need to set the table for four people?

These questions give children the space to answer in whatever way makes sense to them. Person-oriented questions are useful when you want to increase the amount of conversation with and between children or assess what children know about a topic.

To extend children's learning and to guide them toward more meaningful conversations during a STEAM exploration, ask **process-oriented questions** that require children to complete an action (such as observing) in order to respond. For example,

> What do you notice about the leaves? What are some things that you see?

> Could a bridge made of paper be strong enough to hold one of our toy cars? Let's find out!

> How can we find out how many plants will fit in our planter box?

Asking such questions provides children with a strategy to better understand a STEAM topic. Building content knowledge and inquiry process knowledge together is essential for future success in STEAM learning.

Play-Based STEAM Assessment

A powerful benefit of informal play-based assessment is that it leads to new directions for learning both in the moment and over time. For example, you may observe a child counting the number of cars in the block center and make note of the child's abilities. Seeing the child skip from the number 4 to the number 8, you can suggest that the child might want to recount the cars. You might also give support while the child is counting by counting alongside the child or by holding the child's hand and pointing to each object together.

 Methods of assessment should be responsive to children's developmental accomplishments.

After intentionally playing together for several minutes, you will have gathered good information on the child's grasp of numbers up to 10. With this information, you can introduce an appropriate follow-up play-based activity as a fun way to support the child's learning, such as cars in garages, where the child has to count how many cars can fit into a "garage" (small cardboard box) without stacking them, because you can't crush the cars!

Informal assessments become easier if you set up a schedule, have assessment materials ready (a clipboard with a prepared record sheet, a stack of sticky notes), and try to take notes on three to five children a day. Having a schedule can ensure that you observe each child every week and also keep the task manageable. You will also be able to compile your notes to see what patterns might be emerging for small groups or for the whole class's STEAM learning.

After a few weeks of planned observations, you'll have a lot of information on children's knowledge, skills, and interests. Using that information to plan lessons and activities makes it much more likely that you build on children's strengths, meet their needs, and create playful learning experiences that they find engaging.

Sink or Float

The following activity highlights several strategies used by Mrs. Schmidt, a preschool teacher, to support the children's investigations with materials in the water table, assess their learning, and expand on their understandings.

Mrs. Schmidt created a sink-or-float discovery center in the science area using a water table along with a variety of materials for exploration. The children became intrigued with exploring how the different materials responded to being placed in the

water—some sank quickly, some floated, and some appeared to float for a brief time before slowly sinking.

Mrs. Schmidt observed the children's play and supported them in their discoveries by asking prompting questions like "What do you think will happen to the crayon when we put it in the water?" and "Why do you think that?" Together, the children and Mrs. Schmidt created a chart noting which materials floated and which sank. This led to the children wondering more about what small items from their classroom would sink or float.

To follow up on their wonderings, Mrs. Schmidt split the class into two groups to play a STEAM game. Group 1 was asked to collect items they thought would float and Group 2 was asked to collect items they thought would sink. Each group had a small tray to put selected items in and they had about 10 minutes to collect items.

When the collecting time was up, Mrs. Schmidt gathered the children around the water table to test each item together. This provided the children with opportunities to make predictions, test their items, and discuss the results of their experiment. As part of the inquiry process, Mrs. Schmidt also encouraged the children to draw or write (in whatever form they were comfortable) their wonderings and the results of the experiment to support their developing understandings. (A simple science journal with dedicated space for children to draw their observations and record their wonderings works well for supporting children as they work at their own pace.)

Throughout this experience, Mrs. Schmidt was carefully observing, making notes, and gathering children's writing and drawing samples to informally assess children's understanding of the topic. Because the activity involved working with others, she was also able to observe and assess children's peer interactions.

Mrs. Schmidt's observation notes—from both the children's task of collecting items and the testing of the items—together with the children's work samples revealed that many of the children were coming to understand that the weight of an object is an important consideration in deciding if it will sink or float. However, the assessment information Mrs. Schmidt gathered also showed that several children held a belief that larger items would sink only because of their size.

As a key part of science inquiry learning, having experiences that challenge children's misconceptions is an important part of developing their understandings. As a result of Mrs. Schmidt's observation that the children believed size was central to an object's buoyancy, she decided to create a second sink-or-float activity using a variety of larger items in the classroom so the children would be able to explore how size is not the only deciding factor of whether an object will sink or float.

Mrs. Schmidt's flexibility and responsiveness to the children's experiences encouraged them to continue and deepen their explorations. By using observations of children's experiences, Mrs. Schmidt created opportunities for the children to grow their understandings over time.

Conclusion

STEAM experiences that engage children through playful learning also provide teachers with rich opportunities to observe and assess children's understandings of STEAM content and overall development. As you at times play alongside children and ask questions related to their play, you can make observations of their learning and support their developing understandings in a seamless manner, deepening both their learning and your STEAM teaching practices.

ANGELA ECKHOFF is a professor of teaching and learning at Old Dominion University. Her research focuses on STEAM learning in schools and community settings.

SANDRA M. LINDER is a professor of early childhood mathematics at Clemson University. Her research focuses on supporting home mathematics and STEAM environments.

CHAPTER 13

Anecdotal Records

Practical Strategies for Taking Meaningful Notes

Celeste C. Bates, Stephanie Madison Schenck, and Hayley J. Hoover

With so many required assessments in early childhood, it's understandable why the word itself may bring up negative feelings for teachers. But understanding the different types of assessment and how you can use them to support your reflection and planning is important.

Summative assessments are used to gauge children's learning against a standard or benchmark. They are often given at the end of the year and are sometimes used to make important educational decisions about children.

In contrast, *formative assessments* are intended to (1) determine where children are in their learning, (2) understand the developmental continuum and educational expectations, and (3) chart a course to support children's progress (Riley-Ayers 2014). Formative assessments are ongoing and tend to be based on teachers' intentional observations of children during specific learning experiences. Many teachers find formative assessments most useful when planning learning experiences, activities, and environments. Your notes about what children can do while engaged in real-life tasks such as block building, retelling a story, or climbing on a playground structure provide a wealth of information. Getting started with the strategies in this chapter will help you develop a system for taking useful notes. These notes will ground your teaching decisions and enrich children's portfolios with examples of their everyday learning.

From Notes to Records to Planning

Anecdotal records are brief notes teachers take as they observe children (Fiore 2020). The notes document a range of behaviors in areas such as literacy, mathematics, social studies, science, the arts, social and emotional learning, and physical development. When recording observations, it's important to include a concrete description and enough details to inform future teaching strategies. For example, a statement such as "The child was on task" provides no information about the task or the behavior, but a statement like "The child built a tower from colored cubes, creating an AB pattern after looking at a card that showed a similar alternating pattern" provides concrete evidence.

To avoid vague notes, list the associated learning center or content area and include a specific description of what the child is doing. Of course, time is always a concern in preschool classrooms, and children move quickly from one task to the next! Abbreviations can help capture detailed observations in an efficient way.

For example, instead of stating "Leah uses inventive spelling," an anecdotal note could include an abbreviation for the center Leah is playing in and evidence of her inventive spelling: "Leah—DP [dramatic play center]—Wrote grocery list: BACN, aGS, sreL." (If time is short, take a photo of the child's writing and embed it along with the anecdotal record in the child's portfolio.) The evidence in Leah's note gives insight into the consonants and vowels she is learning and the letter forms she can produce. It also aids the teacher in better understanding Leah's progress on the continuum toward standard spelling, helping the teacher be more informed about how to support Leah instructionally.

When taking anecdotal records, it's important to consider word choice. Statements that begin with words like *can't* or *doesn't* promote a deficit view and do not support future instructional planning. For

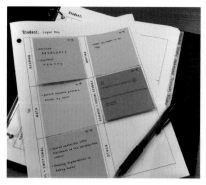

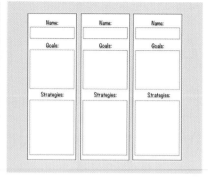

example, the statement "Logan doesn't identify all his letters" is very different from "Logan identifies the uppercase letters A, B, G, N, L, T, Z." Writing what children *can* do ensures that instructional decisions are grounded in children's strengths.

Being a Neutral Observer

It's easy to draw conclusions about a child, especially when you have a history with the family, such as previously teaching a sibling. But no two children are exactly alike, even if they share the same family, community, or culture. Familiarity with children and families may make it easier for you to develop the home–school connection, but it shouldn't affect how you view or treat a child. Similarly, familiarity with a child's community or culture may give you helpful context, but it should not lead to making assumptions—positive or negative. Anecdotal records are intended to be neutral observations of a child's behaviors and interactions, so it's important to guard against assumptions and biases.

It's helpful to periodically review your notes to look for examples of bias. To do this, reflect on ways the notes have been written to see if they're objective. Then look for patterns in the notes to see if subjective comments are linked to any one child or to a group of children. Identifying these patterns can help reveal unconscious assumptions and can assist you in writing more objective notes in the future. You can also ask a trusted colleague to review your notes for the same purposes. Take responsibility for biased actions, even if unintended, and actively work to repair the harm.

Organizing and Managing Your Anecdotal Records

Daily anecdotal notes can be quick to write and easy to file and organize. They should also serve as the basis for reflective practice.

Be selective about the behaviors you observe. Having a specific focus can help you pay attention to the most important details during observations, making your anecdotal records more useful for planning or for individualizing future instruction. In addition, it removes the unreasonable expectation of documenting everything for every child every day.

One suggestion for getting started is to divide the class into small groups of about five students. Assign each group a day of the week, and then concentrate on observing just those five students on their assigned day. Creating daily focus groups helps organize and manage record keeping—and they prevent children from slipping through the cracks. Here are a couple of examples of anecdotal record-keeping systems that use daily focus groups.

Post-it Notebook

A Post-it notebook uses a form for each child that has six boxes. Teachers often choose to label the boxes *Reading, Writing, Math, Science/Social Studies, Social/Emotional,* and *Other,* but the form can be tailored to highlight any content areas or learning domains that you choose! As you make observations, record them on a sticky note and place on a clipboard. At the end of the day, transfer the notes to the child's form in the appropriate category. Keep the forms in a three-ring binder with dividers separating each daily focus group, or organize the forms alphabetically.

Index Cards

The index card system uses individual index cards color-coded by daily focus group (for example, Monday's group is assigned green index cards, Tuesday's group is yellow). Use a binder clip to keep each group's index cards together, then use the cards throughout the day as you capture and record observations on group members' individual cards. At the end of the day, file the cards in a box, and then pull the cards for the next day.

You may choose to record literacy behaviors (or any other content area you're emphasizing) on one side of the card and math behaviors (or another content area) on the other side. Additional cards can be used to capture behaviors in other areas, or a card can be subdivided. Once a child's card is full, issue a new one. You can also take the cards outdoors when observing and recording children's social interactions on the playground.

Reflecting on and Using Anecdotal Notes

A manageable system (like the ones described here) makes it easy to collect the information you need to reflect about what the children are learning. Reflection and anecdotal notes should be tightly linked and should serve as the foundation for instructional planning, helping you think more deeply about children's growth and learning. Also, reflecting on these records allows you to generate questions and hypotheses that fuel additional observations and anecdotal records.

Adopting a child-centered approach to assessment helps you view students from a strengths-based perspective and match teaching to individuals' needs. As a result, children receive more tailored instruction as you become better informed about each child's progress. Reflecting on anecdotal notes can also help you with grouping decisions. Small groups in the classroom should be flexible, and using observational data can assist you in re-forming groups to mirror children's changing needs.

 Recognize individual variation in learners and enable children to demonstrate their competencies in different ways.

You may find it useful to write out your reflections and add them to a child's collection of anecdotal records; as months go by, reviewing both anecdotal notes and timely reflections can be very informative. The data collected from the anecdotal records can also be transferred to more formal assessments, like developmental checklists.

When a challenging situation arises, such as a child not making progress as expected, you can share your notes and reflections with colleagues to generate new ideas about lessons and activities to try. And if a comprehensive or diagnostic assessment seems called for, you have a rich set of records to share with families and specialists.

Anecdotal notes are also a great source of information when meeting with a family. During a family conference, you can use anecdotal notes to provide concrete examples of a child's learning and development and give insight into the child's school day. The information can also assist in collaborating with families to set learning goals and future instructional decisions. In addition, sharing detailed descriptions of a child's cognitive and social behaviors during a conference and in other communications can help families better understand their child's learning trajectory.

Conclusion

Developing a manageable system for taking and using anecdotal notes in the preschool classroom is the foundation for reflective practice and intentional instruction. A well-organized system frees you to focus on the children instead of on the "how-to" aspects of record keeping. Notes with clear language, abbreviations, and evidence provide concrete documentation of children's emerging behaviors, knowledge, and skills, and they also ground your ongoing reflective practices. By monitoring each child's development with daily anecdotal notes and adjusting instructional support accordingly, teachers' perceptions of assessment often shift from assessment for assessment's sake to assessment for the sake of children's growth. This type of intentional, supportive assessment contributes to children's learning and development.

CELESTE C. BATES, PhD, is a professor of literacy education and the director of the Clemson University Early Literacy Center, in Clemson, South Carolina.

STEPHANIE MADISON SCHENCK, PhD, is a project manager for Clemson University's Teacher Learning Progression, an initiative designed to match teachers with focused and personalized professional development. Her research centers on social justice integration in language classrooms and the relationship between language, literacy, and power.

HAYLEY J. HOOVER, MEd, is a doctoral candidate in the Literacy, Language, and Culture program at Clemson University. Hayley has taught in both general education and special education classrooms and studies literacy motivation.

CHAPTER 14

Developmental Moments
Teacher Decision Making to Support Young Writers

Kathryn F. Whitmore and Lori Norton-Meier

Three-year-old Monica lives on a ranch in the southwestern United States. She frequently rides with her father, a cowboy, on his horse named Miss Muffett. It is a developmental moment: Monica is at the kitchen table while her mother makes dinner. She has open access to a variety of writing materials. Monica draws and writes, then reads the message to her mother as she points to the looping lines she's drawn. Across the top of the page, she reads, "Monica!" and down the right side of the page she traces with her finger, "Miss Muffett."

A moment like this, when a young child interacts with writing materials and a reason to write, is an opportunity to understand the child's individual development and literacy development more generally. We think of development as a video or movie—shifting, full of action, and changing too fast to remember or analyze any single moment in real time. We conceptualize developmental moments as comparable to pushing the pause button on a TV remote, creating a still-frame image of movement and change. That image is an opportunity to understand dynamic learning in a preservable anecdote, transcript, or writing sample. We call this framework *developmental moments*. Developmental moments are data gathered through observing, collecting, and reflecting about real writing, reading, and oral language samples to reveal where a child is developmentally at a given point in time. The particular examples in this chapter focus on writing, but the developmental moments framework is applicable to math, reading, and other aspects of children's learning.

Developmental Moments as Instructional Decision-Making Framework

It's in these developmental moments that we pause and ask three questions (see "Developmental Moments Questions" on page 62 for further details):

1. What does the child already know about written language?

2. What is the child currently learning? (What approximations of writing are evident in the moment?)

3. What will best support the child's continued development?

Let's consider these three questions for Monica.

What Does Monica Already Know About Written Language?

In this moment, Monica demonstrates her understanding of written language as two separate systems—drawing and writing. Monica's drawing is conventional enough that it is generally recognizable as an animal. It could be a dog or a cow—it includes legs, a head, and spots. But when Monica reads the writing as "Monica" and "Miss Muffett," the animal shape takes on the additional specific features of a horse, including a saddle, a mane, and a tail, as she explains. (See Monica's horse drawing and writing on the following page.)

Monica's writing is less developed (more approximate) than her drawing, but it shows that Monica already understands that print (in English) is linear and also has shape. Her invented writing marks are not random—they resemble the appearance of English cursive and are clearly comparable to the cursive she frequently observes around her as her parents write lists, sign checks, and leave each other notes. The combination of drawing and writing indicates Monica knows that pictures help a writer tell a story and words help readers read pictures. She understands that illustrated and written texts have a meaningful relationship.

Our developmental moments analysis begins with the recognition that every child comes to school with initial and developing understandings about how language works (Ferreiro & Teberosky 1982). A language community surrounds and defines each child's place, identities, and understandings about how, when, and why language works. Asking ourselves about children's existing knowledge about literacy recognizes that literacy learning is a transactional process, meaning that there is an interactive relationship between the knower (the child) and what is to be known (the text being created) (Dewey 1938; Rosenblatt 1976; Whitmore et al. 2004), within rich sociocultural contexts. Beginning with a transactional perspective of early literacy explicitly reminds us to initiate our analysis of developmental moments with what children know, not what they don't yet know.

What Is Monica Currently Learning About Writing and Drawing?

Monica already knows a lot about written language, and the approximations in this developmental moment are indicators of her future learning. While her drawing is recognizable, her horse has five legs. And while she knows that print is linear, she is comfortable writing vertically as well as horizontally. Moreover, though the form of her writing clearly reflects representations of cursive that she sees around her, she does not form conventional letters. In this moment, Monica reveals her theories and processes about making meaning—by creating squiggly lines of linear text to represent words and an illustration that represents her favorite horse.

Clay (1975) states that two features of the learning process deserve special attention in early writing development. The first is that children's initial writing will be gross approximations of adult conventions that will continue to be refined with time. Clay's point is that when children are learning, they do not write the way adults do, and that it's more productive to think about nonconventional elements of their early writing as developmental rather than mistakes. So loops and lines of print, letters that aren't formed in a standard way or are reversed, and other developmentally acceptable instances of not-yet-conventional writing are called *approximations*.

Second, individual knowledge is very specific. Children construct their own language and understandings about literacy processes for themselves. Although there are common patterns in early literacy development, "children assume agency for their learning and from birth are actively constructing knowledge about literacy; therefore, no two children's paths to literacy look the same" (Whitmore et al. 2004, 298). Some children have a unique and voracious interest in bugs, others in superheroes. Some children move into conventional spelling at a young age, and others take more time in invented spelling. Some children read independently before formal schooling, others not until well into elementary school. In regard to very young children's writing development, Clay says the "characteristics of gross approximation and specificity demand that a teacher knows an individual child's progress to date" (1975, 15).

 Developmentally appropriate assessment recognizes individual variation in learners and allows children to demonstrate their competencies in different ways.

What Are Good Ways to Support Monica's Continued Development?

This developmental moment often evokes recommendations from teachers to "get out some books about horses." Interacting with high-quality literature about horses would fuel Monica's interest in her horse and may provide motivation to continue ongoing demonstrations of letters and words organized in increasingly conventional ways. In addition, an authentic response to Monica's writing and drawing, through conversation ("Monica, you're a writer! Read to me what you wrote"), will support her sense of herself as a writer. The key suggestion for mediation at this developmental moment is to encourage her to keep writing and sharing her stories without worrying about accurate letter formation.

The first two developmental moments questions guide adults to validate children's existing literacy knowledge and to identify the direction their learning is headed. The third question calls on us to consider what to do next. We frame instructional decision making as mediation, drawing on Vygotsky's (1978) premise that children's internal cognitive processes (their thinking,

imagining, and learning) grow only when interacting with people in the environment and in cooperation with peers. Mediation is the action and effect of peers, adults, texts, or other social environmental factors in a child's experiences that extend, challenge, and support learning. It occurs when teachers share and negotiate power and access with children. Such teachers "support children in making connections between the known and new . . . for connecting print and meaning" (Whitmore et al. 2004, 318). Teachers who are mediators help children reach their individual academic literacy potentials at school while maintaining the richness of their sociocultural backgrounds, identities, languages, and community positions.

Young children's development is active and complex, and it is contextualized in the rich physical and social spaces of their homes, communities, and schools (Flurkey & Whitmore 2017). Too often, teachers' unexamined deficit assumptions about children from low-income, multilingual, and ethnically and racially diverse communities influence their decision making in negative and biased ways. Deficit notions of children and families can lead teachers to lower their expectations for children's learning potential (Alanís & Iruka, with Friedman 2021). However, all children bring funds of knowledge to classrooms—areas of expertise and experience that enable them to survive in their communities. We need "to document the funds of knowledge of families and represent them on the bases of the knowledge, resources, and strengths they possess, thus challenging deficit orientations that are so dominant, in particular, in the education of working-class children" (Moll 2019, 131). Our developmental moments framework can help teachers shift from a deficit discourse about children's literacy development to a discourse of strength and possibility.

Developmental Moments Questions

How can the three developmental moments questions be useful and practical for teachers? The first two developmental moments questions remind teachers to focus on strengths and see children in terms of what they know rather than what they need to know.

> Anecdotal records created with the developmental moments lens provide a rich trail of children's learning over time. We find it helpful to immediately jot our interpretations of writing samples on sticky notes or write them directly on the back of a sample. The date and a few words that answer questions one and two are sufficient until the end of the day or week.

> The collection of anecdotal records in the developmental moments framework comprises the ingredients for planning individual and group instruction when teachers turn to ponder question three: What will best support the child's development (individually and collectively)? The answers may be as small as having a conversation or sharing a particular book or material with one child. Or they may be as large as developing a lengthy inquiry curriculum plan for a whole class.

> Many teachers collect developmental moments daily on an ongoing basis to capture writing development when it happens during the class day. Sticky notes with a child's name can then be transferred to a folder as evidence for looking at the child's development over time. Teachers often also make note of their instructional decisions in this folder to document their plans to support each child's continued development.

Instructional Decision Making Based on Developmental Moments

Literacy development, like development across domains, is fluid and dynamic. It occurs as a complex continuum of individual shifts and changes along varied paths, according to personal experiences. Although literacy development is ongoing, developmental moments provide teachers opportunities to figuratively push the pause button and think about an individual child's knowledge and growth to make appropriate decisions about instruction. Rather than basing instruction on a mountain of abstract standardized screening outcomes or determining teaching plans solely on a set of standards or guidelines that have no connection to a particular classroom or child, the developmental moments framework identifies teaching directions that matter in the real learning life of each specific child. The developmental moments framework highlights children's approximations as indicators of their development—ever changing, always evolving, and continuing to grow.

Conclusion

Using the developmental moments process helps teachers think deeply about a child's development, learning, and background. In addition to shaping instructional approaches to fit individual children, it highlights the positive aspects of culture, community, and family that all children bring to school. As a result, families are thrilled to see that teachers know who their children are, what they know, and what they need to know. A child's file of developmental moments, along with teacher analyses—even if jotted on sticky notes—demonstrates to family members that their child is valued and known. A developmental moments discussion between teacher and family helps the family see their child's strengths and opens the door for important questions and conversation. The developmental moments framework helps teachers see learners differently, so learners can say, "This is what I know and here is why."

KATHRYN F. WHITMORE, PhD, is professor and chair of the Department of Special Education, Early Childhood Education and Culturally and Linguistically Diverse Education at Metropolitan State University of Denver in Colorado.

LORI NORTON-MEIER, PhD, is professor of literacy education and director of the Richard O. Jacobson Center for Comprehensive Literacy at the University of Northern Iowa in Cedar Falls.

CHAPTER 15

Authentic and Meaningful Developmental Screening in Early Childhood

Marisa Macy and Stefano J. Bagnato

Magnolia is attending an open house night at Big Smiles Academy, where she is interested in enrolling her son, Mario, in the preschool program. Mario is a playful 35-month-old who loves animals, books, and listening to music. During the open house, Magnolia meets Ms. Angela, a lead teacher, and shares that she is concerned that Mario is not yet grasping small objects like blocks, books, and finger foods during play and routines like mealtimes. Magnolia completes an enrollment packet, and Ms. Angela arranges a time for Magnolia to bring Mario to the center for a developmental screening.

When we engage in screening and assessment practices with children, we observe the child or group of children, and then make sense of what we see using our understanding of child development, each child's individuality, and the contexts in which they are growing and learning.

This chapter addresses screening with meaning. Assessment is authentic when it is meaningful to all involved. Effective practices reflect real life, or authentic opportunities to observe children engaged in their familiar settings, with familiar people, and with familiar objects and materials. Marisa (first author) became interested in this topic as a parent when her daughter experienced screening assessment as a toddler. Stefano (second author) has studied assessments for several years as a researcher at the University of Pittsburgh. In this chapter, we discuss fundamental details about authentic developmental screening—what it is and the purposes it serves, who is typically engaged in the screening process, and how it is effectively used in practice. Then, we revisit the opening vignette to show meaningful developmental screening in action.

What Is a Developmental Screening, and Why Is It Used?

Screenings are a formal way of helping us understand how children are developing. They do so by comparing an individual child's current skills and behaviors to a set of established norms, or a much larger set of same-age peers. Typically, screenings are brief in length and follow specific procedures for each use. Some common tools for a developmental screening in early childhood settings are the Ages & Stages Questionnaire (ASQ), BRIGANCE, and Denver II, to name just a few.

 EQUITY Consider societal and structural perspectives: How might trauma, inequities, and other adverse conditions affect how children respond to their world? What can you do to help each child build agency and resilience?

Developmental screenings are used for at least two reasons and as part of a larger assessment plan and system. Two purposes are

> To assess all children in an early childhood program to identify any concerns or any difficulties they might be having with their development and/or early learning. NAEYC's Early Learning Program Standards, for example, states, "All children enrolled in the program should receive developmental screening within three months of program entry" and that screening should gauge development across domains, from health and physical to cognitive, social, and emotional development.

> To assess an individual child when a familiar caregiver like a parent has a concern about the child's development or learning. For example, a parent notices differences in their youngest child's development compared to their older children. They follow up on this concern by seeking a developmental screening from an early intervention provider in their area.

Whether prompted by an early learning program or a family, authentic developmental screenings can help determine if a more comprehensive evaluation is warranted. Screening should not be used for diagnosis or to determine eligibility for specialized services or therapies. Because developmental screenings do not offer in-depth details about a child's knowledge, skills, or behaviors, teachers rely on other forms of assessment to plan for instruction.

Who Is Involved in a Developmental Screening?

Because of its core purposes, many different professionals are engaged in observing, documenting, and understanding young children through a developmental screening. There are at least four different sectors engaged in developmental screening:

> General education, which includes what occurs in many early learning programs

> Special education, which entails early intervention for infants and toddlers and early childhood special education for preschoolers

> Health care, which includes care provided by pediatricians, nurses, and other health care professionals, such as occupational therapists

> Social work, which includes the services provided by social workers, behavior interventionists, and counselors

For example, developmental screenings play an important role in the care children and families experience at well-visits with pediatricians. It may be the first time a family completes items on a screening, where they might provide information about their child's physical or language growth or their child's emotional responses to different situations.

Families are key participants in the screening process too. They have a unique and sustained view of their child's learning and development. They are often the first to notice if unexpected changes occur or if something does not seem right with their child's development. Family and professional collaboration is essential when children are screened.

How Is a Developmental Screening Carried Out?

Professionals screen children to document their overall growth in a variety of areas. Family-completed measures, like the ASQ, allow a familiar caregiver to consider what they have observed and experienced with the child and share that information through a checklist, rating form, or other tool. Families may not know where to turn if they have a question or concern about their child's development. To address this, early childhood educators can conduct or help arrange for individualized developmental screenings.

Because a screening is an initial formal step into verifying a concern, it is only a snapshot with a limited view. Depending on the results of the screening, a more comprehensive evaluation may be warranted, where a bigger picture will be taken. For example, a child could be screened with the ASQ, which has 30 items. A more comprehensive evaluation could then be done using an instrument that has many more items with a diagnostic purpose and goes deeper than a screener can. Results of the screening compare the child in general to their age-peers. When the results indicate a child falls outside of the expected range for their age, no final decisions or diagnoses should be made. Instead, such results require a referral to a professional for a more comprehensive and detailed assessment of all developmental domains (problem solving, communication, motor skills, and more).

Preschool educators have an opportunity to partner with families and other professionals in the screening and assessment of young children. Sometimes educators begin the conversation with families. For example, an early learning program may include a screening like the ASQ at the start of each program year, then again toward the middle and/or end of the school year to monitor a child's development over time. Before a formal screening, educators can begin

Selected Developmental Screening Tools

Developmental Screening Tool	Age Group	Areas Assessed
Ages & Stages Questionnaires, Third Edition (ASQ)	1 to 66 months	Communication, gross motor, fine motor, problem solving, and personal–social areas
Battelle Developmental Inventory, Third Edition (BDI-3)	Birth to 8 years	Adaptive, personal–social, communication, motor, and cognitive domains
BRIGANCE Early Childhood Screen III	3 to 5 years	Academic skills/cognitive development, language development, physical development, and self-help and social and emotional skills
Developmental Indicators for the Assessment of Learning, Fourth Edition (DIAL-4)	2 years, 6 months to 5 years, 11 months	Concepts, language, and motor areas; self-help and social development
Preschool and Kindergarten Behavior Scales, Second Edition (PKBS-2)	3 to 6 years	Internalizing and externalizing behaviors, social cooperation, social interaction, and social independence

Note: The above list is a brief selection of screening tools, and many more are available. Information in the table is based on publisher websites.

by sharing with families what screening is and what they can expect.

Sometimes educators start the conversation about screening because a family expresses questions or concerns. When this occurs, a teacher can begin by seeking more information, asking questions like the following:

> How would you describe your child, including their growth and learning, to someone who is unfamiliar with your child or family?

> What concerns do you have, and what do you hope to find out from the screening?

> How does your child play?

> How does your child participate in routines (washing hands, feeding, toileting, etc.)?

> How does your child interact with others?

As part of these conversations, early childhood educators can offer support and resources for learning more about the screening goals and process. They can sit beside and get to know families (indeed, this is the

origin of the word assessment, which comes from the Latin *assidere*, meaning "to sit with"). Meaningful conversations with families are the foundation for their child's developmental screening, so it is beneficial to learn more about them in a conversational format before conducting a formal screening.

After these initial conversations and screening, the preschool educator can continue to support the family and the process. A family might need more help navigating the process if a referral was made to another agency for more in-depth diagnostic testing. Checking in with the family to see how it is going and if they need anything could be helpful.

 DAP Assessment is responsive to children's developmental accomplishments, languages, and experiences. Allow children to demonstrate their competencies in different ways.

Another next step for the preschool educator after the initial screening is to assess children's development on an ongoing basis. This can include giving the screening again at specific intervals (every two to three months, every six months). For example, the educator might continue to use a screening with the individual child or a group of children. Screening more than once over time is a useful way to monitor children's development and any concerns when they arise.

On the day of Mario's screening assessment, Magnolia makes sure he is well rested and fed. Magnolia and Mario arrive at the center, accompanied by Magnolia's best friend. Magnolia brings a list of concerns she has written about Mario's development, and an interpreter is present for the screening since English is not Magnolia's home language.

Mario appears to be comfortable and engages in tasks the way he usually does. Magnolia shares information with Ms. Angela, the preschool educator. She also asks questions and explains her concerns about Mario not yet grasping small objects like blocks, books, and finger foods. After the screening, Ms. Angela explains what will happen next in the process, including scoring and interpreting screening results and then follow-up procedures.

Six days later, Ms. Angela calls Magnolia. Magnolia's intuition was right. Mario performed differently from his same-age peers in the fine motor area and how he uses his small muscles and eye–hand coordination. Later, a team of fine motor professionals, like occupational therapists, complete a comprehensive evaluation of Mario's skills. He qualifies for therapeutic services. Mario's preschool educator collaborates with specialists to embed opportunities in the classroom for him to practice fine motor skills. Ms. Angela creates activities that involve ways for Mario to strengthen the use of his hands to perform tasks with his fingers and hands.

Eventually, Mario begins growing stronger in all areas of his development and especially motor. After a year, he exits specialized services. Mario enters kindergarten without a need for special education services. The meaningful screening assessment was instrumental in addressing Magnolia's concerns and in leading to appropriate further evaluation and the right support for Mario's development.

Further Resources

> Learn about the Help Me Grow model for connecting families and providers to community resources related to child development at helpmegrownational.org.

> For information on developmental milestones, see "Learn the Signs. Act Early" from the CDC, cdc.gov/ncbddd/actearly/index.html.

> Discover more about developmental screening on the podcast episode "Developmental Screenings for Young Children: What Parents and Teachers Need to Know" from the Illinois Early Learning Project, illinoisearlylearning.org/podcasts/devscreen-yc.

> For tips on connecting families with community-based services, see *Developmental Screening in Your Community: An Integrated Approach for Connecting Children with Services*, by Diane Bricker, Marisa Macy, Jane Squires, and Kevin Marks, 2013.

MARISA MACY, PhD, is the Cille and Ron Williams Endowed Community Chair of Early Childhood Education at the University of Nebraska Kearney. She is an associate professor in the Department of Teacher Education in the College of Education. Her research interests include authentic assessment of children birth to age 8 with and without delays/disabilities, developmental screening, play, and workforce development.

STEFANO J. BAGNATO, EdD, NCSP, is a developmental school psychologist and professor of psychology and pediatrics at the University of Pittsburgh, Schools of Education and Medicine. He is the faculty mentor/advisor for the Children with Special Healthcare Needs specialization in Applied Developmental Psychology. Dr. Bagnato is the founder and faculty mentor for the Early Childhood Partnerships (ECP) program and a founding and core interdisciplinary faculty member in The UCLID-LEND Disabilities Institute at UPMC Children's Hospital of Pittsburgh, federally funded since 1995.

Learning Stories
A Framework for Authentic Assessment and Critical Pedagogy

Isauro M. Escamilla, Linda R. Kroll, Daniel R. Meier, and Annie White

The Learning Stories approach is a form of observation and documentation that is written in a narrative story format. It was created by educators in New Zealand to highlight children's strengths and improve instruction based on the interests, talents, needs, and rights of children and their families (Carr 2001; Carr & Lee 2019). Learning Stories are told by educators from a strength-based perspective, viewing the whole child as a person rather than fragmenting the child into separate parts based on predetermined assessment measures. The Learning Stories framework honors multiple perspectives to create more complete images of the learners, including the voices of teachers as narrators, the voices and actions of children as active participants in the learning process, and the voices of families who offer their perspective as the most important teachers in their children's lives.

In this chapter we explain the goals, elements, and benefits of Learning Stories for teachers in the United States and how Learning Stories can help link authentic assessment with critical pedagogy.

Authentic Assessment and Critical Pedagogy for All Children and Families

Stories retell information, provide life lessons and morals, entertain, and provide cultural preservation and emotional support. For native and Indigenous peoples, stories are told and retold to ensure that the ontology (what is known of the world) does not diminish; the story is sacred. Indigenous narratives are honest and in tune with the history of the earth, the land, animals, and people. This sacredness around stories entails a certain level of vulnerability for storytellers and audiences, who both must show respect for the privilege of entering into someone else's life, even if for a short period of time. When using Learning Stories in classrooms and other settings, this experience occurs as teachers enter into the intimate space of stories for children, colleagues, and families. In turn, families enter into the thinking space of teachers. When writing classroom stories where children are the protagonists of their own learning, teachers highlight their own personal and community values, such as respect, collaboration, and trust. Perhaps more importantly, they open the door for a meaningful dialogue, exchange, and communication with the intent to get to know children better.

Learning Stories that Embrace Who We Are

Children from culturally and ethnically diverse backgrounds are frequently expected to conform to and learn in cultural settings that vastly differ from those they have experienced in their households, families, home countries, and communities. As is the case with many immigrant families, some children and their families may have never been exposed to the mainstream norms of the dominant US culture, yet they are expected to adapt to those norms and live up to those expectations in early childhood teaching and assessments. For example, regardless of how long families have been in the United States, 4-year-old children in California state-funded preschools must be formally tested in nursery rhyme knowledge based on traditional American children's songs and rhymes such as "Twinkle, Twinkle, Little Star" and

"Teddy Bear, Teddy Bear, Turn Around." In this part of the phonological assessment, the assessor recites lines from 10 different nursery rhymes and pauses, prompting the child to supply the final rhyming words. Usually, children of immigrant families are expected to immediately and successfully engage in dominant and unfamiliar cultural practices to be considered prepared for school, ready or capable (Bennett et al. 2018; Ghiso 2016; Souto-Manning 2009).

Successfully bridging children's emergent bicultural and bilingual identities depends on culturally responsive teaching practices that strengthen teachers' relationships with children and their families through understanding and making visible their interests, language, cultures, beliefs, and customs (Hammond 2014; Ladson-Billings 2014). Teachers can cocreate authentic curricula with children by acknowledging, respecting, and as much as possible including the knowledges, expertise, traditions, and even hopes, expectations, and dreams that children and families contribute to classrooms and programs in what is known as *funds of knowledge* (Esteban-Guitart et al. 2019; Ghiso 2016; Gonzalez, Moll, & Amanti 2005; Licona 2013; Llopart & Esteban-Guitart 2018). These funds of knowledge are the strategies, abilities, practices, and ideas that children and families rely on in their familial networks and for social and cultural authenticity and preservation (Souto-Manning & Mitchell 2010). Learning Stories in many ways may be considered a manifestation of the funds of knowledge that children, their families, and teachers bring with them into their classrooms and school communities. As such, Learning Stories break the traditional unhealthy balance of power between teachers and parents. For example, with traditional observation tools teachers as experts offer their informed opinions on children's development, progress, and growth without room for parents' perspectives on their own child, whereas in Learning Stories teachers as partners offer their points of view and parents contribute by writing or sharing with teachers and their own children what they see as valuable in the learning experiences. The families' words are preserved in their own handwritten notes as a critical component of the children's Learning Stories. In the funds of knowledge and Learning Stories contexts, families are viewed as intellectual resources and competent people, no matter what their social, linguistic, religious, economic, or cultural background may be (Llopart & Esteban-Guitart 2018; Rodriguez 2013).

Foundational Principles for Learning Stories

A Learning Story is first and foremost a story (Carr & Lee 2012). It tells a tale written to the child that is meant to be shared with the family. Each story is based on teachers' daily observations of children at play. It is always written from a strengths-based perspective, and although there is not a universal template or blueprint to create a Learning Story, there are three basic principles (and one optional) at the foundation of any Learning Story:

1. To include written observations and photographs of children in action or of artifacts they created

2. To include a written analysis of the observation from the teachers' point of view

3. To provide a tentative plan to extend children's learning, pending the families' perspective on their children's learning experience

4. Optional: To include specific links to assessment measures

Keep these four basic principles in mind as you collect material for a possible Learning Story, and then again as you prepare for the actual writing and creation of a Learning Story for children and their families.

 Learning Stories are a great example of a system that enables educators to collect, make sense of, and use observations, documentation, and assessment information to guide teaching.

Basic Components in Writing a Learning Story

While the format or structure of Learning Stories may vary in US contexts, as they do in New Zealand and elsewhere globally, we (the authors) have found the following components and structure to be effective yet flexible (Carter 2010; Drummond n.d.):

1. Title: A title that captures the essence of the story

2. "What Happened?" or "What's the Story?": A detailed observation of the event that took place

3. "What Does It Mean?" or "What Learning Do I See Happening?": A paragraph to reflect and interpret the significance of what was observed

4. "Opportunities and Possibilities" or "How Can We Support You in Your Learning": A paragraph to describe what teachers may potentially do to extend the child's learning experiences

5. "What's the Family's Perspective": A question posed to the family to respond with their point of view to what the teacher wrote

6. Assessment measures: At the end, quite often but not always, teachers link the Learning Story to specific evaluative and assessment measures.

Title

Any great story begins with a good title that captures the essence of the tale being told. The title should reflect the child as a competent learner or highlight an aspect of the Learning Story that reveals, as much as possible, the teacher reflecting on their own learning as a result of observing the child and interpreting the learning that took place. In this sense, the Learning Story may serve as a reflection tool for both adult and child where the roles of teacher and learner are not static but interchangeable. Usually, the teacher includes their own first name so the child and the family will know who wrote the story.

"What Happened?" or "What's the Story?"

The teacher begins the story with their own interest in what the child has taken the initiative to do, describing what the child does and says. The teacher writes in the first person directly to the child, which brings a personal perspective that is essential to the tale. For example, "Miguel, yesterday I noticed that you . . ." or "Gaby, today I heard you say . . ." The teacher describes what the child does and says from the perspective of someone who deeply cares and is listening closely to discover what is actually happening and the learning that is taking place.

It is helpful to describe the environment where the events took place, including the time of day, the context, and who was interacting with the child at that particular time. Other information to consider includes the materials the child or children were using, how they were engaging with those materials, and whether there was a practical or intellectual challenge that the children encountered and how they went about resolving it. Describing the process in as much detail as possible, with the aid of a few photographs or brief video and a few anecdotal notes, is quite useful later to help put the story together.

"What Does It Mean?" or "What Learning Do I See Happening?"

"What does it mean?" or "What learning do I see happening?" are questions to encourage teachers to reflect, interpret, and write about the significance of what was observed. The photographs, video or audio recordings, or transcripts of the child in action serve as evidence of the child's resourcefulness, skills, dispositions, and talents. Interpreting the meaning of what children do, make, or say in their daily play is best when the person who writes the Learning Story consults with others—coteachers, family members, classroom assistants, directors, specialists—who know the child in any capacity and are able to offer their perspectives. This richer and multifaceted dialogue for pedagogical purposes may paint a more nuanced portrait of individual children where their talents and strengths are highlighted and specific ways to support their growth are recorded. This can serve as the foundation for a meaningful, authentic curriculum for young children.

"Opportunities and Possibilities" or "How Can We Support You in Your Learning?"

The question "How can we support you in your learning?" is addressed in the "Opportunities and Possibilities" section, which offers a space for teachers to describe what they can tentatively do the next day or during the next few days to scaffold and extend the child's learning. Teachers may offer possible activities to plan with the child or children about what to do next to cocreate a meaningful curriculum connected to an individual child's or group of children's genuine interests. This gives insight to the participants and stakeholders in the school—coteachers, children and their family members, classroom assistants, program directors, specialists—about how teachers actively think about what they do as practitioners to plan meaningful individualized activities, respecting the child's or children's agency. These activities might include gathering books on certain topics, searching for information on the internet, planning a field trip, collecting specific materials, and so on.

"What's the Family's Perspective?"

Ideally, a question is posed to the child's family to respond in writing with their point of view and reaction to what the teacher(s) wrote, but this can also be accomplished in a one-on-one conversation with the parents or even in an email or text message exchange, if the parents prefer. This component is in a way an open invitation for the family to offer their perspective on how they see their child as a competent learner. Quite often, the child's family responds to the teacher and sometimes, when the teachers ask parents to reply directly to the child, they write very personal and heartfelt messages to their children. It is not uncommon for parents to include a question for the teacher, which enriches the dialogue and strengthens the communication between home and school. Occasionally, the child's family even suggests ideas, activities, and materials to use in the classroom to support their child's learning or to enhance the learning experiences for all the children and teachers in the class.

"Ellie's Learning Story" (page 72) provides an example of how the foundational principles and the basic components are integrated into one document. When Learning Stories are told with a strong and authentic voice and draw on rich observations and visuals, they become an integrated mix of authentic assessment and critical pedagogy.

ISAURO M. ESCAMILLA, EdD, is assistant professor in the Graduate College of Education at San Francisco State University. Formerly, he taught in a Spanish/English dual language preschool in the San Francisco Unified School District.

LINDA R. KROLL, PhD, is professor emerita of education at the School of Education at Mills College, Oakland, California.

DANIEL R. MEIER, PhD, is professor of elementary education at San Francisco State University.

ANNIE WHITE, EdD, is assistant professor in the Early Childhood Studies program at California State University Channel Islands.

Ellie's Learning Story: "種植 Planting"

During the COVID-19 health crisis, the teachers at Las Americas Early Education School in San Francisco Unified School District only saw the children in distance learning. Teacher Joanne Yu decided to continue her writing of Learning Stories with her 3-year-old niece, Ellie, with whom she spent time during the COVID-19 pandemic.

Joanne and Ellie planted together in Joanne's backyard, which offered Joanne the opportunity to observe Ellie's interactions, language, and playful actions with the plant materials, with the tools, and with Joanne. Joanne and Ellie spoke entirely in Cantonese, and Joanne first wrote the Learning Story in Cantonese before translating it into English to share with the Las Americas teacher inquiry group (which met online during the pandemic) via email.

In this Learning Story, Joanne's photographs capture at almost ground level Ellie's construction of the flower planting process, from shoveling the dirt to adding decorative rocks to watering the succulent in the pot.

The "What Happened?" section of the Learning Story indicates Joanne's balancing of independent and coconstructed social skills and knowledge and indicates a cultural and familial value underlying their interaction of competence and independence.

In the "What Does It Mean?" section, Joanne extended and deepened her reflections on the social, play, and linguistic value of the Learning Story by noting that "children have the tendency to change their minds about doing an activity after they have seen someone else do it." Joanne effectively moved from the particular observation of Ellie, her niece, to other children with whom she has worked, making an important connection about the value of balancing independent and socially constructed action and play.

The closing section of the Learning Story included a response from Ellie's father, who noted the cultural and familial practice of using rice water to water plants.

In addition to all the precise observations and comments that Joanne included in the Learning Story, you also see Ellie's understanding of the sequence of planting and caring for the plants. She knows what to do first, second, and last. She is independent in her actions, reflecting a solid schema for this particular sequence of events. Sequencing events is a common acquisition in the preschool years. It is interesting that Joanne noted that at first Ellie was reluctant to help. It is as if she needed to watch and understand the sequence before she would act herself.

種植 Planting

Las Americas EES Joanne Yu

7/12/2020

瞳瞳用鏟子鏟一些泥土放到花盆裡. (20年7月12日)

Ellie is shoveling dirt into the flowerpot. (July 12th, 2020)

瞳瞳把肉質植物種在盆內.

Ellie is planting the succulent in the pot.

瞳瞳把裝飾石頭放在花盆內.

Ellie is placing the decorative rocks in the flowerpot.

瞳瞳澆剛種好的植物.

Ellie is watering the plant after planting and decorating.

背景：

自從20年3月17日起，因新冠肺炎疫情，我必須宅家，我花額外的時間在後花園裡．我的侄女瞳瞳Ellie現在3歲半，多數講中文．她喜歡戶外活動和玩水.於是她常常跟著我.這個"學習故事"是這樣開始的.

Background

Due to COVID-19, shelter in place has been effective since March 17, 2020. I have been spending this extra time at home, working in our backyard. My niece Ellie is three and a half years old and speaks mostly Chinese. She enjoys being outside and playing with water, so she often accompanies me. This is the start to my "learning story."

發生的事情：

瞳瞳，今天早上當你看見我種花後，你說你也想種，於是你拿起鏟子鏟起泥土，放在花盆內.你說你自己能做，不用我幫，我說："很好，証明你很獨立."然後，你問我："這花花放在哪裡？".我教你怎樣放入泥內，你把花種入泥內後，然後用裝飾石頭壓住泥土，最後，用花洒澆水.

What Happened?

You saw me planting flowers and wanted to try it this morning, so you shoveled the dirt into the flowerpot. You said you were able to do it with no help. I said, "That's good, you're very independent." And then you asked me, "Where does the flower go?" I taught you how to plant the flower within the dirt. After you put the flower into the dirt, and then you placed decorative rocks on the top, finally you watered it.

這意味着什麼：

在後花園，瞳瞳開始只想玩水，不想跟我種花，當我種完花後，叫她澆水，她很樂意，澆完水後，瞳瞳問我："我可不可以種花花？"小孩子有時是這樣，當有機會看到你做的東西後，覺得有興趣，就有可能改變主意，想做她原來不想做的東西.她只有三歲半，能運用整句句子來問，說明她有好的語言能力．她說她自己能用鏟子鏟泥，不用我幫，她把泥裝在盆內，這說明她有表達自己想法的能力.然後她學我那樣，將植物種入盆內，把小石頭壓住泥土.這說明她有模仿能力.

What Does This Mean?

When we first started going out into the backyard, she only wanted to play with water. She didn't want to plant flowers with me. She liked to help me water the plants after I finished planting them. After helping me water the succulents, she then asked, "Can I plant a flower?" Children have the tendency to change their minds about doing an activity after they have seen someone else do it. Just like in this situation, she didn't want to plant flowers in the beginning, but after, decided she wanted to try. She is 3 and a half years old and she can ask me what she wants to do. That means she has good language skills. She said she was able to shovel and do it by herself. That means she can express her idea. She followed the process of planting the flower with me. She remembered to plant the succulent in the pot, and then put the rocks on the top of the dirt. She was capable of imitation and has a good memory.

下一步計劃：

1. 學詞語：泥土，肉質植物，種
2. 數學：學數1至10
3. 培養種花興趣
4. 植物需要水

Next Steps:

1. Learn Vocabulary: dirt, succulent, plant

2. Learn to Count from 1 to 10

3. Gardening as a Hobby

4. Plants Need Water to Survive

家長看法：

我告訴瞳瞳的爸爸媽媽，瞳瞳今天種花，并澆水。她爸爸很高興，熱愛花草樹木，是好事，他說洗米水很好，以後會叫瞳瞳一起去後院用洗米水澆檸檬樹，花和她種的肉質植物.

Parent's Comment

I told Ellie's parents that Ellie planted and watered a succulent today. Her dad was happy to know Ellie was engaging with nature. Her dad said rice water is good for plants, he will bring her with him to water the lemon tree, flowers, and the succulent that she planted in the backyard.

Teaching to Enhance Each Child's Development and Learning

RECOMMENDATIONS FROM THE DAP POSITION STATEMENT

Recognizing play as critical for children to experience joy and wonder, early childhood educators incorporate frequent opportunities for play in their teaching strategies. They plan learning environments that provide a mix of self-directed play, guided play, and direct instruction. Educators maximize opportunities for children to choose the materials, playmates, topics, and approaches they use throughout the day for all children. . . . Educators support and extend children's play experiences by providing materials and resources based on careful observation of children's play choices. Adult-guided activities provide for children's active agency as educators offer specific guidance and support to scaffold and extend children's interest, engagement, and learning.

Teachers Patricia and Vera are making great efforts to embed literacy practices in the context of science in their dual language preschool classroom. There are open books at the science table and a stack of writing journals and magnetic letters on an adjacent science shelf. The children's journals are filled with visual representations of their recent explorations of the natural world. In the carpeted area, there is an easel displaying a shared writing experience that took place after a field trip to a museum a few days earlier. Alongside the teacher's writing is a string of letter-like markings that one of the children contributed to the list. (From "The Power of Science: Using Inquiry Thinking to Enhance Learning in a Dual Language Preschool Classroom," page 78)

This example captures an essential component of developmentally appropriate practice: teaching to enhance each child's development and learning. The materials in Patricia and Vera's setting enable children to make rich, meaningful connections between content areas. The teachers have introduced engaging, stimulating ideas and experiences for the children

to explore. Intentional teachers integrate choice and agency with well-planned learning environments and experiences (NAEYC 2020). This is not play *or* learning but rather play *and* learning!

Teaching is bound and connected to a program's early learning curriculum. The curriculum provides the framework for learning, the structure for ensuring that all relevant goals are covered in a logical way, but teaching practices are the means by which children experience learning. Because relationships are at the heart of development and learning, effective preschool educators model a caring community in their interactions with children. They scaffold learning, as appropriate, helping preschoolers to further their thinking. Effective preschool teachers ensure that they get to know each child and their family and use that information to plan the physical environment and activities in ways that promote healthy development within the learning domains and subject areas. In short, teaching practices are the actions that intentional teachers take to facilitate learning for, and connection with, the children.

Equitable teachers consider each child's unique abilities, identities, temperament, and other characteristics and adjust their teaching behaviors and interactions to best support each individual. The position statement on advancing equity in early childhood education states that early childhood educators should "consider the developmental, cultural, and linguistic appropriateness of . . . teaching practices for each child" (NAEYC 2019a, 7). This consideration is crucial because teaching practices are relevant, meaningful, and most effective when they are based on and informed by children's lived experiences, ways of knowing, and ways of being.

Educators profiled in the chapters in this section make intentional decisions about teaching strategies and approaches depending on the particular children, the content, and the setting. You will read about teaching methods such as

- Demonstrating and modeling a commitment to a caring community of learners

- Using knowledge of each child and family to facilitate meaningful, accessible, and responsive learning experiences

- Implementing a curriculum with individualized goals for all domains and subject areas
- Intentionally planning the environment, schedule, and daily activities
- Using a variety of strategies to facilitate learning
- Scaffolding learning
- Strategically using different learning contexts
- Differentiating instruction (NAEYC 2020)

Effective teachers possess a tool belt with many tools. Knowing about and utilizing different approaches and strategies help to ensure that all children will build knowledge and master content in the context of joyful, playful learning experiences. By being familiar with many ways to facilitate learning and the needs of each child, preschool teachers help to ensure that all children reach challenging and appropriate learning goals.

Part 4 illustrates teaching that is inclusive, individualized, and reflective of the diverse world in which children live and develop. The chapters address different aspects of teaching, including daily routines, group activities, indoor and outdoor play, and interactions with children that encourage deeper thinking.

READ AND REFLECT

As you read the chapters in this section, consider and evaluate your own classroom practices using these reflection questions.

"The Power of Science: Using Inquiry Thinking to Enhance Learning in a Dual Language Preschool Classroom" discusses the ways the teachers use "an extensive repertoire of skills and teaching strategies" (NAEYC 2020, 23) as they engage children in a variety of joyful, integrated science experiences. **Consider:** What teaching strategies promote creative thinking and problem-solving skills and help to develop lifelong, confident learners through joyful learning experiences?

"A Guided, Exploration-Based Visual Arts Program for Preschoolers" presents a great example of teachers using their professional judgment to determine appropriate levels of scaffolding while honoring the individuality and creativity of each child (NAEYC 2020). **Consider:** How could you modify visual arts instruction to teach techniques and also encourage children to be creative?

"Supporting Positive Racial Identity with Literacy-Based Math" demonstrates how educators can "use their knowledge of each child and family to make learning experiences meaningful, accessible, and responsive to each and every child" (NAEYC 2020, 21), in this case,

Black children. **Consider:** How can teaching strategies influence child learning and development within learning domains as well as children's view of themselves, people like them, and people different from them?

"Meaningful Talk: The Importance of Using Sophisticated Language at Preschool" explains how early childhood educators can help expand young children's vocabularies and support linguistic development—a key factor in school success—by creating "language-rich environments that focus on the diversity and complexity of language" (NAEYC 2020, 22). **Consider:** In what ways can you incorporate sophisticated language into your setting?

"Using Nature Contact to Support Children Under Stress" describes specific ways the educators "differentiate instructional approaches to match each child's interests, knowledge, and skills" (NAEYC 2020, 24). **Consider:** What contexts for learning exist in your setting? How might you strategically use these contexts to meet the diverse needs of your children in an individualized way?

"Timing Is Everything: Understanding the Importance of Timing, Length, and Sequence of Activities" illustrates how teaching to enhance development and learning is not only about the strategies or the types of experiences but also involves planning "the environment, schedule, and daily activities to promote . . . learning" (NAEYC 2020, 22). **Consider:** Think of your daily schedule, classroom environment, and learning activities. Where might you make adjustments to better meet the needs of your preschoolers?

CHAPTER 17

The Power of Science

Using Inquiry Thinking to Enhance Learning in a Dual Language Preschool Classroom

Leanne M. Evans

When preschool teacher Patricia speaks about her childhood in Mexico, she reminisces about exploring and playing outside. She describes digging up the dirt in her yard to look for worms, watching the growth of seeds she planted, and catching lightning bugs. "I want the children in my classroom to have the same opportunities to explore, to feel, to touch, and to open up their imaginations. That's what's really going to help them learn," Patricia shares. Fellow teacher Vera remembers the days she spent as a child finding ladybugs, chasing butterflies, and helping with the cattle and chickens on her family's Mississippi farm: "I think about everything I did as a child. I try to bring it to the classroom as much as possible."

Patricia and Vera teach alongside one another in a dual language Head Start classroom. Ninety percent of the children come from homes where Spanish is the primary language, and the young learners have varying degrees of Spanish and English proficiency. Patricia takes the lead on Spanish days, and Vera takes the lead on English days. They alternate the language of instruction weekly, with the goal of creating a pathway for children to become bilingual, biliterate, and multicultural. The teachers have found that coteaching in two languages requires weekly planning sessions and daily conversations filled with reflections on how they nurture children's language development and effectively support each other during instruction.

As a literacy and language researcher and former early childhood reading specialist in a dual language school, I partnered with Patricia and Vera to examine the relationship between science, literacy, and language learning. The teachers believed that science and literacy could be connected in effective ways, and they were ready to explore how this could be done as they worked with the children in two languages.

Why Focus on Science?

Inquiry-based science instruction in early childhood classrooms is, essentially, doing science (Worth 2019). It involves the many ways learners study the natural environment in a process that develops new knowledge (Gillies 2020). The inquiry learning cycle begins with time for children to observe, explore, and wonder about a specific natural phenomenon. They are given the space to question and share what they notice. From there, the teacher guides them in a deeper exploration of aspects of the natural phenomenon that sparked their interest. This process involves predicting, planning, and organizing, while information is collected through interactions with others. Teachers support children in their construction of new knowledge, and a cycle of learning develops as new questions emerge.

Interactive science inquiry offers emergent bilingual learners highly motivating, conversation-rich environments where children ask questions and search for answers together—creating lots of authentic opportunities to develop their language and literacy skills (Evans & Avila 2016). In particular, partner and small group settings offer dual language learners—and all learners—nonthreatening situations where they have freedom to share observations, questions, and discoveries with each other.

"Sometimes It's Hard for Us to Talk About Science"

Early in our discussions, Patricia revealed one of her challenges: "Sometimes it's hard for us to talk about science. I worry if I'm using the correct language.

The words are so technical." I prompted Patricia and Vera to reflect on the ways that early literacy and science exploration are similar.

We began by thinking about questions the teachers often pose during read-alouds—questions that are similar to those they use when they ask children to observe the steps of a science experiment. As a guide, I shared a list of scientific process skills (observing, questioning, describing, predicting, investigating, planning, recording, interpreting, and sharing ideas) (Hamlin & Wisneski 2012), then developed a list of questions to help Patricia and Vera think about how to bring scientific thinking into their read-aloud discussions. (See "Questions Linking Book Sharing and Scientific Inquiry.")

Questions Linking Book Sharing and Scientific Inquiry

What do you notice about . . . ?
(¿Qué nota usted acerca de . . . ?)

What do you think will happen next?
(¿Qué sucederá después?)

Have you ever experienced . . . ?
(¿Ha tenido alguna experiencia con . . . ?)

What happened first? Next? At the end?
(¿Qué sucedió primero, después, al final?)

What if . . . ?
(¿Qué pasaría si . . . ? ¿Qué tal si . . . ?)

How did _____ change from the beginning to the end?
(¿Cómo cambio _____ desde el principio hasta el final?)

How are _____ the same/different?
(¿En qué se parecen/se diferencían _____?)

What happened that caused _____?
(¿Qué fue lo que causó?)

Through this conversation, Patricia concluded that the same types of graphic organizers used in repeated read-alouds (e.g., T-charts, Venn diagrams, cause-and-effect illustrations) could also be used to connect literacy objectives within a science context. Vera wondered how the science center could become more literacy rich and how journals could be used as a regular part of recording observations as science and literacy were merged. Patricia wanted to explore the connections between science and literacy in an upcoming lesson she was developing on the school's theme, Alike and Different. She invited me to return to the classroom in two weeks to observe her lesson with her new focus on integrating science and literacy.

Somos parecidos, somos diferentes/We Are Alike, We Are Different

Returning to Patricia and Vera's classroom, I noticed an open book at the science table. I also took note of a stack of writing journals and magnetic letters on an adjacent science shelf. The children's journals were filled with visual representations of recent explorations of the natural world. In the carpeted area, there was an easel displaying a shared writing experience that appeared to have taken place after a field trip to a museum a few days earlier. Alongside the teacher's writing, I saw a string of letter-like markings that one of the children had contributed to the list. It was evident that Patricia and Vera had made great efforts to embed literacy practices in the context of science.

Guided by her well-defined lesson objectives (see the chart on the following page), Patricia began the *alike* and *different* lesson by seating the children in a circle and showing them two eggs—one brown, the other white. Vera sat on the far side of the circle in a position of support. Patricia demonstrated how to pass the eggs around the circle gently. She asked the children to observe the eggs using their senses of sight, touch, and smell. As the children passed the eggs, they spoke to each other about what they noticed. I recorded their observations:

Child 1: Esta frío. (It's cold.)

Child 2: Mi mami hace huevos. (My mommy makes eggs.)

Child 3: Son chiquitos. (They are very little.)

Child 4: Uno brown y uno blanco. (One brown and one white.)

Child 5: I don't have eggs at my house.

Child 6: Son de pollitos. (They are from chickens.)

Parecidos y diferentes/Alike and Different—Lesson Objectives

Science	Literacy	Language
Children will	Children will	Children will
■ Demonstrate knowledge of the concepts of alike and different through the exploration of physical properties (color, shape, size) ■ Use scientific inquiry skills (observing, describing, predicting, and recording) to explore the concepts of alike and different	■ Explore the initial syllable /pa/ as they are introduced to the key word parecidos (alike) (Note: Spanish phonological awareness instruction centers on vowel sounds and is taught through an exploration of initial syllables. This is in contrast to the focus on initial consonant sounds taught in English phonological awareness instruction.) ■ Demonstrate shared reading skills (observing, describing, and predicting) as they engage in a read-aloud experience exploring the concepts of alike and different ■ Engage in shared writing/drawing as they explore the concepts of alike and different	■ Express and receive language to gain an understanding of the concepts of alike and different ■ Interact with the language of science: observe, describe, predict, and record (at all levels of language development)

The children made connections to their own lives and prior knowledge as they used their senses to explore the eggs. When all the children had a chance to examine the eggs, Patricia made a T-chart with the title "Huevos" (Eggs) and two columns, "Parecidos" (Alike) and "Diferentes" (Different). As she wrote the word *parecidos,* she said, "Pa . . . pa . . . pa. ¿La palabra *parecidos* empieza con . . . ?" (The word parecidos begins with . . . ?). Several students said "pa." She asked, "¿Puede usted pensar en otras palabras que empiezan con la /pa/?" (Can you think of other words that begin with /pa/?). The children contributed words that included papa (potato), papá (dad), pasta, and papel (paper). I was sitting close enough to hear one child quietly say to another, "Pa . . . pa . . . pato" (duck).

Returning to the chart, Patricia placed the eggs in the center of the circle and asked the children to stand up if they thought the eggs were *alike.* Four children stood up. She wrote their names on the chart, asking the children to help her with the initial sound and initial letter of each name. She then did the same with the concept of *different,* for which seven children stood up. Patricia asked the children to help her *describe* the eggs. She led the students in sharing and communicating their ideas using the sentence frames, "Los huevos son parecidos porque _____. Los huevos son diferentes porque _____." (The eggs are alike because _____. The eggs are different because _____.) Most of the children focused on the different colors of the eggs. One child (who

knew *iguales* [equal], but was just starting to learn *parecidos*) responded, "Iguales, porque van a cocinar." (Same, because they are going to be cooked.) Another quietly stated, "Dos cosas." (Two things.) Through a brief exchange, Patricia supported the child in the conclusion that they were alike because they were the same size and shape, but they were different because of their colors.

When it was time to crack the eggs, Patricia prompted the children to *predict* what was inside. One child looked at another and said, "Hay pollitos adentro." (There are chickens inside.) The second child replied, "I think there is oil inside. Some eggs have baby chicks, but the ones we eat have oil inside." Patricia eventually broke the eggs onto two plates and asked, "¿Qué observas?" (What do you observe?) A choir of voices rang out: "¡Iguales! They are the same!" Patricia explained to the children that she wanted to *describe* and *record* what she saw. She used the easel paper to draw one brown egg and one white egg. Underneath each of the eggs she drew a yellow yolk surrounded by a clear circle, suggesting to the children that she *observed* that the eggs were the same on the inside. She then *shared* her ideas: "Observo que los huevos están parecidos adentro." (I observe that the eggs are alike inside.) I noticed the children were using the word *iguales* as a synonym for parecidos; Patricia directed the children back to the lesson's vocabulary in her use of *parecidos* as she prompted the observation of the similar insides of the eggs.

Patricia next picked up the book *Shades of People,* by Shelly Rotner and Sheila M. Kelly, from the table and showed the children the cover. She said,

> Miss Patricia y Miss Vera somos diferentes afuera, pero por adentro, todos somos parecidos como los huevos. Mira eso: la gente tiene características diferentes, pero todos somos seres humanos y todos somos únicos e importantes. Adentro, todos tenemos un corazón y un cerebro. Todos parecidos. (Miss Patricia and Miss Vera are different on the outside, but on the inside we are alike, like the eggs. Look at this: the people have different characteristics, but all of us are humans and we are unique and important. On the inside, we all have a heart and a brain. We are alike.)

Although the book was written in English, Patricia read it using her own Spanish translation. As she moved through the pages, she asked the children to *observe* and *describe* the similarities and differences between the people (mostly children) shown in the photos. At one point, she asked the children to *share* their ideas with a partner, providing the sentence starter, "Me di cuenta que . . ." (I noticed that . . .). Their responses touched on many different elements of the photos:

> ❭ Ella tiene pelo largo como yo. (She has long hair like me.)
>
> ❭ There are boys and girls.
>
> ❭ Hay uno brown y uno blanco. (There is one brown and one white.)
>
> ❭ Es la mamá y papá. (It's the mom and dad.)
>
> ❭ Fui a la beach como ellos. (I went to the beach like them.)

When Patricia finished the book, she asked the children to move their circle closer and for everyone to put one hand in to meet the other hands in the center. One last time, she asked, "¿Qué observas?" (What do you observe?) The children were amazed at the spectrum of color in their circle of small hands. She said, "Somos parecidos en muchos aspectos, pero en algunas cosas también somos diferentes." (We are alike in many ways, but with some things we are also different.)

The components of the lesson described in this chapter provided extended time for children to explore, investigate, and use their language skills. This multipart lesson is a great example of developmentally appropriate practice as it shows how intentional and thoughtful planning can promote children's learning and development.

Post-Lesson Thoughts

Patricia and Vera had successfully engaged children in the natural world while simultaneously providing myriad opportunities for the children to engage in activities in which language and literacy development flourished in English and Spanish. They had introduced new vocabulary in a meaningful context and had fostered early literacy skills by finding spaces to work on the alphabetic principle, name writing, and conventions of print. This lesson was Patricia and Vera's first step in purposefully integrating science thinking and emergent literacy development.

Scientific explorations are an ideal place for fluid and dynamic literacy and language practices. When free to observe, think, and create in both languages, dual language learners enhance their linguistic repertoires. In turn, this provides the children with more language to use when engaging in further explorations and inquiry.

Patricia, Vera, and I summarized key strategies that could be incorporated into any lesson designed to integrate science inquiry with emergent literacy objectives:

> Connect the science topic to your own life and tell children what you are wondering ("I wonder . . .").

> Guide the children in connecting the science inquiry to their own lives ("Have you ever . . . ?").

> Model the language of noticing ("I noticed . . .").

> Become intentional observers of the natural world throughout the day by using the language of inquiry.

> Connect children to books that will give them another perspective.

> Offer many opportunities for children to visually represent their inquiry experiences (e.g., science journals).

> Make language central to each learning experience and nurture peer interaction and talk.

> Provide language supports throughout instruction. Use visuals, realia (actual objects of study, such as real leaves instead of felt leaves), hands-on activities, actions, and oral sentence starters to guide a combination of science and language exploration.

> Value the entirety of children's language resources (in English and other languages) as they engage in observations and experiences of inquiry.

Conclusion

All young children are learners of language, and the practices emphasized with dual language learners in this chapter are beneficial for all learners. Guiding children in thinking about how they use words to inquire about the natural world can build their understanding of inquiry and how inquiry thinking and language can lead them to new discoveries. These discoveries will shape who children are as science thinkers and, just as powerful, will foster their language and literacy identities.

Author's Note

The author extends thanks and appreciation for the opportunity to participate in Patricia and Vera's classroom. This research study was supported by a US Department of Education grant (number T365Z120147).

LEANNE M. EVANS is an associate professor and Early Childhood Education Program Chair at the University of Wisconsin–Milwaukee. Her teaching and research interests include literacy and language development in the lives of young children; culturally and linguistically responsive pedagogy; and the experiences of teachers and teacher educators in urban education.

CHAPTER 18

A Guided, Exploration-Based Visual Arts Program for Preschoolers

X. Christine Wang, Keely Benson, Corinne Eggleston, and Bin Lin

It is the first day of our visual arts guided play session. An easel with *The Starry Night*, by Vincent van Gogh, is set up on the rug, and the visual-artist-in-residence, Jeannet, finishes facilitating a discussion about the paint and color choices van Gogh used in the painting. The children begin working on their own canvases in small groups. Some work at tables while others choose to paint at easels; Jeannet, Keely (the classroom teacher and curriculum coordinator), and student interns walk around discussing ideas and artistic techniques with each child.

"I mixed them! I mixed them! I mixed them! I like to mix my colors," Sawyer, a 3-year-old, excitedly shrieks as he creates his own representation of the soft blue and purple sky. Looking back at *The Starry Night*, he seems to contemplate what he will paint next.

At our school, guided explorations of the visual arts for preschoolers are planned jointly by Keely and Jeannet to make the most of their knowledge of instruction, children, and art. Jeannet is a visual artist-in-residence. While having a visual artist-in-residence may not be possible for all settings, there are artists who are members of communities of different demographics. Early childhood educators can seek to partner with community artists to experience the same collaboration and goals from an arts and early childhood expertise and background. The goal is to introduce young children to the beauty and joy of the visual arts through a combination of examining selected masterpieces, building children's knowledge of key features of those masterpieces (including painting techniques and subject matter), and engaging in exploratory art experiences, including art planning, making, viewing, and appreciating.

Facets of a Visual Arts Program Based on Guided Exploration

In early childhood classrooms, the two most common visual arts approaches either offer little intervention or focus on production (Bresler 1993). The little-intervention approach gives children freedom to explore and create with minimal guidance or scaffolding from teachers, while the production-oriented approach emphasizes children following teachers' directions and creating art based on a model prescribed by teachers (Bresler 1993). While both of these approaches have value—the first supports self-expression and the second can offer a playful context for developing fine-motor and executive function skills. Learning about well-known works of art and artists in a hands-on manner offers opportunities to learn about and develop background knowledge and vocabulary (which are essential to their future reading comprehension). Having an understanding about those painters' techniques, especially by practicing them, helps children more deeply understand the paintings and better develop a broad set of artistic skills.

Our guided-exploration approach, which is based on work by Bressler (1993), does the following:

> Encourages children and teachers to use an aesthetic lens in planning and creating art

> Positions teachers as facilitators who provide "guidelines that help children observe things carefully, use their sensitivities, and express their ideas when they create artwork" (Bae 2004, 248)

> Fosters children's observation, listening, and communication skills through the arts

> Enhances children's enjoyment of aesthetic art experiences as it helps them develop their identities as artists (Eckhoff 2013)

To achieve these goals, we set up our visual arts program to incorporate art viewing and appreciation, art discoveries and play, planning, and art-making opportunities, all of which are described in the following sections.

Our visual arts program consists of sessions that take place once a week and are led by both the visual artist-in-residence and an early childhood teacher. Through both large- and small-group activities, children are introduced to different artists and specific art elements (such as color, style, form, and content).

The Teacher's Role

The guided-exploration approach to visual arts teaching values the joint activity of both the teacher and the student; teachers mediate children's meaning making with art. This mediation can take on many forms, such as modeling, facilitating, and playing with the students. Teachers facilitate three main activities to guide children's explorations.

> **Introducing a model artwork.** Teachers illustrate techniques and demonstrate an appreciation for the art. They encourage children to make connections and discuss their own experiences in relation to the artwork. Teachers also model during art making, using their own canvases to demonstrate different techniques influenced by the artwork being examined.

> **Guiding individual interests and choices.** During art making, teachers encourage children to integrate their own interests into their paintings or help children build and elaborate on their initial ideas. Teachers' knowledge of and connections with each child are critical.

> **Guiding discussions and documenting children's understanding.** Teachers talk about children's artistic decisions, observe as they use new vocabulary and describe their work, and evaluate and scaffold children's development.

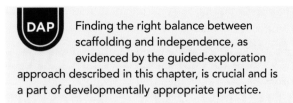 Finding the right balance between scaffolding and independence, as evidenced by the guided-exploration approach described in this chapter, is crucial and is a part of developmentally appropriate practice.

Art Viewing and Appreciation

One small-group activity invites children to look at famous artwork with magnifying glasses and discuss what they notice. Teachers model discussions about the artwork, focusing on aesthetic appreciation of the color, technique, and balance that the artist portrayed and on children's personal connections to the art. Teachers' sophisticated conversations about the artwork guide children to discuss the pieces in a similar manner. We also use the game I Spy to help children interpret the work in a whole-group setting—they identify specific objects, images, and artistic techniques in the painting (McClure et al. 2017).

Art Discoveries and Play

The focus of our visual arts program is on play-based learning and helping children to discover qualities of art through play. For each session, we plan activities that enable children to play with the materials that are highlighted by each focal piece of artwork. For example, when studying *The Starry Night*, by Vincent van Gogh, children took part in activities focused on the aesthetic qualities of the sky and how to represent them visually. Children then engaged in music and movement activities to embody the swirls in the sky, and they discussed how their movements compared with the movement in van Gogh's brushstrokes. This play gave children an understanding of the resources they would later use for their paintings.

Planning

Teachers encourage children to brainstorm and plan before visual arts activities. This "quiet think time" lasts for approximately 30 seconds. Teachers offer a prompt related to a recent read-aloud or an observation—such as "We learned that people often see constellations, like the Big Dipper, in the stars as they look at the night sky. Will your stars also form constellations?"—and children are asked to think rather than talk about it. Children's literature is essential to our planning process, as children are encouraged to look through illustrations and photos in fiction and nonfiction books; this also gives them an opportunity to discover their interests. Children can use other media, such as online photos and videos, to examine their interests as well. Planning time encourages children to make decisions about the painting they will create.

Art Making

Each session, children have an extended period of time to create meaning through painting. We end the session with approximately 30 minutes for children to paint their ideas and understanding. Children each have their own canvas and build on their artwork each week, adding dimension and interest. Each child chooses the amount of time they spend painting each week and where they feel comfortable painting. Children sit at tables in small groups, three or four to a table, to encourage collaboration and discussion of ideas during painting. (Since children choose to spend different amounts of time painting, they are free to move to different learning centers when they are ready.)

Program Planning and Implementation
Selecting Model Artwork

Before implementing the program, teachers find well-known artists and works that the children can identify and connect with. It is important to consider the background and historical context of the artist and art that is selected, intentionally choosing artists with diverse backgrounds each session. We considered artists' subject matter, painting techniques, and mediums. For example, Vincent van Gogh intrigued us because of his expressive style and pronounced brushstrokes. His swirling and circling strokes are reminiscent of children's early explorations with paint and paintbrushes. Such considerations can be adapted to include diverse art styles, such as pop, abstract, and representational art. No matter the style, the most

important aspect of teachers' guidance in this program is helping children connect their lives and interests to the art.

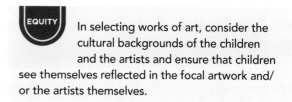

In selecting works of art, consider the cultural backgrounds of the children and the artists and ensure that children see themselves reflected in the focal artwork and/or the artists themselves.

The focal artwork provides a starting point for the children and a valuable structure for children to use in exploring their own creations. It is important to note that it is *not* used for replication. Children learn about techniques the artist used and adapt those techniques to create their own art. Children's free expression is emphasized during art making. The focal artwork and children's final creations tend to diverge greatly.

Choosing Mediums and Materials

Rather than using oil paint, as our focal artists often did, we worked with acrylic and watercolor paints since both are easier for young children to manipulate and offer different color-mixing properties. To provide children with an authentic exploration of the visual arts, we invested in high-quality materials. We supplemented those quality supplies with many affordable household materials. For example, we filled two yogurt cups with paint and placed them side by side so children could mix and compare different shades. We also made smocks out of small towels by cutting a hole in the middle so they could fit over children's heads.

Preparing the Classroom

Essential to our planning is configuring the layout of the classroom. We want the children to have ample room to create their individual artworks as well as opportunities to discuss and engage with their peers and view each other's pieces. We feel that large tables seating groups of three to four children—with enough room for individual workstations—permit children both to work independently and to collaborate.

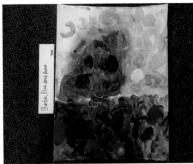

Guidance for Educators

As you create a guided visual arts program for your setting, keep these suggestions in mind.

> **Model appreciation for artwork.** To encourage children to identify with and discuss famous pieces of art, it's important that you model an interest in and curiosity about the qualities of the artwork. Begin by talking about its colors, shades, lines, shapes, and subject. "I love how van Gogh used different shades of blue. I see both light and dark blues. What do you notice about the colors he chose?"

> **Guide children to think deeply as they paint.** Find opportunities while children are painting to sit next to them and discuss their artistic decisions. Give them space to explore but also look for moments to ask questions and prompt them to think about their decisions. "I see that you are making circular brushstrokes to show movement in the sky. Tell me how you make those strokes."

> **Scaffold conversations between peers.** Children are used to answering adults' close-ended questions. Give them opportunities to discuss painting with each other. "It looks like you and Juan are using the same color! I wonder what Juan is using it for? Why don't you ask him?"

> **Encourage free expression.** The model piece of artwork is a guide for artistic technique—not necessarily the subject children need to represent. Some children will focus on mixing colors and create more abstract works, while others will have the fine-motor skills and interest to paint something representational. Encourage children to express themselves and make connections between the painting and their own lives. If a child prefers to paint a sun rather than a moon or explore mixing colors during the study

of *The Starry Night*, support the idea. "How can you use your paintbrush to create a sun in the same way that van Gogh used his paintbrush?" and "I see that you have a new color on your canvas. What colors did you mix together to make that color?"

Finishing with a Culminating Class

The culminating class of each unit engages the children in finishing their artwork the way a professional artist does—children title, sign, and present their artwork to their peers. To help the children come up with titles, we read some of their favorite books and view some of their favorite paintings; then we discuss why the authors titled them, or named them, the way they did. Children independently write their names on their pieces, an act that encourages them to be proud of their accomplishments and work.

Essential to the conclusion of each visual arts unit is the presentation and discussion time. In small groups, children explain their paintings to each other, and their peers are encouraged to ask questions and make comments about the artwork. In addition, children invite their families to the school art gallery, which is put together at the end of each unit.

Student engagement and interest has driven the continuation of this program at our center. As one 4-year-old child explained, "I'm happy. I feel happy because I like to paint!" Teachers' anecdotal records have illuminated the progress that children in the program have made, such as improving their artistic techniques and elevating their discussions of artwork. The children have truly begun developing their identities as artists.

Swirling Skies: Children Create Their Starry Nights

Interpreting and reimagining widely known works of art is a thought-provoking process. Prior to each session, teachers break down an aspect of each focal piece of artwork, in this case *The Starry Night,* and continually scaffold children's learning about both the painting's contents and the artist's techniques.

Here, we share our outline for the first of the six sessions we developed on *The Starry Night.* (To see the other sessions, visit NAEYC.org/dap-focus -preschool.) Our hope is that teachers will find our ideas useful for creating their own guided explorations of artwork and artists. By basing your explorations on the children's interests and drawing connections with other aspects of your curriculum, you'll boost children's learning and creativity.

Session 1: Introduction to the Night Sky

Observe the Sky During the Day and at Night

This activity helps children develop observation skills and probes their prior knowledge. While we looked outside the window at the day sky, we had to rely on photos on our classroom computer for the night sky. We then compared the day and the night on a Venn diagram, titling one side, "What do we see in the day?," and the other side, "What do we see at night?" It's important to look at real (not altered or enhanced) photos of the daytime and the nighttime, and facilitate discussion with questions such as

› What colors do we see?

› What is in the sky?

› What do we do during this time?

> Objective: Children make observations of both the day and night skies while observing the outdoors and/or referring to real photos regarding colors, shapes, and objects. (Whole group for 5–10 minutes)

Introduce the Painting and the Artist

We looked at the painting *The Starry Night* as a whole group. We used a Vincent van Gogh puppet to make connections to the night sky, saying that Vincent (represented by the puppet) was really impressed by the night sky, so he chose to paint it.

Children then had time to discuss the painting as we asked them a variety of questions, including

› What do you see?

› What do you notice in Vincent's interpretation of the night sky?

› Does the painting look the same as or different from the photos we looked at? Why?

> Objective: Children discuss, using both statements and questions, van Gogh's painting. (Whole group for 5–10 minutes)

Model and Explore Artistic Techniques

We first modeled, using a large sponge brush, making back and forth strokes to create a background on the entire canvas. Next, we modeled how to use a paper towel to soak up the watercolor paint to create clouds. (Crinkle the paper towel and place it in a cup of water. Wring it out and hold it down on selected places in the painting for five seconds, each time counting "1, 2, 3, 4, 5" aloud.) Finally, we engaged the children in exploring these materials and techniques.

> Objective: Children observe artistic techniques and then use the techniques to create their own artworks inspired by the night sky. (Small groups at the tables for 5–10 minutes)

Paint the Sky

Children chose from several paint colors—different shades of blue and black—to create their own skies. While the children painted, we discussed with them which colors they chose and why. We encouraged children to use black and/or white paint to make shades and tints of the colors they chose.

> Objective: Children mix in black and/or white paint to create shades and tints for their representations of the night sky. (Small groups at the tables for 20 minutes, or as long as the children need)

X. CHRISTINE WANG, PhD, is professor and the director of the Fisher-Price Endowed Early Childhood Research Center at the State University of New York at Buffalo. Her research interests include technology and young children, early science and literacy, and early education in international contexts.

KEELY BENSON, PhD, is the associate director of the Fisher-Price Endowed Early Childhood Research Center. Keely has more than 10 years of preschool teaching experience, and her interests include visual arts in early childhood.

CORINNE EGGLESTON, PhD, is the associate manager of early childhood development research at Fisher-Price, Inc. Her research interests include parent–child joint engagement with electronic literacy and visual arts in early childhood.

BIN LIN, PhD, is an adjunct instructor at the State University of New York at Buffalo. She is pursuing a second PhD in curriculum, instruction, and the science of learning. She is a former research assistant and teacher at the Fisher-Price Endowed Early Childhood Research Center.

Supporting Positive Racial Identity with Literacy-Based Math

Toni Sturdivant

It's center time in Ms. Alma's and Ms. Christine's prekindergarten class. Stacey, a 4-year-old Black girl, and Elisa, a 4-year-old Latina, are playing with dolls. Elisa sits down with her doll and opens a hairstyle book.

Elisa: Which one should I make? (*Flips to the page with an illustration of a girl wearing her hair in an afro.*) I don't want to make that hair.

Stacey: Why not?

Elisa: Because I'm going to make a hair that is beautiful.

Stacey looks over at the picture Elisa was referring to and sees that the character is wearing a style very similar to hers. She pauses her play for a bit, frowning as she looks to the floor.

Ms. Alma and Ms. Christine know that young children talk about human differences like hair, skin color, and eye color. Without proper adult support, the children may make hurtful or stereotypical comments about other people that make it difficult for some children to feel good about who they are. These teachers know how critical it is to address such comments. And they also know that they can integrate learning across the curriculum while advancing equity.

 By taking the time to center aspects of Black children's identities and experiences in a meaningful way, preschool teachers work against notions of Blackness being inferior and teach children to feel pride in their social identities. (See principle 5 of child development and learning.)

There are many ways early childhood educators can help ensure that children are confident in themselves and their families and see the value in one another's differences. As noted by the 2020 position statement on developmentally appropriate practice, educators make every effort to ensure that "each child hears and sees their home language, culture, and family experience reflected in the daily interactions, activities, and materials in the early learning setting" (17). When messages that celebrate humanity's differences are woven together with and across academic content, we can

> Show just how important these ideas and attitudes about diversity are

> Increase engagement as children see themselves reflected in the activities

> Save some planning time and help children learn more effectively by creating learning experiences that integrate across content areas and developmental domains

> Ensure that content instruction is relevant to children's lives

Children's literature is a great way to affirm and support the positive development of each child's identities and their acceptance of others' identities. This chapter offers a few math activities based on children's literature that send positive messages to children about diversity in hair textures and styles as well as in skin color. They also foster early math learning! Rich with text and visual details, these books—and the associated math activities—will engage and benefit each and every child.

Visual representation is important in the classroom. While only a few examples of hands-on math activities are included here, use these ideas as inspiration to create your own activities to deepen children's acceptance, understanding, and joy surrounding diversity. Two of the activities use dolls with tightly coiled hair, which is a common texture for Black hair. If dolls that look like this aren't readily available, it is a good idea to get some by purchasing from the store (if budgets allow), looking for dolls at garage sales, or asking friends or family if they have well-cared-for dolls to donate.

Children are naturally curious about human differences and often ask questions about physical appearance. When preschool teachers bring physical characteristics to the forefront such as during the math lessons described here, they make space for children's curiosity and ensure that learning is more meaningful to each child. By focusing on Black physical characteristics, preschool teachers are being responsive to a group of children that is too often not represented. As children play, it is important to pay attention to the topics that interest them and any emerging or explicit negative feelings regarding race. Use this information to create learning experiences that not only teach academic skills but further children's accurate and positive understandings about race.

I Love My Hair

by Natasha Anastasia Tarpley. Illus. by E.B. Lewis. 2001. New York: Little, Brown Books for Young Readers.

I Love My Hair tells an authentic story of a young Black girl getting her hair styled by her mother. The mother takes readers on an imaginative journey of comparing hair styling to yarn being spun in a spinning wheel and crops being planted in rows in a garden as she explains the versatility and beauty of afro-textured hair to her daughter. The daughter expresses the joy she experiences from her hair and celebrates it with a beautiful metaphor of her afro style being free and round as the Earth in our solar system.

Make It Math! Bead Patterns. A common hairstyle among people of African descent is to wear braided hair adorned with beads. In *I Love My Hair*, Keyana delights in hearing her beads clink as she walks about. Early childhood educators can use this iconic hair accessory as a math manipulative for patterning: provide children with a doll and hair beads (such as pony beads) of different colors or sizes, and encourage children to practice stringing on the beads to make patterns. This bead pattern activity also supports the development of fine motor skills.

Princess Hair

by Sharee Miller. 2018. New York: Little, Brown Books for Young Readers.

This rhyming book celebrates different natural hairstyles for children with afro-textured hair. The narrator describes the diverse hairstyles appropriate for a princess to wear under their crown as they do things they love and as they love their hair. From kinks to Bantu Knots to blowouts, each style is suitable for a princess.

Make It Math! Matching Numerals and Afro Puffs. One of the featured hairstyles in *Princess Hair* is afro puffs (afro-textured hair sectioned into ponytails). After reading the book together, teachers can prompt children to replicate this hair style using classroom dolls with tightly coiled hair. Hand out numeral cards to each child based on their counting skill level (if you don't have any on hand, you can make your own using index cards), and ask them to match the quantity of afro puffs on the dolls with the number on their cards. If there are a limited number of dolls with tightly coiled hair available, print pictures of each style and present them to children with the numeral cards. These photos can be used later to discuss human differences in a social studies unit, to diversify the physical space of the classroom through displays, or to use for other math activities such as patterning or sorting.

Don't Touch My Hair

by Sharee Miller. 2019. New York: Little, Brown Books for Young Readers.

Aria, a Black child, loves her hair but does not like it when people touch it without her permission. After finally setting a personal boundary by yelling "Don't touch my hair!" to all who can hear as she is walking through town, she gets to enjoy her free-flowing afro-textured hair without having to worry about unwanted touches. Friends and community members begin asking to touch her hair and accepting her response, rather than reaching in to touch it without her permission as they did before.

Make It Math! Roll the Dice/Find the Matching Hands. In *Don't Touch My Hair*, Aria describes the many hands trying to touch her hair. In this math activity, provide children with dice and pictures of hands holding up fingers to show quantities ranging from one to five. Children will roll their number die, then look for the number of fingers that match. For example, if a child rolls four, they will search for the hand holding up four fingers. If they roll a six, children might find ways to match different finger values that add up to six, such as four and two fingers or five and one fingers. This matching activity can also celebrate dark skin tones if the pictures of the fingers include dark skin tones and the hands are turned where the children can see the hue of the skin rather than simply the palm.

For added engagement, early childhood educators can use pictures of the hands of children in the classroom. Children will enjoy trying to guess whose hands they are matching with their dice. As the activity comes to an end, remind children of the importance of getting permission before touching people's bodies.

All the Colors We Are: The Story of How We Get Our Skin Color/ Todos los colores de nuestra piel: The Story of How We Get Our Skin Color/La historia de por qué tenemos diferentes colores de piel

by Katie Kissinger. 2014. St. Paul, Minnesota: Redleaf Press.

This informational text features photographs of real people. Using child-friendly language, Kissinger explains the scientific and historical reasoning for differences in skin color. The narrator explains that skin color comes from three sources: our ancestors, the sun, and melanin (the pigment that makes skin a certain color).

Make It Math! Color Match Recipe Cards.
A commonly used diversity activity in early childhood programs is to have children mix paint to find their exact skin color. Teachers can extend this art activity into a math activity focused on quantity, counting, and writing numerals by having children create recipe cards as they make their own unique shade. Provide children with spoons, a bowl, and paints in various skin-tone colors. Help children count and document the number of spoonfuls of each color they use to make their unique color. Laminate these recipe cards for children to use throughout the year to create the shade that matches their own skin color and their classmates'.

TONI STURDIVANT, PhD, is vice president of early education at Camp Fire First Texas.

CHAPTER 20

Meaningful Talk

The Importance of Using Sophisticated Language at Preschool

Tracy Weippert

In a multiage preschool classroom, children gather at a table where a plastic terrarium serves as a worm habitat. They cover the table with sandpaper and bits of grass, then remove a worm from its home to feed it.

"It's crawling!"

"It's slithery. Our snake did that."

"Catch it 'fore it gets 'way!"

"It won't get away. It's trying to get the fruit. It's hungry; that's why we gave it melon."

This nature study gave the children opportunities to observe the actions of live worms, to read books, to talk with teachers and classmates about knowledge gained and new questions to explore, and to form hypotheses regarding what their worms might need to survive. These kinds of conversations and interactions are laced with language-supporting activities, including activities that promote vocabulary and world knowledge accumulation—some of the key building blocks of reading comprehension.

Vocabulary Matters

If left to their own devices, almost all children growing up in language-rich social environments will automatically learn a lot of words. However, incidental word learning alone is not enough to promote success in later grades. Children also need many well-crafted opportunities to learn sophisticated vocabulary that will enable them to think, talk, and write about academic topics—including worms, habitats, nutrients, and more.

Studies have found that preschoolers' vocabulary knowledge—particularly the words that they understand (*receptive vocabulary*) and use appropriately (*expressive vocabulary*)—predicts their reading comprehension development in early elementary school (e.g., Burchinal et al. 2016; Dickinson & Porche 2011). Some studies suggest that at kindergarten entry, children who had smaller and less sophisticated vocabularies (e.g., those who knew fewer academic words related to content areas, such as *mist* for science or *cube* for math) struggled more with listening and reading comprehension; they also had less vocabulary growth in kindergarten and beyond (e.g., Durham et al. 2007; Neuman 2011; Wasik & Hindman 2014). This has important long-term consequences.

Sophisticated vocabulary allows children to understand advanced texts, which offers increased learning opportunities and even more vocabulary growth. A sizeable, academic vocabulary provides significant advantages that tend to keep growing as children progress through school. Even more important, a sizeable, academic vocabulary is something that preschool teachers can help virtually all children develop!

 Intentionally focusing on sophisticated vocabulary regardless of children's economic, cultural, or linguistic backgrounds promotes equity by giving all children the necessary background information to be successful academically.

Enhancing Vocabulary Development

Here are several strategies you can use throughout the day to boost children's vocabulary knowledge—and set them on a path to develop and learn strong language and literacy skills.

Read Frequently

› **Read with children daily.** Find different texts that reflect the "Goldilocks principle": just the right amount of new words mixed with familiar ones. Observing children closely will help you determine what is the right amount; notice when the children are engaged or seem confused, and adjust accordingly (Bennett-Armistead, Duke, & Moses 2005). Also, share texts that have a theme, a topic, or an idea in common: reading many different books (and other texts) will teach children new, sophisticated words in relation to big ideas. Encourage children to notice themes (and the words associated with them) and to make connections between books and their lives.

› **Reread and talk about favorite books.** Multiple exposures to a text aid in children's comprehension. Encourage the retelling of stories or dramatic play episodes in which children depict story events. Promote the use of sophisticated vocabulary from the story as a part of these activities. For example, children retelling a story about butterfly life cycles could be encouraged to use terms such as *cocoon* or *chrysalis* in their retelling or dramatic play event.

› **Offer a wide variety of fiction and nonfiction texts**—including interactive, educational media—that children find interesting and motivating, that reflect their identities, and that connect to a common theme or idea. Provide classics in addition to texts tied to topics that children are curious about and are investigating, ensuring that similar words and ideas overlap in these varied texts.

› **Teach new and sophisticated words during read-alouds.** Before reading a book aloud, review it for words that may be unfamiliar to children and will be important for understanding the story or topic. These are good words to target, spending time talking about and showing what these words mean when you encounter them while reading aloud. Be sure to follow up after the read-aloud to keep the word-learning going. See the sidebar below for ideas on how to make your read-alouds more interactive.

The Benefits of Interactive Read-Alouds

Interactive read-alouds, which are a staple of many classrooms and homes, are a great way to build children's academic vocabularies, among other key early literacy and language skills. They engage children and teachers (or family members) in sharing quality children's books by discussing and questioning the ideas and themes in fiction and nonfiction texts. Effective interactive read-alouds include high-quality talk, such as using complete sentences and sophisticated vocabulary; avoiding "baby talk"; asking open-ended questions to probe children's ideas; expanding on children's comments by adding ideas or information; and restating children's thoughts in complete sentences using standard academic English.

In addition, effective interactive read-alouds embed vocabulary instruction to support children's overall language and literacy growth. When you intentionally use high-quality talk during interactive read-alouds, you give children opportunities to learn the meaning of new words. You can give visual (an illustration) and verbal (the text and your explanation of it) clues about a word's meaning. Through this reading, questioning, and discussing, you create vocabulary-building experiences that mix incidental learning and explicit teaching. The interaction is crucial: merely reading a text aloud to children does very little for the development of vocabulary skills. Children need opportunities to engage with words in texts in a supportive environment and with intentional instruction.

Use and Encourage Sophisticated and Academic Language

> **Provide natural and authentic conversational opportunities to foster sophisticated language use** by pairing books with activities and explorations (such as after a read-aloud). Intentionally say words that are less common in everyday situations and offer child-friendly definitions as needed. The worm *terrarium* and related books and discussions in the opening vignette are a great example! Taking advantage of natural openings to teach new vocabulary words is a way to challenge children just beyond their current level of knowledge.

> **Foster *word consciousness* (a curiosity about words) throughout the day.** You can model an interest in words by pointing out when you come across a word you don't know, and you can recognize and reinforce when children notice and ask about a word.

> **Introduce advanced topics.** When children are immersed in a topic for several weeks, they develop understanding, knowledge, and vocabulary that enable them to think about and discuss the more advanced aspects of those topics. With time and support, children appreciate conversations on thoughtful issues and themes.

> **Promote *disciplinary vocabulary.*** Young children can learn new and challenging words that are important or specific to a content area through texts, lessons, and conversations, whether about nature, the arts, mathematics, technology, or any topic they find engaging and motivating. Use multiple modes (pictures, sounds, gestures, print) to help children learn the meaning of content-specific words.

> **Encourage dramatic play.** Children use significant language skills during episodes of dramatic play, including rehearsing vocabulary words that they will later use in other situations. Provide props that will encourage specific language (for example, play tools and wood scraps to encourage building and construction play or eye charts; eyeglasses frames, lab coats, and a pointer for optometrist play) to enable children to rehearse complex themes and ideas. By providing vocabulary targeted props during dramatic play, you can support children in using their home languages as they learn important academic vocabulary.

Preschoolers are capable of participating in intense and thoughtful conversations. The more you engage them in meaningful talk using sophisticated vocabulary, the more they will benefit!

TRACY WEIPPERT, PhD, was formerly a teacher educator.

CHAPTER 21

Using Nature Contact to Support Children Under Stress

Becky L. DelVecchio, Susan Ferguson, and Wesley Knapp

All children experience stress at one time or another, and effective early childhood programs have people, strategies, and systems in place to guide them through stressful situations and emotions. As adults working in the field of early childhood education, we have the responsibility to help children develop positive ways to manage a variety of emotions and reactions to stressful events in their lives. To do so, we can think both widely and creatively to tap into and share tools and resources, including in nature.

Contact with nature can help mitigate the negative effects of stress and can help boost resilience across one's lifespan (Chawla 2015). Through nature-based encounters, we can provide children with strategies to use while they are in our care and beyond. Indeed, by using readily available natural materials or environments, these techniques have the added benefit of being accessible indoors or out, at home or away, and within or outside of early learning programs.

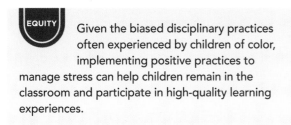

EQUITY Given the biased disciplinary practices often experienced by children of color, implementing positive practices to manage stress can help children remain in the classroom and participate in high-quality learning experiences.

In this chapter, we share several scenarios depicting children experiencing stress in two different classroom settings. After each one, we describe nature-based strategies that an early childhood educator used to offer support and encourage resilience in those children.

Stressful Situations and Nature-Based Supports

> Three-year-old Lenny wants to play with Sandeep. He chooses a spot to play near Sandeep, looks over at him several times, and offers toys to Sandeep three times. Sandeep does not return any of Lenny's social overtures. When asked by his teacher, Mr. Ortega, if he wants to play with Lenny, Sandeep shouts no. When Lenny hears this, he becomes increasingly anxious and desperate for the attention of his classmate and shouts loudly, "No! No! No!"

Lenny was trying, unsuccessfully, to connect with another child. Although each of his and Sandeep's behaviors were appropriate given the situation, Lenny experienced stress. Lenny became overwhelmed with his "big" emotions and needed the support of his teacher to help him cope with them. To support Lenny, Mr. Ortega took several steps, including incorporating natural objects into the support he offered.

To begin, Mr. Ortega was careful to encourage Lenny's independence while giving him the time and space he needed to feel better. For example, Mr. Ortega verbally described Lenny's feelings and actions, so he could begin to do the same. He said, "Lenny, you are upset. You were yelling when Sandeep did not want to play with you. That must have felt very hard to hear. I can help you find a way to feel better. I remember that you like the fish."

Then, Mr. Ortega offered Lenny the responsibility of a "very important classroom job." That job was to feed the class pet, a fish, and to check that the water pump was still running. While Lenny was feeding the fish, he and Mr. Ortega observed and chatted about the aquatic plants that were anchored underneath the rocks, which grew upward and swayed with the movement of the water.

Finally, Mr. Ortega invited Lenny to further extend the experience by taking pictures with the classroom camera for the art wall. Lenny could take as many photos of the fish as he liked. Later, he chose one to print and display for his classmates to enjoy.

Mr. Ortega took Lenny's social and emotional development quite seriously, as evidenced by his efforts to support Lenny. The teacher's sustained commitment to this goal illustrates the importance of the social and emotional domain. Ultimately, feeding, observing, and photographing the class fish helped Lenny to focus on something other than the attention he was not receiving from his classmate. It redirected his energy to another task, and it helped mitigate his feelings of disappointment or anxiety by fostering his sense of independence. Over time, and with similar supports, Lenny will be able to redirect his energy more efficiently when he is feeling stressed.

> Four-year-old Fabiola misses her family when she is at school. She stays near her teacher, Ms. Paul; her voice shakes; and she is often close to tears. She does not play. Instead, she primarily clings to Ms. Paul as she watches the other children play and engage in activities.

Fabiola was struggling with separating from her family and the feelings of missing them throughout the day. Ms. Paul noticed that when she became involved in a specific task, especially one with concrete objects, Fabiola demonstrated fewer anxious emotions and behaviors. Ms. Paul started to plan nature-based activities to offer Fabiola upon her arrival each morning.

For example, Ms. Paul began with a nature-based scavenger hunt for Fabiola to complete. The scavenger hunt included items that Fabiola could find on the playground or around the school building. Fabiola then presented the items to her family at pickup time. Ms. Paul made sure to include a variety of natural objects with different characteristics: some were soft plants like lambs-ears and pussy willows; some were spiky like pinecones, burdocks, and cacti; some were aromatic like roses, mint, and lavender; and some even liked to hide in cracks like mosses and lichens. Several days after Ms. Paul implemented this strategy, she noticed Fabiola making scavenger hunts for other children.

Fabiola's introduction to natural materials and her ensuing fascination with finding them helped to reduce her stress and to demonstrate resilience. She took on a leadership role in the classroom while sharing one of her passions with other children. Building these positive connections with others, through her own connection to nature, aided Fabiola in feeling more in control of herself and her environment.

> Five-year-old Maya is attending an early learning program during the COVID-19 pandemic. She often becomes angry during the day. For example, her school requires social distancing when children do not wear face masks, and if her parents do not pack her favorite mask, Maya refuses to wear one altogether. This causes her to have to play in one-person spots away from the other children, which frustrates Maya further.

Maya's teacher, Mr. Ortega, noticed that several children needed mask breaks throughout the day. Wearing masks was challenging for some children, and the requirement to wear them caused stress for both children and teachers. To alleviate the isolation of the one-person play spots, Mr. Ortega created a classroom garden just outside the classroom door, where mask breaks were allowed. Although the area outside the school was mostly paved, the teacher brought in large pots and potting soil for children to use for gardening. Mr. Ortega planned several adult-directed planting activities that ensured the plants would grow, but Maya's favorite part of outdoor gardening was the independent garden pots. There, children planted and nurtured whatever they liked in their own pots. Maya planted morning glories and sunflowers, which grew quickly. Maya's frustration and anger eased because she had a task that gave her some control and agency, helped her redirect her focus, and enabled her to feel more independent while connecting with nature, a pastime that she could access at home, at school, and in most other environments.

> On the playground, 4-year-old Rosalie struggles with body coordination during play. For example, she often crashes her scooter into the shed and fence as she rides. Today, she slides headfirst down the large slide and bumps into other children who are near her. The other children decide to leave their play with Rosalie and play somewhere else. This is not the first time this has happened. Other children try to play with her, but when she starts to get "too crashy," they seek other activities without her. Rosalie expresses stress and hurt feelings when they do.

Rosalie loved to climb. Although the trees around them were not conducive to safe climbing, Ms. Paul

recommended that she try to "grip and hold" a tree in their playground area. In this activity, Rosalie put her arms around a large tree, like a hug. Then she (magically!) lifted her feet off the ground. The other children were impressed and wanted to try too. Rosalie found an activity that helped her feel more in control of her body, that was easily accessible, and that other children could do with her. This helped Rosalie feel more accepting of her own abilities and acknowledge the limits set for her at school.

EQUITY Providing the right support for a particular child, rather than using a one-size-fits-all approach to guidance, is an important equitable practice.

BECKY L. DELVECCHIO, PhD, is a longtime early childhood educator and adjunct faculty member.

SUSAN FERGUSON, MEd, PMC, is a preschool teacher at the Wellesley College Child Study Center in Wellesley, Massachusetts.

WESLEY KNAPP works as the chief botanist for NatureServe, a leading conservation nonprofit based in Arlington, Virginia.

Conclusion

NAEYC's 2020 position statement on developmentally appropriate practice states, "Early childhood educators . . . support *all* children's learning by recognizing each child as a unique individual with assets and strengths to contribute to the early childhood education learning environment" (7). Teachers can use nature contact to connect to each child's strengths and build the child's recognition and regulation of the stressful feelings they may experience in a moment and over time. These stress management strategies do not require special materials that can only be found in the classroom. Rather, they make use of natural materials that children can access in most environments. This is a critical feature of helping children develop coping strategies that can be internalized and accessed throughout their lives, no matter the environments and situations in which they find themselves.

CHAPTER 22

Timing Is Everything

Understanding the Importance of Timing, Length, and Sequence of Activities

Monica Lesperance

Every classroom has its own daily schedule and routines: morning circle, centers time, snack, outdoor play, and so on. You probably have a schedule clearly posted for visitors and one in picture format for children to see. Most days you follow it closely—or at least you try to! But have you ever considered how the daily schedule impacts the behavior of the children in your classroom?

Classroom Environments: Space and Time Both Matter

Classroom environments influence the way children behave. From the acoustics (how a room's shape or size impacts being able to hear sounds clearly) and lighting to the furniture layout and organization, the *physical environment* affects how children behave and learn. The timing, length, and sequence of activities—sometimes referred to as the *temporal environment*—also influence children's behavior and learning.

You change the classroom setup throughout the year, tweaking it to create a more comfortable and functional space for you and the children. Adjusting the schedule can be more challenging, though, since there are factors you can't control. Arrival and departure times, shared outdoor space, and your program's curricular expectations all need to be considered.

The ideal amount of time to allocate to different activities depends on the ages and developmental range of the children in the classroom, as well as the learning goals. For example, we might expect a typical fifth-grade student to sit at a desk and stay

engaged in a writing activity for up to 30 minutes. But asking a preschooler to do the same is not developmentally appropriate and would certainly lead to some behaviors that an educator finds challenging! Expectations for younger children are different, and the classroom schedule and routines should reflect that.

In a preschool setting, there are likely children at various levels of development, including some with delays or disabilities and those who are dual language learners. Having a schedule that considers the development and needs of all children is key in creating an inclusive environment where all children can thrive.

How Do You Know if Your Schedule Is Working?

Sometimes it's obvious that the timing of specific activities leads to challenging behaviors. For example, if your schedule calls for a late lunch and many of the children become easily frustrated during activities right before they eat, you might add a snack break into the schedule. Other times, it's not so clear that the schedule is the issue.

If you notice more challenging behaviors at certain times of the day or during certain activities, it might be time to modify the schedule. Here are some things to consider.

Length of Structured Activities

Children's attention spans vary depending on their ages, interests, and development (and also depending on more day-to-day factors, like whether they got enough sleep the night before). A long circle time or extended read-aloud may cause some children to become disruptive. When children have exhausted their focus on one activity, they often begin to fidget, make disruptive noises, or get up and walk away! Their behavior tells you that they've had enough.

When one child behaves this way, consider an individual accommodation, such as providing an alternative, quiet activity for that child. But when several children are having trouble paying attention or remaining engaged—and a simple reminder or redirection doesn't help—consider ways to alter your schedule:

> Shorten the activity by a few minutes.

> Incorporate more movement or sensory breaks into activities. (A sensory break is a short pause from an activity that includes brief movement or another physical activity to help children refocus. Examples include deep breathing and stretching, jumping jacks, hopping on one foot, dancing, finger games, and squeezing stress balls.)

> Add breaks for calming and focusing, such as everyone standing up to stretch and taking three deep breaths.

 Play promotes self-regulation, which helps children engage in nonpreferred tasks for an extended time. Given the necessity of play for children's development, educators must plan ample amounts of time for play. In addition, evidence suggests that some Black and Latinx children are not provided as much time for play as White children; educators working with these populations should advocate for the right and need for *all* children to play.

Transitions Between Activities

Ah, transitions. For many children (and teachers!) these are the most challenging times of day. Long transitions or too many transitions can lead to disruptive behaviors. Even within an activity, too many transitions can be difficult for some children—particularly those with developmental delays or disabilities. If you notice that a child's challenging behavior occurs mostly during transitions, try modifying or providing extra support during those times:

> **Allow the child to transition first.** If you know it takes Shaun longer than others to put on his coat, give him extra time to get started before the rest of the group lines up.

> **Add structure to transitions.** If Mara has trouble keeping her hands and body safe while waiting for the class to line up, give her a job, such as holding the teacher's coat or holding the door for her classmates, so she has less idle time.

> **Cut down on transitions.** Do you have to walk the whole group to the bathroom for a break? Or can you send a few children at a time with a classroom assistant? Find places in your schedule where you can streamline activities so there are fewer transitions during the day.

Sequence of Events

The time of day when activities take place can also impact children's behavior. Different classroom activities require different levels of attention and energy. Asking a child to do a high-attention task just before lunch or at the end of the day could result in resistance, disengagement, or disruptive behaviors. Build in extra support for children by thinking strategically about their day:

> Provide a balance of teacher- and child-directed activities. Sustaining attention during circle or story time takes a lot of effort for preschool children! They have to keep their bodies still, focus on the speaker, and process what they see and hear. These activities are appropriate and beneficial for children, but they should be kept short, with most of the classroom time devoted to active play, interactions with peers and adults, and exploration. A schedule that includes back-to-back circle, story time, and teacher-directed group activities can be too much for many preschoolers to manage. Alternating free- or guided-play activities with teacher-directed, large-group activities gives children a chance to recharge and promotes their development and learning.

> Build in quiet time to transition children from high-energy activities. It takes a while for young children to calm their bodies after running outside or playing an active game. Try an age-appropriate mindfulness activity, like a few simple child yoga poses. Or ask children to sit with their legs crossed and shrug their shoulders up and down. This helps them prepare to shift their focus to a new activity.

> Plan for children with specific needs. Make sure there are ways for children with physical or medical conditions that affect their energy levels to participate in high-energy activities. You might schedule activities at times when those children have the most energy.

> Allow children to take breaks. When frustration levels start to rise, give children the option of taking a break. Sometimes getting a drink of water or taking a short walk down the hallway is enough to help a young child get back on track. Some children benefit from spending a few minutes talking one-to-one with an adult or drawing a picture to express their feelings.

Consider implementing an individual schedule for children who need more time, fewer transitions, or a different order of activities. You might have a child who entered your program midyear or a child with a disability who is not ready to sit for a full story time, even with accommodations like sitting on a special seat cushion or holding a fidget (squishy ball or weighted stuffed animal). This child may need a more individualized schedule that includes a sensory break after five minutes of focusing so that they are able to sustain attention for longer periods of time.

Conclusion

Once you start looking at the schedule through the lens of children's behavior, you'll see places where small changes can have a big impact on children's engagement.

MONICA LESPERANCE is the deputy director of the DC Special Education Cooperative in Washington, DC, where she developed the INCLUDE DC teacher training program.

Planning and Implementing an Engaging Curriculum to Achieve Meaningful Goals

RECOMMENDATIONS FROM THE DAP POSITION STATEMENT

The curriculum consists of the plans for the learning experiences through which children acquire knowledge, skills, abilities, and understanding. Implementing a curriculum always yields outcomes of some kind—but which outcomes those are and how a program achieves them are critical. In developmentally appropriate practice, the curriculum helps young children achieve goals that are meaningful because they are culturally and linguistically responsive and developmentally and educationally significant. The curriculum does this through learning experiences that reflect what is known about young children in general and about each child in particular.

Learning through play is a central component of curriculum. . . . A well-designed developmentally and culturally relevant curriculum avoids and counters cultural or individual bias or stereotypes and fosters a positive learning disposition in each area of the curriculum and in each child.

Our center began a Seeds of Change Initiative to raise awareness about the health crisis affecting our local and global communities and to build agency among the children. Children researched and actively contributed to the creation of practical solutions to the challenges. We started an edible indoor garden to supplement the nutritional and physical needs of our community. As the children learned about their community and themselves through themes such as "My Community and Me" and "5 Senses," they expanded their knowledge and skills by learning how fresh food is planted, grown, cultivated, distributed, and prepared. They also

learned about their place within a local and global community. (From "Never Too Young to Champion a Cause: Supporting Positive Identity Development Through Social Justice Curriculum in Preschool," page 104)

The above excerpt from a chapter in this section shows how educators can create plans that help children reach "desired goals that are important for young children's development and learning in general and culturally and linguistically responsive to children in particular" (NAEYC 2020, 25). Curriculum planning is an important part of how educators make sure they address key concepts and skills using strategies that can maximize children's engagement and progress.

When preschool teachers know and understand the children, their families, and their cultural backgrounds, they can use and adapt the curriculum as a framework for relevant teaching. The goal is to build on knowledge that diverse children bring with them into the preschool classroom to lead children to new understandings and abilities that they might not have arrived at without the support of a well-planned and responsive curriculum. The fourth edition of *Developmentally Appropriate Practice* states that "when coupled with engaging instruction, a culturally and linguistically responsive curriculum helps teachers and children achieve success and develop as confident learners" (Masterson 2022, 215).

Rather than rigidly follow the adopted curriculum, intentional preschool teachers make adjustments and plans that fit the interests and experiences of the actual preschoolers in the classroom. Teachers facilitate learning and development in all domains and subject areas while providing the necessary supports for each child. Intentional teachers do all this actively and thoughtfully as they use the curriculum as a guide in ways that are responsive to the specific children they teach.

The curriculum may look different depending on a program's philosophy; however, all developmentally appropriate curricula and experiences share certain commonalities:

- Responsive goals have been identified and articulated.
- The curriculum includes the identified goals and accounts for them within all learning domains and subject areas.
- The curriculum framework is used by educators to plan for learning and development.
- Educators are intentional about making connections between the curriculum and the lives of the children.
- Educators collaborate with educators from other age groups to ensure continuity across ages and grades.
- All age groups have a written curriculum in place. (NAEYC 2020)

While preschool teachers may not be able to choose the program's curriculum, they use it as a framework to ensure that all learning goals are covered in a deliberate matter. With their knowledge of children and families, they make additions and modifications as necessary to intentionally center the lives of the children, ensuring that learning activities are culturally and linguistically relevant. In addition, where possible, preschool educators seek to collaborate with toddler and kindergarten teachers to help ensure that, at each step, learning goals are identified and properly addressed for each child.

Part 5 illustrates thoughtful curriculum planning across content areas by diverse educators in a range of settings. The educators create environments and plan experiences that consider individual differences, building on each child's culture, home language, experiences, and other assets and characteristics The result is joyful, engaged learning.

READ AND REFLECT

As you read the chapters in this section, consider and evaluate your own classroom practices using these reflection questions.

"Never Too Young to Champion a Cause: Supporting Positive Identity Development Through Social Justice Curriculum in Preschool" illustrates that preschoolers can learn about and act on local and global issues while gaining essential knowledge and skills across the curriculum. These educators "make meaningful connections a priority in the learning experiences they provide each child" (NAEYC 2020, 27). **Consider:** How could you plan a curriculum that involves multiple learning areas, as the authors describe in this chapter?

In "Diverse Children, Uniform Standards: Using Early Learning and Development Standards in Multicultural Classrooms," the educators illustrate how to carefully examine early learning and development standards with a critical eye to establish meaningful goals for children's development and learning. They emphasize ensuring that plans are culturally and linguistically responsive to the children in the classroom. **Consider:** How can you modify preexisting curricula to make room for joy (if it is not present) and to reflect the lived experiences of the children in your classroom?

"Preschool in the Park: Place-Based Learning in Unexpected Spaces" demonstrates how thoughtful curriculum planning can take place in joyful, play-based outdoor settings and provide integrated learning experiences in content areas such as math, literacy, and science. Such integrated learning is a key practice in developmentally appropriate curriculum planning. **Consider:** What types of learning experiences could occur in your outdoor spaces?

"Metamorphosis: Life Cycle in a Box" looks at the importance of including in-depth, hands-on learning experiences in the curriculum to build "on ideas and experiences that have meaning in the children's lives and are likely to interest them" (NAEYC 2020, 27). The approach described also provides a tangible anchor to the learning to support dual language learners. **Consider:** What are other opportunities for tangible and tactile learning in your classroom?

"Listen to What We Hear: Developing Community Responsive Listening Centers" describes how educators invited family and community members to record a story or song in their home languages as a way to make the program's listening centers better reflect the children and families attending the program. These educators effectively planned "curriculum experiences to build on the funds of knowledge of each child, family, and community in order to offer culturally and linguistically sustaining learning experiences" (NAEYC 2020, 27). **Consider:** In what ways can you involve the community in the education of the preschoolers in your setting?

"Walk With Us: Indigenous Approaches to Developmentally Appropriate Practice" describes how preschool educators can consider the wealth and depth of knowledge and ways of being that Indigenous children of the Americas bring into the classroom. Making meaningful connections between the learning and the lives of children is an essential practice (NAEYC 2020). **Consider:** How can you use intentional curriculum planning to build on the children's diverse cultural and linguistic strengths?

CHAPTER 23

Never Too Young to Champion a Cause

Supporting Positive Identity Development Through Social Justice Curriculum in Preschool

Veronica Benavides, Roxanne Ledda, and Maimuna Mohammed

At the Garden of Learning and Discovery Pre-K Center in Highbridge, Bronx, we have chosen to focus on instilling a sense of social responsibility and advocacy into our teaching to enhance children's learning and development. Our belief is that we must go beyond the current status quo to drastically change outcomes for our most marginalized children; we also believe that our children are never too young to champion a cause. Because disparities in school performance can often be traced back to early childhood, growing appreciably during the primary and middle school years (Grodsky et al. 2017), we embraced a pedagogical stance that focuses on social justice, that is knowledge rich, and that promotes positive identity development. It is leading to fundamental changes within the district, which "[s]ince 2010 . . . has been the poorest . . . House district in the country" (Santiago 2019).

In this chapter, we provide a look into our community and the contexts in which young children are growing and learning. Then, we describe our journey toward social justice advocacy and the process through which we developed a knowledge-rich curriculum to support positive identity development of our children and our beloved Highbridge community.

The Highbridge Community

In 2015, a New York City mayoral initiative led to more than triple the amount of prekindergarten spots available to NYC students and families. To meet this need, the Garden of Learning and Discovery Pre-K Center opened its doors as the sole Community School District 9 stand-alone center in Highbridge, Bronx. Highbridge is located in NYC Community District 4, and its residents are 96 percent families of color. While our community contends with a plethora of long-standing, systemic issues impacting quality of living (high levels of homelessness, minimal quality nutritional sources, and increased levels of disease), we found strength in concentrating on our communal cultures that are inclusive of resiliency and social capital. From a strengths-based perspective, we were able to "challenge inequity and disrupt unfair circumstances and situations" (Howard 2018, 28). We understood that we could not ameliorate all these structural inequities immediately, but we came to the conclusion that promoting justice and knowledge in our youngest learners (and ourselves) could lead to lasting and deep community engagement, empowerment, and evolution.

Our Journey into a Social Justice and Knowledge-Rich Curriculum

Our journey began in the fall of 2018, when the Garden of Learning and Discovery center partnered with the Center on Culture, Race & Equity (CCRE) at Bank Street College of Education. The CCRE and our staff embarked on a yearlong professional development series that guided our staff's learning about knowledge-rich curriculum, families as partners, culturally responsive practices, and children's identity development. This work resulted in our staff having a research-informed plan to engage children and families in a critical discussion about social justice and advocacy. (For additional ways to engage in professional development around diversity and equity, see the chapters in Part 6.)

Knowledge-Rich Curriculum

In exploring aspects of knowledge-rich curriculum, we examined the interdependent relationship between concepts, content, knowledge, and skills. For example, we looked at how a lesson on water could be used to build knowledge of history, science, geography, art, literacy, social justice, and music. Through intentional curriculum mapping and careful planning of activities like read-alouds, we learned to support the children in deepening their critical thinking skills and knowledge base.

 The knowledge-rich approach to curriculum planning described here also uses an integrated learning approach, supporting meaningful connections between new learning, the children's lives, and various content areas. The integrated approach to curriculum planning is an important component of developmentally appropriate practice.

In exploring the possibilities of a knowledge-rich curriculum, we also discussed the importance of teaching subject knowledge that foregrounds social justice. The knowledge we introduce to children should be powerful, equipping children to liberate themselves. According to Robertson (2016), "A radical curriculum would be knowledge-rich, and would leave its students empowered by the knowledge they were taught at school, not perplexed, years later, as to why nobody thought to introduce them to it while they were at school."

Families as Partners

As we participated in this professional development, we gained insights into what the research shows about positive, reciprocal partnerships with families. We learned the following:

> Authentic home-school partnerships result in better student performance, healthier behavior, fewer behavior problems, and higher levels of enjoyment in school (The Fatherhood Project 2015).

> Authentic family engagement is a cornerstone of culturally responsive teaching (Bennett et al. 2018).

Equipped with this perspective, Garden of Learning and Discovery committed to enhancing an already-strong foundation of family engagement. We sought to engage the families of the children and the entire Highbridge community that surrounds and supports our youngest learners.

Culturally Responsive Practices

Our yearlong study also revealed key elements of culturally responsive practices:

> Using families' funds of knowledge as educational assets to help children learn (Gonzalez 2010). Integrating funds of knowledge, or the cultural assets of children's home lives, into school-based learning experiences means understanding and applying a strengths-based lens to each child and their family. This approach can enhance educators' efforts to engage and empower families.

> Partnering with local organizations devoted to social justice initiatives that serve the communities of children and their families in specific ways. These organizations can help to target issues and promote solutions that are in conjunction with the desires, perspectives, and assets of the community.

> Using curriculum that places importance on text that draws from minoritized cultural capitals can be used to empower children by allowing them to express themselves in ways that align with their current ways of being and knowing (Goldenberg 2014).

According to Robin DiAngelo (2016), "*Minoritized* [refers to] a social group that is devalued in society. This devaluing encompasses how the group is represented, what degree of access to resources it is granted, and how the unequal access is rationalized. The term *minoritized* (rather than *minority*) is used to indicate that the group's lower position is a function of active socially constructed dynamics, rather than its numbers in society" (82).

To deeply understand and internalize the tenets of culturally responsive practice, we began by exploring our own cultural practices and norms, including from "the positions of privilege we occupy—such as being White, having grown up in an economically comfortable household, speaking Mainstream American English, being heterosexual, or being Christian" (Souto-Manning 2013, 12). Then we could more deeply explore how our own upbringings and experiences influence the classroom and school climate, the content taught, and the methods used at our center. Certain research helped guide us to examine the impact of White middle-class norms on school culture and standards, for example:

> When students of color are rewarded (or sometimes chastised) for conformity to white norms and standards, whiteness becomes an alienable property. This can specifically be seen in what is often referred to as students "acting white," or in depictions of Asian Americans as "model minorities," because they adhere to an array of characteristics endorsed by white society and attributed to whiteness." (Rector-Aranda 2016, 7)

Too often, schools have sought to prepare students for the "real world," stripping away cultural assets that could support children in navigating and thriving in life (a second language or code-switching). In examining the origins and functions of typical academic standards for "success," we peeled back the layers of deeply ingrained schoolwide cultural beliefs and sought to create a learning environment that nurtured and built upon the existing cultural assets of our children and families.

Identity Development in Early Childhood

Finally, our yearlong professional development included research about identity development. The following is some of what we learned:

> Children develop conceptions of race at a young age, beginning with knowledge of color categories, to a conceptual awareness of racial categories, to ultimately an awareness of group identity (Farago, Davidson, & Byrd 2019).

> Understanding oneself is inexplicably tied to understanding where one fits into a group (Baldwin, Brown, & Hopkins 1991).

> The concept of "stereotype threat" is about "being at risk of confirming, as a self-characteristic, a negative stereotype about one's group" (Steele & Aronson 1995, 797) and about its impact on the academic performance of students of color. For example, the threat that the judgments of others or their own actions would negatively stereotype them resulted in underperformance of Black participants taking a standardized test.

> Children as young as 5 years of age are susceptible to stereotype threat—predicting, for example, that an Asian student would outperform a White student on a math exam (Galdi, Cadinu, & Tomasetto 2014).

> A child's sense of self is correlated with the development of cognitive and noncognitive abilities and academic outcomes (Ladson-Billings 2009). Too often, the stereotypes of children from minoritized communities shape their feelings of academic inferiority and uncertainty about whether they belong (Walton & Cohen 2011), adversely impacting their motivation to learn.

While we believed that most of the children at our center felt a sense of belonging, we dove deep into questions about identity and belongingness for children who stood outside of the margins. We wanted to ensure that all of the children felt included, represented, and empowered in our center, including children whose social identities are not typically reflected in school.

Because there are few examples of developmentally appropriate approaches that address all of the above areas of the curriculum and learning environment, Garden of Learning and Discovery decided to develop a school-wide social justice project to support children's positive identity development through a knowledge-rich curriculum. This is outlined below.

Seeds of Change: A Social Justice, Knowledge-Rich Approach

With the understanding that identity-affirming spaces for our children and families contribute to positive child outcomes, the Seeds of Change

Initiative was born. This initiative aimed to build individual and collective agency among children by bringing awareness to the local and global health crisis affecting our community. Children researched and actively contributed to the creation of practical solutions to local and global challenges. Our goal was to positively connect with and support our families and bring wakefulness to micro- and macro-instances of environmental and social injustices. We began by exploring the nutritional deficiencies present within the community of Highbridge, and we decided that we had to address the lack of affordable and nutritional food options.

To launch our Seeds of Change Initiative, we organized a planting party for our community. Over half of the families of our children attended the planting party, and many of them led the organization of the event, supported the event with food donation, offered assistance with program design, and provided translation of materials. Families discussed their own experiences with environmental injustice and learned about ways they could support their children in making a difference. Families and children took their first step in making change by painting pots and planting seeds for the indoor garden. This initiative strengthened a sense of belonging, engagement, and activism among children and families.

DAP Focusing on increasing a sense of belonging is an important step in designing a curricular experience because this sense allows children to feel that they are a part of the learning and not just the recipient of knowledge. Children are more likely to connect with the knowledge and their peers, feel valued, and be excited to learn. (See principle 6 in the developmentally appropriate practice position statement.)

Based on the energy of our launch event, our center inaugurated a wide-ranging edible indoor garden in May 2019 to supplement the nutritional and physical needs of our community. As the children learned about their community and themselves through themes such as "My Community and Me" and "5 Senses," they expanded their knowledge and skills by learning how fresh food is planted, grown, cultivated, distributed, and prepared. They also learned about their place within a local and global community.

Our center understood that we needed to integrate social justice practices into our thematic units throughout the school year. We decided to introduce global issues such as water accessibility and conservation by holding informative sessions for families and participating in a whole-school, reusable-water-bottle challenge. Our desire was to raise awareness about the scarcity of water throughout our international communities, making sure our children knew that there are 3-, 4-, and 5-year-olds who have to walk miles every single day for a luxury our children just had to turn the faucet to obtain. As the children became more knowledgeable of the factors that plagued others, we began to see an increase in the level of empathy shown toward their peers and a desire to bring change to their community as a whole.

The Garden of Learning and Discovery Walk for Water

On June 12, 2019, our center concluded the first year of our social justice, knowledge-rich approach to teaching and learning with a televised Walk for Water. With children, staff, families, and community members, we walked across the High Bridge, a historical aqueduct that once transported water between Manhattan and the Bronx, to bring awareness to the global water crisis. The school partnered with the We Movement, a social activism organization who contends that more than 840 million people worldwide are living without access to clean water and 40 percent of the world's population is affected by water scarcity. As we walked and chanted on that June afternoon, our community supported us with cheerful applause and genuine surprise and delight at the thunder of preschoolers' feet that passed their buildings. At that moment, the children at our center joined the ranks of other young social justice organizers in history. One community member reflected, "The children may be small, but their message is big!" A teacher commented, "The transformation in engagement and agency is clear. Kids are never too young to learn about activism. Our children now know their voices matter and that they can make a difference."

Reflecting Back and Looking Ahead

This process of collective investigation and action allowed us to further support children in critically understanding their identity and how it intersects with the world. They were able to see themselves as authors of their own narratives, empowered to create change in the face of challenge. Looking back at the four key elements learned during our professional development work—knowledge-rich curriculum, authentic family engagement, community partnerships, and understanding the importance of identity—we found that they, indeed, contributed to our success in implementing this social justice advocacy process.

Through this work, we realized that early childhood is the perfect time to begin the establishment of a collective and empathetic mindset. Young children can hold the complexity of two powerful ideas at the same time: sometimes unfair things exist in this world (there is a lack of access to healthy food options in our neighborhood) and we can make a difference and change things (we can build an indoor community garden). As early childhood educators, we need to introduce this work organically, to weave it throughout our instruction and interactions, and to ensure it is developmentally appropriate. A knowledge-rich and action-oriented education lays the foundation for an indestructible and more equitable society.

VERONICA BENAVIDES, EdLD, is passionate about building a more just and equitable world. She is an experienced educator, facilitator, change management strategist, and leadership development specialist.

ROXANNE LEDDA, MSEd, MBA, is the former director of early childhood in NYC CSD 9 and the principal of The Max P.S. 70 elementary school in Bronx, NY. She is committed to the provision of culturally responsive educational experiences and ensuring social justice project-based learning is integrated throughout the elementary school trajectory.

MAIMUNA MOHAMMED, MSEd, is an early childhood educational equity consultant and practitioner. She is an experienced diversity, equity, inclusion, and belonging (DEIB) content developer and facilitator. She has more than 30 years of teaching experience and more than 22 years working as an early childhood educator in community-based programs in New York City.

CHAPTER 24

Diverse Children, Uniform Standards

Using Early Learning and Development Standards in Multicultural Classrooms

Jeanne L. Reid, Catherine Scott-Little, and Sharon Lynn Kagan

Ms. Robinson, a teacher in a pre-K classroom, places a variety of materials on the floor and asks her students to solve a problem. Using any of the materials they want, can they build a bridge across the space between two tables? The purpose of the activity is to foster the children's problem-solving skills, sustained attention, and social and communication skills—areas described in the early learning and development standards Ms. Robinson uses to guide her teaching.

As Ms. Robinson observes the children, she sees that some are building on their own while chatting with their peers about unrelated topics; some are watching their peers and then quietly trying to build their own bridge; and still others are exchanging ideas with peers and then building a bridge together. Are the children who are working together not able to do the task alone, or are they demonstrating collaborative skills? Are the children who are trying to do it alone unable to seek help from their peers, or are they demonstrating individual initiative? Are the children who are chatting about other topics distracted from the task, or are they demonstrating social skills? Are the children who are silent lacking the verbal skills to engage their peers, or are they demonstrating keen attention skills? What can Ms. Robinson learn about the children in this context?

This example demonstrates how thoughtful teachers seek to understand children's behaviors, motivations, approaches to learning, and individual differences. In an early educational environment characterized by youngsters from increasingly diverse backgrounds, teachers know that children differ and seek to tailor their teaching to build on children's behaviors, preferences, prior experiences, and funds of knowledge. Fully understanding children's words

and actions in the classroom, which are shaped by the many assets they bring with them from their unique cultural and family experiences, is a goal that practitioners and scholars are pursuing with new intensity (NASEM 2018).

 The opening vignette and the explanation that follows exemplify curriculum planning that considers each child as an individual. This consideration is essential for meeting the needs of each child in the classroom. See principle 4 of the developmentally appropriate practice position statement.

In addition to understanding children's different approaches to learning, almost all teachers of prekindergartners are expected to follow their state's early learning and development standards (ELDS), which define uniform expectations for what children should know and be able to do before kindergarten. Standards commonly describe, for example, how children should demonstrate initiative in the classroom, how they should focus their attention on tasks and activities, and how they should use verbal skills with their peers. Yet, as we see in Ms. Robinson's class, the ways children express knowledge and skills differ, and these differences may have roots in how children have been socialized to organize their own learning.

This chapter explores one critical dimension of such differences: the role that culture plays in affecting how children learn. In particular, this chapter considers some specific areas of children's learning commonly addressed in ELDS, with an eye toward how they do—and do not—honor cultural diversity.

Many teachers are already aware of the importance of learning about children's and families' social norms, such as the appropriateness of making or avoiding eye contact with adults. But recent research on the cultural nature of early learning has shown that cultural variation affects not only social norms but also how children learn across multiple developmental domains. Significant advances have been made in our understanding of how children from different cultural backgrounds vary in how they focus their attention, organize themselves to learn, and engage in classroom activities. When these advances are not well represented in ELDS, the expectations described in ELDS may disadvantage children from some cultural groups.

The Cultural Nature of Learning and Development

Culture has traditionally been thought of as a set of values, beliefs, norms, and practices shared by a group of people and communicated from one generation to the next. While we often focus attention on the markers of culture that are easy to see, such as food, fashion, holidays, language, crafts, and music, recent scholarship has focused more on the invisible workings of culture as an inherent part of the process of learning and development (Bang 2015; Rogoff, Najafi, & Mejía-Arauz 2014). With this perspective, culture influences not only children's personal preferences and behaviors but also how they think, feel, and learn. Instead of seeing culture as an external influence on children, it is viewed as a process in which children use cultural "tools" or "artifacts" (values, symbols, objects, technologies, words, norms, traditions, schemas, scripts, and practices) to make meaning of their daily experiences. Culture and the development of cognition are therefore inseparable (Sasaki & Kim 2017).

Children learn from their cultural experiences, and each child uses that learning in a unique way to develop a new understanding of the world. In addition, culture is no longer thought of as a label that is rooted in a child's race, ethnicity, or country of origin. Rather, a child's culture is a rich set of practices and tools acquired from the many cultural communities each child navigates (e.g., home, early learning program, neighborhood, doctors' offices, and religious institutions). Although racial and ethnic groups share common values and traditions (and are often referenced in research on cultural variation), each child's unique mix of multiple cultural experiences helps to shape that child's individual development. Culture is thus a dynamic and complex process in which cultural perspectives vary at the individual level.

Cultural Variation and ELDS

Paradoxically, as our understandings of the diversity in children's learning and development have advanced, ELDS that seek to standardize learning outcomes are increasingly used to guide the content of teaching and learning in early childhood settings. Within the United States, every state has adopted ELDS for preschool-age children (National Center on Early Childhood Quality Assurance 2017). ELDS have become one cornerstone of a systematic approach to early childhood education quality in the United States, guiding curricular and assessment decisions, pedagogy, and professional learning. Yet how can teachers use these standards in classrooms with ever more variation in the ways children learn? How can teachers be guided by ELDS without standardizing their teaching?

To consider these questions, we have identified specific dimensions of child development that are both commonly addressed within ELDS and particularly subject to cultural differences in how they are expressed. The areas relate to standards commonly found in ELDS that are often broadly defined with limited descriptions of how children demonstrate the skills when, in reality, children from varied cultural backgrounds may demonstrate mastery with a variety of behaviors. As such, the descriptions in ELDS may tilt the lens on what is considered typical or appropriate behavior that demonstrates the standard.

Here, we highlight three of these dimensions of development. They are intended to provide a starting point for teachers to consider the varied behaviors they see within culturally diverse classrooms and the ways expectations for children's behaviors are expressed within state ELDS. (For additional examples of cultural differences in learning, please see NAEYC.org/dap-focus-preschool.)

Dimension 1: Concentration and Attention Control

❯ Children who are accustomed to learning a skill or solving a problem by observing others may be more likely to keep track of multiple events simultaneously, while other children may be more likely to focus their attention on one event at a time.

❯ Some children may be skilled at demonstrating a narrow focus of attention when presented with an object or activity, while other children may divide their attention to consider contextual information about objects and activities.

❯ Some children may pay close attention to their peers when they are learning, while other children may direct their attention to a teacher and then to their own work.

❯ Children who may not appear to be paying attention to an activity, such as a read-aloud, may in fact be paying close attention while their eyes—and even their bodies—wander.

Dimension 2: Initiative and Persistence

❯ Children from cultural contexts that emphasize individual initiative may eagerly begin interactions with peers and adults, while children from cultures that emphasize deference to the leadership of adults may prefer to wait for them to initiate social interactions.

❯ Some children may speak up quickly when they need help, while others may patiently wait for assistance and show a great deal of persistence in trying to solve a problem on their own.

❯ Children who are accustomed to a cooperative approach to learning may demonstrate initiative by helping with group projects and freely sharing ideas, while children who are accustomed to a more individual approach may initiate activities that reflect their own interests.

Dimension 3: Curiosity and Exploration

❯ Some children may satisfy their curiosity within adult-directed activities, while others may demonstrate curiosity and motivation to learn by asking lots of questions and exploring the environment on their own.

❯ Some children may eagerly approach teachers with questions, demonstrating their expressive communication skills and motivation to learn, while others may exercise a more restrained approach, waiting to hear what teachers say and do.

❯ Children who are accustomed to a cooperative approach to learning may be motivated to learn by mutual affection and pride in their group, while children who have been socialized to value individual accomplishments may be motivated to learn more by personal acclamation and reward.

❯ Children who have been socialized to direct their own learning may be more likely to demonstrate their motivation to read by exploring books on their own, while children accustomed to more communal approaches may be more likely to engage with books in concert with their peers.

While ELDS have become an important guide for instruction in early childhood classrooms, there has been only limited consideration of how highly susceptible they are to potential cultural biases. For example, a standard that describes the expectation that children sustain their attention despite distractions from peers may privilege a cultural perspective that values self-contained, individual learning over more collaborative learning. Children from more collaborative cultures may understand that observing peers and attending to their ideas is an integral part of paying attention and learning. Another example might be a standard that includes the expectation that children demonstrate willingness to try new things by suggesting or beginning a new activity on their own; this privileges a cultural perspective that values children trying new things independently over one that favors children trying new things within activities structured by adults. To identify effective teaching practices, educators may need to reconsider the content of the standards, indicators, and the examples that often accompany them.

Implications for Culturally Responsive Practice

A clear implication of these new understandings is the need to recognize that all ELDS have an implicit cultural perspective. Moreover, there is an urgent need to help teachers use standards more effectively with children from diverse heritages. To this end, we offer the following recommendations.

Develop a Deeper Understanding of How Culture Shapes Learning

To develop a deep understanding of how culture and learning are intertwined, teachers need to learn about the cultural nature of early learning, about themselves, and about the children in their classrooms.

First, supported by quality professional learning opportunities, teachers can gain new understandings of culture as an array of dynamic tools and practices (rather than a stable entity) that helps children make meaning of experiences in the context of multiple communities and activities.

Second, supported by quality professional learning opportunities, teachers need to identify their own cultural perspectives and biases, which may unconsciously shape their pedagogy, practice, and the ways they evaluate children's behavior and progress.

Third, teachers need to study each child to gain an understanding of each one's cultural experiences and development. Beyond simply respecting or acknowledging cultural differences, teachers need to build on the varied cultural assets that children inherently bring. The critical foundation for this approach is a secure and trusting relationship with each child in which both teachers and children are learners.

Learn Meaningfully and Systematically from Parents and Families

To work with children in ways that truly build on, rather than simply acknowledge, their cultural experiences, teachers create rich, diverse opportunities to learn from families. Family members can serve as cultural leaders, helping teachers gain deep understandings of children's cultural capital and the learning goals and pedagogies that the family values. These, in turn, can be used in the classroom to inform teaching practices and support children's positive identity development as well as their learning (Durden, Escalante, & Blitch 2015).

Nurturing constructive partnerships with families requires diverse approaches. Beyond making families feel welcome in classrooms, teachers (and other program staff) should initiate multiple strategies to engage parents and families who may have varied and unpredictable work schedules, such as emails, texts, or communication apps; weekly curriculum letters that describe daily activities in the classroom; invitations to share their cultures in the classroom; questionnaires for all primary caregivers; phone calls and/or home visits with family members to exchange ideas about a child's behaviors and accomplishments; progress reports; and family–teacher conferences. Teachers can also help family members learn about and understand the ELDS that guide what and how they are teaching. Families need to understand the teaching practices used in the classroom and how they are being adapted to their children, particularly if the practices differ from their own approach at home.

 Using multiple ways to connect and collaborate with families is an essential practice for applying early learning standards in a culturally informed, equitable way. This is also an equitable practice on its own. See recommendation 4 under "Establish Reciprocal Relationships with Families" in the advancing equity position statement.

Examine State ELDS to Consider Cultural Biases

With knowledge about the cultural nature of early learning and the children in their classrooms, teachers can review the content of ELDS for standards or indicators that might be culturally laden and consider how any potential biases might support or deter the learning of their students. Armed with this perspective, teachers can then plan different types of learning experiences, consistent with the expectations within ELDS, that will engage diverse children and provide robust opportunities to promote their learning.

In summation, ELDS must be thoughtfully used with a thorough understanding of the cultural nature of early learning. With fresh perspectives on the content of ELDS and the children, families, and themselves, teachers can find new ways to create time and space for all children to think and act on their curiosity and ideas. In a community of diverse learners, when difference is celebrated, learning can increase.

JEANNE L. REID is a research scientist at the National Center for Children and Families at Teachers College, Columbia University. She has worked on multiple studies on the content and quality of early learning and development standards, and on socio-demographic diversity in young children's development.

CATHERINE SCOTT-LITTLE, PhD, is a professor in the Department of Human Development & Family Studies at the University of North Carolina at Greensboro. Catherine has worked with several states to develop and implement their early learning and development standards.

SHARON LYNN KAGAN is the Virginia and Leonard Marx Professor of Early Childhood and Family Policy and codirector of the National Center for Children and Families at Teachers College, Columbia University. She is a professor (adjunct) at Yale University's Child Study Center and a former board member and president of NAEYC.

CHAPTER 25

Preschool in the Park
Place-Based Learning in Unexpected Spaces

Rachel J. Franz

It's midweek at a park on Beacon Hill, in Seattle's south end. It's rainy, and only a few brave walkers are out, wearing raincoats and bending their heads low against the wind. But if you peek through a small patch of trees in the corner of the park, there, with no buildings or walls, is a preschool.

Tiny Trees Preschool is just one of many all-outdoor preschools in Washington, the first state to license outdoor and nature-based child care programs. Each morning, children from ages 3 to 5 come to a tiny corner of a public park—rain or shine. It's a space populated with log circles, stumps, and storage for materials for outdoor play, learning, and exploration. Some of these materials include traditional arts tools like scissors, paint, and paper. We also include outdoor tools like binoculars, wheelbarrows, and hammers to add to the possibilities for exploration. Schools like Tiny Trees that offer place-based education rely on the surrounding landscape to teach life skills, such as staying warm and contributing to the community. In addition, outdoor activities address preschool content standards, like counting, alphabet recognition, and spatial awareness.

What Is Place-Based Education?

Place-based education uses local cultures, heritage, landscapes, opportunities, and experiences to create a curriculum in which literacy, mathematics, social studies, science, and arts learning occur in the context of place. That is, learning focuses on local themes, natural resources, and content; it is relevant to children's daily lives and experiences. (Learn more at promiseofplace.org.)

 Connecting children with the community around them promotes equity as it builds on the knowledge that children and families bring with them to the program. See recommendation 5 under "Create a Caring, Equitable Community of Engaged Learners" in the advancing equity position statement.

Educators can use aspects of their program's site—urban, suburban, or rural—to inspire the curriculum and to launch learning projects that follow the children's interests. At Tiny Trees, we engage in place-based education mainly by focusing on outdoor experiences; this could include studying fish at a park where salmon spawn in a nearby stream or experimenting with angles and inclines at a local skate park.

Learning Is Everywhere

As my colleagues and I have learned at Tiny Trees, moving beyond the walls of a classroom can be tricky. Obstacles include weather, gear, access to outdoor space, safety worries about strangers or wildlife, and teachers' and families' comfort level with nature and the outdoors. Educators can find opportunities for teaching everywhere and in almost any weather, but it does take intention, effort, and persistence. In this chapter, you will find activity ideas and learning opportunities for math, science, and literacy and some tips for getting started!

Place-Based Math

Children learn best when they experience new concepts in familiar contexts. For example, children are more motivated to recognize numerals (or number symbols) when they relate to the children's daily lives and experiences—such as identifying the numbers on a neighbor's apartment door or examining prices on items in the grocery store. By integrating children's new learning with familiar contexts like this, educators make learning more relevant and help children make meaningful connections.

In the many different parks that serve as Tiny Trees' homes, numerals are everywhere: they're used as trail markers, they're embedded in the sidewalk and on signs, and they're even tagged in street art! Educators point out numerals as they walk, play, and explore with children. One activity to try:

Getting Preschoolers Outdoors: Where to Start

Need some help getting started with place-based education? Here are some ideas.

> **Identify the parks and outdoor spaces that the children's families frequently visit.** Plan trips to those spaces, if possible. Explore the school's neighborhood together and help the children create a neighborhood map.

> **Think beyond the playground.** While parks are often attractive to families because many have playgrounds, they have much more to offer in the natural spaces beyond the playground. At Tiny Trees, teachers intentionally avoid the playground in favor of other landscapes that children might not use with their families outside school hours. Instead, we use natural areas and neighborhood resources to engage in math, science, and literacy explorations.

> **Find the cracks (and numbers, letters, and slopes) in the sidewalk.** Practice noticing these details in your personal life, and then work on introducing them to children. Use phrases like these:

- "Oh! I see that there are numbers on this sign! I see the number three. I wonder what it refers to" and "What other numbers can we find on our walk, and what do they tell us?"

- "I see some footprints across the concrete. I wonder who made them. Can we think about where they might be going?"

- "I spy with my little eye . . . a triangle on the basketball court. Can you find other shapes on the court?"

Giant dice: A set of giant dice is useful when helping children learn to associate numbers with quantities. A fun game to play in the park is to roll the dice and find the same number of objects nearby, such as six stepping stones in a path or four birds on a telephone wire. As children further develop their concept of numeracy, they can look for numerals in the environment, such as on signs or license plates.

Science on the Sidewalk

While outdoor preschools are fortunate to have access to green space, many early education facilities have limited outdoor space. Especially in urban environments, teachers have to be creative: cracks in sidewalks with grass shoots and puddles that shrink in the sun offer rich learning opportunities. Even schools that have concrete lots for outdoor spaces can promote science learning. Here are some ideas:

Ecology: One feature in our urban park is storm drains. For children, storm drains hold a lot of mystery. One day, the children in our program noticed that things had been dropped into the storm drain. We discussed the impact this has on our watershed, and the children—adamant that they would help keep the water clean by catching lost objects—decided to create fishing rods out of sticks and string. It was a fantastic cooperative play opportunity for the group: they came together to practice problem solving, turn taking, and sharing space as well as to learn about environmental stewardship.

Physics: Another surprising outdoor learning activity was a visit to a skate park, which is fairly empty during school hours. It provided amazing opportunities for using spatial vocabulary (*up, down, around, sideways, diagonal*) and for talking about speed ("Wow! That ball moved even faster down this side!"), inclines and angles ("Which side is the steepest?"), and other physics-related topics. Children explored the skate park with their bodies and with balls, acorns, and other items that roll and move in different ways.

Literacy Is All Around

Promoting early reading and writing skills is great fun outdoors. Our world is full of signs; they are perfect for scaffolding emergent reading skills, like letter recognition. Some activities to try:

Street sign scavenger hunt: Looking at signs as the group walks through the neighborhood helps children appreciate that written words and symbols have many important purposes—to keep us safe, to help us work together, and to spread essential information. Try prompting children's thinking with questions like "Oh! What signs do we see? I wonder what the clues are to tell us what this sign says?"

Can you write in the rain? Outdoor preschools show that learning outside is possible even in sloppy weather. Think outside the box: writing doesn't need to rely on pencils and paper. Instead, children can write with water or sticks in mud, gravel, and snow. We have even used water to

write on the sidewalk! Children can also form letters using twine, twigs, and other objects found in nature.

Conclusion

Children deserve to have childhoods that connect them to their neighborhoods and provide outdoor experiences that get them excited about learning, no matter where they live. Educators can feel empowered to get children outdoors and into the world around them. Children, in turn, can find learning opportunities wherever they go—even in their neighborhood park!

RACHEL J. FRANZ, MEd, is the founder of Twig & Thread Consulting, which offers training and support to programs who want to take learning outside. She is also the education manager at Fairplay, where she works to help families and children navigate our technology-driven world with child development in mind.

CHAPTER 26

Metamorphosis
Life Cycle in a Box

Sara Starbuck

What could be more captivating than watching a caterpillar transform into a butterfly? Countless teachers purchase larvae or collect caterpillars to give young children a chance to observe this magical process. However, butterflies are fragile, so children are usually warned to look but not touch. Tiny fingers on delicate wings could easily bring the study to a tragic end.

But what if there were a sturdier option than butterflies for learning about metamorphosis—one that children could hold? Good news! This is possible when you study mealworms.

Mealworms aren't really worms, though they do look like small worms. They are the *larval* (juvenile) form of mealworm beetles, a type of darkling beetle. (Beetles go through four stages of life: egg, larva, pupa, adult.)

They are about the size of an inchworm but have six jointed legs. You can buy them at pet stores or bait shops. (Do not buy giant mealworms; they have been hormonally treated to delay their development.)

When you introduce mealworms, children can become more deeply engaged in investigating metamorphosis than they can with caterpillars and butterflies. They can safely interact with mealworms throughout the transformation from small, worm-like larvae to wiggly, alien-looking pupae, and finally to adult beetles.

At every stage, these insects are hardy, and children can handle and examine them with little worry that the insects will be injured. In addition, mealworms are inexpensive and easy to obtain. They make ideal classroom pets because they require minimal care and children can help build their homes and replenish their food and water.

Caring for Mealworms

Mealworms have simple needs. All they require is grain to eat (oatmeal is my preference) and some moisture. I like to use a critter cage to house them because it has a clear plastic bottom, a lid with holes, and a handle. But you can use a plastic shoebox if you put some holes in the top. Fill the box about half full with dry oatmeal.

Mealworms need liquid, but putting water in the oatmeal will cause it to grow mold. A potato can provide the needed moisture—cut it into halves or thirds so the mealworms can easily get to the inside. (To learn more, visit mealwormcare.org.)

Supporting Dual Language Learners

Active, hands-on exploration—such as the one with mealworms that teacher Robin Koetting and her preschoolers engaged in—is ideal for dual language learners because it lets them investigate through their senses and share language with peers and adults. Provide books and charts that have lots of photographs of mealworms during different stages of the life cycle. These images give children an opportunity to identify and name the mealworms' current stages.

In Robin's class, Royce and Carolyn, two children whose primary language was Mandarin, were fascinated by the mealworms. At one point, Royce went to the writing center to get an English-language picture encyclopedia. He turned to the page in the book that had a photograph of a cobra. Royce laid a mealworm on the page next to the cobra. The cobra looked a lot like the mealworm! He pointed at the photo and then looked at the teacher with a big smile on his face.

Metamorphosis

When you buy mealworms, they are actually larvae, the second stage of the beetles' life cycle. They will grow over the next several weeks, shedding their hard outer shells, or *exoskeletons*, multiple times as they do—a process called *molting*. (This is all great vocabulary for children to learn!) During their last molt, mealworms stop growing and turn white. They are becoming pupae—entering the one- to three-week stage in which the adult form develops.

The pupae don't move most of the time, but sometimes, when held or disturbed, they will jump or wiggle a bit. Unlike butterfly chrysalises, pupae are not delicate and do not need to stay in one place—children can touch and actively explore them. After a couple of weeks, a darkling beetle will emerge from each pupa. The beetles are harmless—you can invite children to handle them!

DAP Use your early learning standards to help choose activities related to a study of mealworms. For example, what math concepts do preschoolers need to know? How can you tie counting into the study? What other subjects can be integrated?

Tips for Exploring Mealworms

> **When you introduce mealworms, show them to the children in their original container.** Ask the children what they notice about the mealworms. Have they seen insects like these before? You can use books and a life cycle chart to show how a larva turns into a beetle. Guide the children in filling the container with oatmeal, cutting up the potato, and moving the mealworms into their new habitat (critter cage or shoebox), explaining the purpose of each action.

> **Facilitate children's closer examinations** by setting cafeteria-style trays around a table and putting a handful of mealworms and oatmeal on each. The children will be interested in holding and observing the mealworms. Add magnifying glasses so children can see them in more detail.

> **Get the mealworms out as often as possible.** Leave them out for extended periods so children can explore them in depth. Be sure that all children have an opportunity to move to the table for a while. Some may spend 30 minutes or more a day exploring mealworms! Set out rulers or other tools (like beads of different sizes) so the children can measure the mealworms.

> **Provide materials like paper and writing instruments to deepen children's investigations,** so they can record their observations and draw pictures of the mealworms. Help children write down what they observe each day in a journal or on a roll of paper that can later be used for a documentation panel.

> **Take photographs of the children with the mealworms as the insects grow and change.** The children can use the photos to document their work.

> **Encourage the children's investigations.** They will notice early on the exoskeletons that the mealworms have shed. Soon, the mealworms will turn into pupae. Give the children the scientific language to describe what they see—and use it

frequently yourself—including words like *habitat, molting, metamorphosis, exoskeleton, larva,* and *pupa.*

> **Watch for beetles to emerge from the pupae.**
The children can hold the beetles, and they typically delight in feeling the tickly insects moving on their hands. The beetles move fast enough that sometimes they will wiggle under a shirtsleeve, causing giggles, but not so fast that you can't catch them. Some children are hesitant but will hold the beetles with encouragement. Never force a child to hold an insect if the child is reluctant.

> **Keep the beetles in the container with the mealworms, and keep watching.** (Your package of mealworms is likely to have larvae of different ages, so some will transform into pupae and beetles sooner than others.) Remind children to observe the potato closely. Are the mealworms gathering there? Often, there will be big holes in the potato. Ask the children what they think happened to make the holes. Replace the potato as it dries out.

If children keep watching and continue to tend to the mealworms, pupae, and beetles, they will eventually be rewarded with baby mealworms. It is unlikely that the children will see the eggs that the darkling beetles lay, which are smaller than a grain of sand. But if they look carefully, they will one day find very tiny babies, about the size of the letter *l* on this page.

SARA STARBUCK is a retired associate professor of child development from the Department of Child and Family Studies at Southeast Missouri State University, in Cape Girardeau, Missouri.

CHAPTER 27

Listen to What We Hear
Developing Community Responsive Listening Centers

Emily Brown Hoffman and Kristin Cipollone

Jasmine's eyes light up as she hears her mother's voice read a book in Arabic through the class tablet. Her teacher, Ms. Bloom, holds open the matching book as Jasmine and three of her classmates crowd around to see the pictures in *Al-Alwan, Al-Ashkaal, Al-Arqam: Learning My Arabic Colors, Shapes, & Numbers*, by Asma Wahab. "That's Jasmine's mommy reading to us," squeaks Grace, one of the children crowded around the book.

"It is! We can listen to your grandma read next, Grace," says Ms. Bloom.

Jasmine's class is one of seven at the Rainbow Center in east-central Indiana that is taking advantage of new listening centers. Thanks to a 14-week partnership with Ball State University's Early Childhood, Youth, and Family Studies Department, children at the Rainbow Center can now hear recordings of books read by members of their families and the community who share their cultural heritage.

The goal of this partnership was twofold: to offer a unique learning experience to future and current educators and to support the center's efforts to enhance its literacy and language resources to be responsive to the children and families it serves. Together, we created listening centers that aimed to achieve responsiveness through practices and materials supported by emergent literacy theories and current research.

Books and other texts have the potential to reflect identities, experiences, and communities (Sims Bishop 1990). When they do, they can appeal to readers of all ages and prompt literacy enjoyment and growth. However, inequities exist in who is represented in these books and how they are portrayed. This disparity extends to the materials and learning centers found in early childhood classrooms.

Community Responsive Early Literacy: The Value of Listening Centers

When children have access to culturally relevant literature, academic achievement significantly increases (Clark 2017). However, the landscape of children's literature remains remarkably resistant to change. While Latino/a, Black, Indigenous, and Asian American children surpass the number of White children in America's public schools (NCES, n.d.), children's literature remains overwhelmingly White (SLJ, n.d.).

Early childhood educators can offer inclusive language and materials that actively represent all children and families while simultaneously fostering the critical thinking and early literacy skills connected to academic success in kindergarten and beyond. These practices need to encompass all foundational early literacy skills, including oral language development (Dickinson, Nesbitt, & Hofer 2019; NAEYC 2020; Paris 2005).

The field has consistently recognized that enacting engaging, well-conceived listening centers is an effective way to promote these early literacy skills with young children (Fisher & Frey 2019; Schickedanz & Collins 2013). Listening centers are physical areas (or stations) in classrooms. They are designed to help children work collaboratively (in large or small groups) as they listen to oral stories, songs, rhymes, or books through technological means and then engage with what they listened to through exploring, discussing, or creating with others. Sometimes, children look at a written text that matches what they are hearing. Sometimes, they engage solely through listening, talking, and moving.

Planning and Implementing Community Responsive Listening Centers: One Program's Journey

The children at Rainbow Center have a variety of interests, strengths, needs, and characteristics. Because of this and the number of languages spoken, each listening center had to be unique. We wanted to create centers based on the specific children at this center rather than on the generic, monolithic, identity-based assumptions or stereotypes that can occur in early education settings (Gilliam et al. 2016). An example of such an assumption might be creating a learning center around camping because you consider the rural community in which your students live "outdoorsy" instead of intentionally exploring whether families are interested in outdoor activities.

Each team interviewed families, explaining the idea behind building listening centers in the classrooms. Families excitedly shared about their children, what they (the adults) would like to see in a new listening center, and how they would best like to be involved. Besides interviewing families at drop-off and pickup times, informational fliers and questionnaires were sent home with children to encourage families to offer additional ideas.

Designing the Listening Centers

Each team first assessed the strengths and gaps in their current classroom materials, then began planning the design and content of their listening centers. As the overseers of this partnership, we (the authors) asked the teams to consider several factors, including

> Children's progression in early literacy and language development

> Current classroom resources

> Family interview results

> Children's interests

> Effective literacy practices

> Effective community responsive practices

We wanted the centers to be inviting spaces for children. We also requested that teachers offer a wealth of materials, including oral stories, songs, rhymes, and both digital and print books. The latter needed to include board books, interactive books, and wordless books, all from a variety of genres.

Acquiring Funding

We (the authors) applied for and obtained a grant through the university to purchase materials and resources for the listening center. This grant allowed each room to buy a 12-inch tablet, $400 in furniture (tables, rugs, and storage), $100 in interactive materials (scarves, puppets, felt boards, and balls), $100 in technology supports (tablet stands, tablet covers), and $400 in books. While the funding was useful and exciting to all participants, listening centers can be created with fewer resources. All that is really needed is a recording device (cell phone, inexpensive voice recorder), the public library, and community connections.

With their budget in mind, each team developed a plan for their listening center that would best fit the needs of their particular children, including the physical layout, technological needs, and interactive materials. However, the most important item could not be purchased. For the voices that would narrate our books, we turned to the community.

 While centers may have varying access to technological devices, using digital technology for a culturally responsive listening center is a great example of responsible and intentional ways to use technology as a learning tool. (See principle 9 of the position statement on developmentally appropriate practice.)

Finding Storytellers

To incorporate effective literacy practices and ensure community responsiveness, listening center content must be inclusive and unique to each classroom. Before purchasing reading material, our teams of teacher candidates and classroom teachers compiled lists of potential books using well-established and respected lists of quality children's literature. These included the American Library Association Youth

Media Awards, the International Board on Books for Young People Honour List, and the Social Justice Books Booklists.

Books were evaluated using several criteria, including the extent to which the books

> Reflected the children's experiences and identities

> Reflected the families' interests

> Offered new windows into the experiences of others

> Were written in "own voices"

Teams then searched for developmentally appropriate, high-interest, and community-relevant materials for each listening center. For instance, because the barbershop was a central meeting place in this community, teachers intentionally selected *Crown: An Ode to the Fresh Cut*, by Derrick Barnes. Yet as they searched through book and song recordings available online or from commercial vendors, our teams noticed that the majority of items available were read, talked, or sung by people who did not look or sound like the children and families of Rainbow Center. Given what we know about the lack of representation of diverse social identities in children's books, this discovery was expected. We decided to ask families and community members to record the listening center content on our tablets.

To attract community interest and involvement, Rainbow Center set up an open house at the adjacent elementary school. Teacher candidates and classroom teachers transformed the library into a book display and recording studio.

As people mill about at the open house, one of the teacher candidates approaches an adult she does not know. "Hi! We are creating listening centers for all the classrooms at the Rainbow Center next door. Would you like to read a book or tell a story? I'll record it on the tablet, and then the children will get to hear it as they look at the book."

The adult stops and looks at all the books, a small smile on her face. "I can read any of these, and the kids will get to hear my voice reading?" She picks up *I Love My Hair*, by Natasha Tarpley. "You have my favorite book."

She then turns to her school-age children, who are browsing the tables full of books. "They can read too," she says, thereby extending Rainbow Center's outreach to community members of all ages.

Teacher candidates held recording sessions at Rainbow Center, the local community center, and the elementary school. Community members selected books from a diverse collection of high-quality children's texts to read and record (see "Choosing Books for Listening Centers" on page 125 for a sampling), or they brought a favorite book to read. We encouraged them to read in their home language. Some also generously and spontaneously shared oral histories of the neighborhood and sang songs. Families and community members were thrilled to be involved—treated as partners who can significantly and meaningfully participate in children's learning. (See "How to Create a Community Responsive Listening Center" on the next page.) The listening centers would now be filled with meaningful content shared through the voices of family and community members rather than people with whom the children had no connection.

If there is not a way to collect recordings in person, educators can ask families to send in videos or audio of them greeting the class or reading their favorite books from home or the classroom library. Alternatively, they might send a tablet home and ask families to make recordings, then return the tablet.

DAP Using the expertise of families and community members in curriculum planning is crucial. These listening centers were special not just because of the materials that were selected but also because they utilized the community's knowledge, which must have been evident in the way the individuals read, sang, and spoke their recordings.

Launching the Centers

Once the centers became part of the classroom, they were predominately used with an adult to coincide with each classroom's curriculum themes, schedules, and student requests. At the end of the project, families and community members were invited to browse through the listening centers during an open house, where the teaching teams showcased their centers and offered opportunities for families to use the materials with their children.

How to Create a Community Responsive Listening Center

Action Steps	Supporting Resources
Get to know and connect with the community where your school is situated.	Visit community spaces, meet community members, and learn and explore where students and families spend time. For example, do your shopping in the community or attend community meetings.
Refresh your knowledge about developmentally appropriate literacy practices and resources for your children by considering commonality, individuality, and context (NAEYC 2020).	Michigan ASCD Literacy Essential Modules michiganascd.org/literacy-essential-modules Developed for leaders and classroom teachers, these free resources show practice in action in real early childhood classrooms. Children's Literature Blog *A Fuse #8 Production* blogs.slj.com/afuse8production This blog supports adults in staying up to date on children's literature, from board books to chapter books. NAEYC position statements NAEYC.org/resources/position-statements
Assess your materials.	Inventory the resources you have. What resources do you need and/or want to create a community responsive listening center?
Solicit children's and families' ideas and expertise.	Interview children and families about their interests, home languages, and favorite books and songs; ask them what they want in their listening center.
Design your listening center area and prepare content.	Consult reputable websites and lists to find books. This is one source: diversebooks.org/resources/where-to-find-diverse-books Ask families and community members to vet the materials. Create multiple opportunities for community members to record content, including in their home languages. Select a final set of materials, including high-quality, hand-picked children's texts and a recording device.
Launch your new listening center.	Gather a small group of children and tell them you are going to listen to a story read by someone they may know. Ask the children to follow along in a book or use materials to creatively respond to the story. Push play and share the recording with children. Watch them react to hearing familiar voices.

Listening Centers as a Community Reflection

So often, we may forget that families are experts in their own right. This project influenced how current and future early childhood teachers thought about and engaged with their community as an asset to children's development and learning. The listening centers they created were uniquely reflective of the children in a particular classroom: each listening center authentically incorporated classroom families and the larger community while effectively applying emergent literacy theories and research-based literacy practices.

 A listening center with books and recordings in the children's home languages is a wonderful way to support literacy and strengthen family-school connections. Encourage families to read to their children at home in their home languages, and share information with them about how this supports literacy development.

Teacher candidates and classroom teachers came to understand the political nature of early literacy, taking seriously the potential and real harm done to children when literacy practices—and schooling more broadly—attempt to separate children's funds of knowledge and cultural wealth from their learning (Freire 1970 [2000], 1985; Moll et al. 1992; Yosso 2005b). As one of the teacher candidates participating in this partnership said, "Early literacy has everything to do with linking school and culture together in meaningful ways. We wanted there to be a space where the children could hear their community represented inside the classroom as well as the different cultures within their families."

As they seek to promote genuine literacy learning experiences, effective educators become knowledgeable of and responsive to the strengths, interests, values, and needs of a community. They are attuned to children's and families' cultures, identities, and home environments. In practice, this means that educators affirm, introduce, value, and reinforce multiple forms of literacy and refrain from normalizing only dominant ways of knowing (Kirkland 2013; Paris & Alim 2017). It also means that educators get to know the community and work to build authentic and deep relationships with families. As one teacher candidate said, "It is an ongoing process that needs constant attention and adjusting. All of these ideas and philosophies and strategies need to be something that is not only a part of who I am as a person and a teacher and a part of my belief system, but something I do and enact in my day-to-day life and in the classroom."

Choosing Books for Listening Centers

When evaluating books for inclusion in a listening center, it is important to ask three key questions:

> Does this book reflect the children in my classroom?

> Does it offer an important window into a different perspective that they may not have experienced?

> Is it responsive to children in my class and the surrounding community? Is it available in the home languages spoken by children's families?

Here are some book suggestions to help you start your own list:

> *Baby Goes to Market*, by Atinuke (2017). Set in a busy Nigerian marketplace, this beautiful book offers rhythmic language, humor, and an introduction to numbers.

> *Love Makes a Family*, by Sophie Beer (2018). By showing simple, joyful activities done by many different kinds of families, this inclusive book demonstrates that the most important part of a family is the love they share.

> *Danbi Leads the School Parade*, by Anna Kim (2020). Danbi starts school in America after moving with her family from South Korea. Overcoming language and cultural barriers, Danbi shines as she makes friends and finds joy in school.

> *Maybe Something Beautiful: How Art Transformed a Neighborhood*, by F. Isabel Campoy and Theresa Howell and illus. by Rafael Lopez (2016). A story about how one neighborhood transformed a neighborhood through art, this book will inspire children to create murals through pictures, colors, and shapes that represent their own community.

> *What Is Light*, by Markette Sheppard and illus. by Cathy Ann Johnson (2018). A lyrical book that emphasizes the salient moments and simple pleasures in children's lives, this text reveals all types of light in the world.

> *Holi Colors*, by Rina Singh (2018). In this board book of bright photographs and playful rhymes, Holi (the Hindu celebration) is featured as a magnificently fun way for children to explore colors.

EMILY BROWN HOFFMAN, PhD, is an assistant professor in early childhood education at National Louis University in Chicago. Her research examines how early childhood educators can implement equitable curriculum and instruction to provide genuine learning that affirms children and all their identities.

KRISTIN CIPOLLONE, PhD, is assistant director for Professional Learning and Consortium with the University of Buffalo Teacher Residency Program (UBTR). Her research interests include the development of equity-focused educators, preservice teacher dispositions, and the ways in which inequality is (re)produced in and through schooling.

CHAPTER 28

Walk with Us

Indigenous Approaches to Developmentally Appropriate Practice

Trisha L. Moquino, Joshuaa D. Allison-Burbank, Rebecca Blum-Martinez, and Katie Kitchens

The following vignette is about learning experiences in Cochiti Keres, an oral, unwritten language.

"Children, which direction shall we walk?" our Elders ask in a voice tinged with the sweetness of our Cochiti cookies. The children eagerly yell, "To the east!" They quickly pull on their bulky jackets. One child carefully pulls on her shoe, pushing the Velcro flaps in place. "I'm ready!" she exclaims and darts to the door. All the children line up by the classroom exit, anxiously awaiting the outdoors and trying not to step on one another. The Keres-speaking Elder and the Keres-speaking Montessori guides (teachers) scan the room one more time to see that everybody is ready. The children, ages 2½–6, all head out the door and down the hill. They are well on their way when Hunter stops and says to Rainbow, "Look at the cactus. It has a flower." Our Elder stops and reminds the child of the Keres name of cactus and introduces a new word, the word for the prickly pear and the flower. In Keres, he says, "You have to know how to pick the prickly pear so you don't hurt yourself with the cactus spines."

Another child walks over to the small little plants full of purple flowers and tries to pick one. One of the guides gently reminds him, "If you don't need to pick it, you should leave it. You can admire its beauty, though." The child takes a deep breath in, smelling the beautiful flowers that are as purple as the fields of lavender up north on the Ohkay Ohwingeh's Tribal Nation. The Elder stops the children and says, "Look at the clouds. Let's call them to bring us rain. Then we will have even more flowers to admire." In Keres, all the children yell humbly to the clouds to bring us the rain that is always much needed here in the high desert in our ancestral homelands of our beloved people, the Cochiti.

Nature Walks at Keres Children's Learning Center

Intergenerational nature walks at the Keres Children's Learning Center (KCLC) have been a cornerstone of the Indigenous Language Immersion (ILI) primary (2½–6 years old) classroom since its inception in 2006 and its official launch in September 2012. The integration of nature is not a new idea; the people of Cochiti have been practicing what might now be termed *land-based childrearing* for millennia. These practices, however, have been intentionally disrupted by the devastating forces of settler colonialism, white supremacy culture (Okun, n.d.), and capitalism that have relentlessly conspired to separate our people from our lands. They have attempted to turn the land into something lifeless to be conquered and commodified. In a world shaped by consumerism and settler colonialism, one of our paramount aims is to use our Indigenous language to reconnect our children with our lands, our ancestors, and our culture. Schooling in the settler colonial United States emphasizes individualism over the collective, productivity over relationships, and passivity over critical consciousness. Factory models of education separate and silo subjects, betraying the interconnected nature of being that is foundational to many Indigenous epistemologies, or ways of knowing (Grande 2015). Nature walks offer an opportunity for holistic integration that supports the development of the whole child. They also allow the children to experience learning through their heritage language and make immediate connections to concepts in an integrated and holistic manner. The sections below explore the ways in which nature walks serve as a healing, connective, and decolonizing approach to developmentally appropriate practice as defined by Pueblo educators at KCLC.

Relationships and Social and Emotional Development

At their core, nature walks at KCLC are about building, strengthening, and sustaining relationships. They offer the opportunity for authentic interaction between Elders and children that mirrors their lives at home, reestablishing an intergenerational pillar. Nature walks also encourage children to explore their relationship to the plants, animals, and land that surround them. For instance, in the vignette above when the Elder reminds the children to take the fruit of the prickly pear only if it is needed, the children practice a core Cochiti value: plants are beings with whom we are in relationship. This value stands in direct opposition to capitalist values, which turn plants, animals, and land from beings into commodities to be consumed. If the children were to pick the prickly pear, they would do so in a way that aligns with the values of Cochiti. They would take only what they needed, and they would return to the school to prepare the prickly pear with KCLC's food educator and cook. These nature walks also offer the children the space to deepen their relationships with themselves. As people who belong to a place, Cochiti children's way of understanding themselves and their people cannot be separated from the land and language of their ancestors.

In many conventional early childhood settings, it is rare to see Elders authentically integrated into the learning environment. This lack of intergenerational connection between the youngest and the eldest members of the community stands in direct opposition to traditional Pueblo communal structures, where Elders play an integral role in childrearing. Nature walks at KCLC arrest that narrative by inviting the involvement of our Elders, who then share their experiences with and on the land while connecting our children to our language. Providing opportunities for Elders to hold substantial roles in an early childhood setting is crucial to having children learn empathy, compassion, respect, and understanding of their own responsibility for taking care of others. Additionally, centering Elders in classroom instruction and field experiences allows children to take advantage of their unique sensitivity for language acquisition by encouraging proximity to Elders who are fluent in our Indigenous languages. Time spent with the children allows Elders to respond to the particular needs of the children in a natural, culturally, and linguistically appropriate manner. Western schooling has removed Elders from children's lives; establishing Elders as an integral part of the KCLC experience reestablishes this important relationship.

Enhancing Executive Function

In addition to the development and maintenance of strong relationships, nature walks encourage the cultivation of executive functioning skills, including attention, memory, mental imaging reasoning, and concept acquisition. Children develop their attention by being drawn in by captivating phenomena, such as a hummingbird sipping nectar from a cactus flower. They exercise their working memory as they learn new Keres words, phrases, and sentences, and then use them the next day during their nature walk. The children are exposed to a variety of plants, animals, and landscapes that strengthen their ability to create mental representations of the world around them. They also begin to categorize these impressions, extending their reasoning by thinking about how the seasons connect to the changing or falling leaves, noticing how green buds begin appearing on branches as the temperature rises. All of this executive function development occurs on Cochiti land, in Keres, through the Cochiti worldview.

Sensitive Periods

KCLC utilizes the Montessori method as a framework for supporting culturally sustaining, humanizing language immersion learning environments. One of the foundational tenets of the Montessori method during birth through age 6 is what Maria Montessori termed *sensitive periods*. During these sensitive periods of early learning, the child is temporarily highly attuned to the development of specific skills (Montessori 2012). Two of the most prominent sensitive periods during the birth-to-6 age range are language and movement. Nature walks authentically integrate the heightened sensitivities children experience during these periods, aiding development.

Language

During our ILI planning lessons at KCLC, we work with a variety of generations to continually develop a curriculum that supports children in deepening their understanding of the Keres language while considering their developmental levels. These lessons are the bedrock of instruction at KCLC, as it is through our language that children build an understanding of the world that is rooted in our values. While we diligently plan lessons that guide our nature walks, we are also mindful that we cannot plan for the spontaneous learning that occurs when a robin unexpectedly appears or we happen upon Indian tea growing alongside the KCLC building. These invaluable unplanned moments give vital space for further learning, often uncovering new opportunities for spontaneous, rich Keres language transmission from our Elders to both the children and to our guides, leading to learning across the generations. Furthermore, these experiential activities allow for naturalistic and collective learning, which have long been core teaching values and strategies in the rearing of Indigenous children. This intergenerational approach restores the ancient traditional methods of teaching young children essential life skills and fostering community and land fluency that lead to strong Indigenous language exposure in naturalistic settings and opportunities for developing academic foundations through various learning settings like the outdoors.

There is power in Indigenous languages. There is love in Indigenous languages. Indigenous language revitalization efforts at KCLC have shown that young children can be effectively taught Western academic concepts while building strong dual language skills, such as receptive and expressive skills, in the two languages of Keres and English.

Movement

Pueblo people are runners. During the Pueblo Revolt of 1680, runners ran from pueblo to pueblo, often traveling for hundreds of miles, to orchestrate this monumental act of resistance. Pueblo ancestors have known for millennia of the importance of physical development and the ways in which it supports holistic health (Yellowbird 2021). This is also reflected in our communal Pueblo dances, which integrate physical, spiritual, emotional, and communal wellness. Centering movement as a way of knowing during nature walks is a purposeful act of decolonization in early childhood programming, where notions of *school readiness* dictate what is most valued. Often, this school readiness is defined by intellectual development, or skills that are cultivated in the pursuit of academic achievement, and does not address the importance of physical development. The Montessori approach reminds us that the preschool years are defined by a period of rapid physical development and that the need for children to increase their gross and fine motor coordination must be tended to as a part of the prepared environment. Nature walks provide the opportunity to practice these skills in a joyful, culturally nourishing way.

Culturally Sustaining Practice as Developmentally Appropriate

The KCLC is a model of culturally sustaining/revitalizing pedagogical (CSRP) teaching that returns to the traditional Indigenous ways of teaching young children. We choose to use the term CSRP to describe our work, as it centers the importance of language revitalization within Indigenous communities (McCarty & Lee 2014; Paris & Alim 2017). Further, it empowers us to consider equity as defined by our Tribal Nations.

 Culturally and linguistically sustaining learning experiences build on the funds of knowledge of each child, family, and community.

Developmentally appropriate practice seeks to support the cultivation of children's fullest potential, emphasizing each child's strengths while centering joy (NAEYC 2020). To truly implement a practice that reflects these lofty goals, early childhood educators must wrestle with the ways in which white supremacy culture, settler colonialism, and capitalism inform and shape mainstream approaches to early childhood education. Equitable practice in early childhood learning environments must recognize the role that the ongoing legacy of settler colonialism has played in establishing violent, inequitable schooling practices (Moquino & Kitchens 2021). Before Spanish contact, children in Cochiti learned in ways that were joyful, humanizing, and culturally sustaining. Among other colonial constructs, the introduction of boarding schools disrupted ancestral childrearing practices, introducing schooling environments that ripped children from their land, their languages, and their people. Truly developmentally appropriate practice is

a practice of healing, a practice of equity, a practice of return. KCLC strives to come home to the practices of our ancestors that revered children, holding them as sacred beings. These are practices of respect, of joy, of deep connection, and most important, of love.

TRISHA L. MOQUINO, MA, is the cofounder/education director/Keres-speaking elementary guide at Keres Children's Learning Center. Her daughters and grandparents were the original inspiration for the work of KCLC. She is from the Tribal Nations of Cochiti, Kewa, and Ohkay Ohwingeh.

JOSHUAA D. ALLISON-BURBANK, PhD, CCC-SLP, is a speech and language pathologist and developmental scientist at Johns Hopkins Center for Indigenous Health. He is Diné and Acoma Pueblo.

REBECCA BLUM-MARTINEZ, PhD, is professor emerita at the University of New Mexico. She specializes in bilingualism, second language development, and language revitalization in Latinx and Indigenous communities.

KATIE KITCHENS (they/them) is a queer, white, Jewish educator and researcher. Katie is the English-speaking elementary Montessori guide at Keres Children's Learning Center and a doctoral student at Chapman University.

PART 6

Demonstrating Professionalism as an Early Childhood Educator

RECOMMENDATIONS FROM THE DAP POSITION STATEMENT

Developmentally appropriate practice serves as the hallmark of the early childhood education profession. Fully achieving these guidelines and effectively promoting all young children's development and learning depends on the establishment of a strong profession with which all early childhood educators, working across all settings, identify.

Viewing videos of their teaching across a range of instructional contexts provides opportunities for teachers to self-reflect and identify key areas in which practice can be enhanced and offers powerful ways to engage in personalized professional development. When watching a video of herself leading a cooking activity, Amanda observed, "I probably didn't give them [the children] the opportunity to really answer my question. I could have waited a little longer for them to answer that." Amanda's noticing that she needed to leave more for children to respond to her question is a powerful self-reflection. (Adapted from "Personalized Professional Development: How Teachers Can Use Videos to Improve Their Practice," page 135)

This example demonstrates the value of self-reflection, an important aspect of demonstrating professionalism as an early childhood educator and something that enhances teaching for new and seasoned educators alike.

Early childhood education lays the foundation for later school learning and lifelong success beyond the classroom. Remaining committed to professionalism in our everyday practices as early childhood educators is essential. Developmentally appropriate practice necessitates that educators are committed to the work, to developing their knowledge, and to the profession.

Preschool educators' interactions with children, their families, the community, and fellow colleagues have

a profound impact. Because educators can affect the ways preschoolers see themselves, their own abilities, and others for years to come, they take care to create healthy learning environments that support rather than undermine development and learning. Therefore, professional educators understand and abide by ethical guidelines, including the Code of Ethical Conduct (NAEYC 2011), to ensure that children and colleagues thrive in safe and healthy environments. Professionalism includes a commitment to equity, a commitment to learning how to best support each individual child in a way that considers and celebrates their cultural background, language, interests, abilities, and developmental levels.

Professionalism also means that colleagues within the field work together to create environments that promote the safety, care, and growth not only of children and their families but also of the staff. Early childhood educators also understand that the actions and decisions they make in the community reflect on the field and that a commitment to children includes engaging in professional development, self-reflection, and advocacy.

While early childhood education is a field with many different job titles and areas of focus, there are key principles that apply to educators no matter their specific role. These principles include the following:

- Identify as an early childhood educator; participate within the field; and advocate on behalf of children, their families, and the profession as a whole.

- Learn about and abide by the ethical and other regulatory guidelines affecting the work, including the Code of Ethical Conduct (NAEYC 2011).

- Communicate in a professional and effective manner through all forms of communication to meet the needs of children and their families and to work well with other early childhood professionals.

- Remain committed to learning as a means of improving professional practice.

- Engage in reflection and commit to intentional and purposeful practices (NAEYC 2019b).

Professionalism is an essential part of meeting the needs of children and those who aspire to work with children, yet there are different considerations depending on a professional's particular role. For this reason, this section on professionalism includes suggestions and personal reflections from researchers, early childhood classroom teachers, higher education faculty, and a community-based early childhood program owner.

READ AND REFLECT

As you read the chapters in this section, consider and evaluate your own classroom practices using these reflection questions.

"Becoming Your Best: Building Professional Competencies" details nine vital practices to help early childhood educators be the best professional version of themselves. Centers and programs should ensure that early childhood educators are "given appropriate autonomy in their settings to make sound professional judgments" (NAEYC 2019b, 27) that will allow them to implement the suggested practices as appropriate for them. **Consider:** As you reflect on your practices, what opportunities for improvement exist, and what resources do you have access to that might facilitate this improvement?

"Personalized Professional Development: How Teachers Can Use Videos to Improve Their Practice" examines an approach to professional development in which teachers evaluate themselves and update their practice based on their self-critiques. These critiques represent reflective and intentional practice (NAEYC 2019b). **Consider:** As you read this chapter, think about what parts of your daily schedule might benefit from recording and reflection.

"Leading with LOVE: Leveraging Our Value Every Day" discusses ways to create an overall commitment to love as an action in daily practices. It illustrates the ways in which one center ensures that "professional communication skills . . . effectively support their relationships and work [with] young children, families, and colleagues" (NAEYC 2019b, 24). **Consider:** What issues affect young children in your community, and how can you use your knowledge and skills as an early childhood professional to work toward solutions?

"Beginning (or Continuing) the Journey to a More Equitable Classroom" demonstrates that "equity in education begins in early childhood and that early childhood educators have a special opportunity and responsibility to advance equity in their daily classroom work with children and their work with families and colleagues" (NAEYC 2019b, 24). The chapter describes the ways in which educators can enact change to work toward a more just future for diverse groups of children and their families. **Consider:** After reading this chapter and engaging in the steps laid out by the authors, reflect on whom you might share your journey with to encourage others to participate in a similar process.

"Incorporating Anti-Racist Approaches for Asian American Children" describes the importance of engaging in difficult conversations with young children and demonstrating cultural competencies in understanding, appreciating, and interacting with people from cultures that are different from one's own. Communicating effectively is an essential part of professionalism (NAEYC 2019b). **Consider:** What steps can you take in your setting to gain more cultural competence in working with specific groups of children and families, such as Asian Americans?

CHAPTER 29

Becoming Your Best
Building Professional Competencies

Meghann Hickey

My career in early childhood education has been an unexpected adventure, giving me an expanded view of life outside the classroom. Before my current role supporting early education programs that are implementing technology in their classrooms, I was a preschool teacher for five years. As much as I loved teaching, I also had a passion for policy that brought me to Washington, DC. Now, I'm honored to help teachers have a voice in education policy and support high-quality programs for children.

While the primary focus of your job as a teacher is educating and caring for young children, there's growing momentum for teachers to take charge of their profession. I've gathered the following be-your-best ideas for busy teachers regarding competencies, professionalism, and support from my time as a teacher, an advocate, and a trainer (and continuous learner!) working with programs from coast to coast.

Be Knowledgeable

While many teachers don't focus on their program's general employment policies—sick leave and vacation, coverage and break times, and health care benefits—these things directly impact how you practice in the field. For example, knowing that NAEYC calls for staff to have planning time built into the schedule, as opposed to the common expectation that teachers will do this work in their personal time, can help you advocate for work–life balance. Make sure you understand policy implications and participate in staff meetings in which policies are reviewed. If you don't know when the program policy reviews occur, ask for a schedule and to be included.

Be Self-Aware

In a typical office job, you can step away for a coffee break if you feel stressed, but the pressures of coverage and teacher-to-child ratios can quickly make a teacher feel overwhelmed. Take time for your mental health and ask for breaks away from the classroom when needed. You'll be a better teacher for the children when you're at your best.

Be Vocal

Working at an advocacy organization in Washington, DC, I saw that classroom teachers had the greatest impact when they addressed issues like teacher salaries or class size from their unique perspectives and experiences. I became much more passionate about speaking for the field when I found that leaders listened to the real-life challenges I had faced in my classroom. I also saw how many opportunities to influence policy we miss by not speaking up. You know (and research demonstrates) how crucial your role with children is, so find ways to advocate for the importance of early childhood education and increase support at local, state, and federal levels. It can be as simple as posting on social media about your work or having the children in your classroom draw and write messages to mail to your representatives!

Be Ethical

Part of what defines a profession is having a set of ethical guidelines for practice. Doing what is right for children starts with agreed-upon guidelines for interactions in your classroom, with your fellow educators, and with the families you serve. We focused on partnering with families to understand their specific preferences for their child's feeding, napping, emotional support, and more. I used the NAEYC Code of Ethical Conduct (NAEYC 2011) to guide me as I developed relationships with families. It reminded me that it's important "to acknowledge families' childrearing values and their right to make decisions for their children" (I-2.6), especially when I felt tension between meeting the needs of an individual child and supporting all the children in my care.

Be Educated

While a degree alone does not make a high-quality teacher, it's important to have knowledge of child development. For example, through studying child psychology as part of child development coursework, I've learned that toddlers act out, such as by biting, because of some sort of emotional trigger. Biting is a way to communicate distress, so instead of punishing the child, it's important to figure out the action or situation that causes the biting. If college seems out of reach, you can start by taking a course or even attending a single lecture at a local college. In addition, you can seek out professional development via NAEYC conferences, webinars, and publications, which are based on current research in early childhood education and child development. You'll support the children better in their learning by being a lifelong learner yourself.

Be Passionate

An easy way to start your own higher education or professional development path is to find what motivates you to teach. For me it was American Sign Language (ASL), which became a core part of my teaching practice. In college I minored in communication disorders, which is how I learned ASL. From there, I used it with infants and toddlers. Whether or not the children had diagnosed needs, ASL helped the children communicate better, which decreased their frustration when communicating needs to adults and interacting with peers. Find classes you enjoy—children's literature, STEM, or even puppetry—that you can put directly into practice to make your learning useful and fun!

Be Mentored

Aside from deepening your knowledge, gaining experience is a large part of becoming a successful teacher. I was blessed throughout my career to have mentors to guide me and inspire me to be my best. My first mentor in the field—who continues to support my career today—challenged me to leave my comfort in the classroom and use my voice to become a full-time policy advocate. Invest in yourself by learning from experienced members of the profession so you can continue to develop our field.

Professionalism as an Early Childhood Leader

Cashelle Johnson

As an early childhood leader, I must consider the ethical responsibilities I have toward this profession, including emphasizing the importance of diversity, inclusion, and equity. Our center has an equity cohort that meets weekly to discuss how educators can acknowledge diversity in the classroom. As a member of the cohort, I lead a discussion on ways to encourage children to discuss or ask questions about gender, race, or ethnicity (using children's literature, photographs of the children's families, children's artwork, etc.).

Our goal is to nurture a more diverse and inclusive generation of young children who thrive through their experiences of equitable learning opportunities in early learning programs. We commit—both individually and collectively—to continuous learning based on personally reflecting on how our beliefs and actions have been shaped by our experiences of the systems of privilege and oppression in which we operate and based on respectfully listening to others' perspectives (Yoshikawa et al., 2013). Knowing that all children have the right to equitable learning opportunities, I must continue to provide a work setting that embraces diversity not only for the children and their families but also for the educators. Educators are supported through collaborative meetings that reflect on equity concerns and are made aware of resources to strengthen our relationship with the students.

CASHELLE JOHNSON is an early childhood doctoral candidate at Capella University.

Be Accountable

Take charge of your professional development. Your program's leaders should be providing you access to curriculum materials and professional development opportunities. If they aren't, take it upon yourself to find learning opportunities that inspire you. I am passionate about child-driven lesson planning, so I sought out articles, books, online sessions, and conferences—anything I could get my hands on—so I could learn more and share with my colleagues. Many conferences offer great scholarships to make attending affordable!

Be Equitable

I'm extremely grateful that I learned early in my career the importance of connecting with families to understand their preferences and beliefs before making judgments about how a child was behaving. This framed my understanding of cultural differences and gave me a strong foundation for educating children equitably. For example, my colleagues and I had a few children in class who struggled to settle at nap time. This was frustrating for us—as most programs do, we used nap time for planning and meetings. The children would not settle, wanted individual attention from their primary teachers, and quite often were exhausted (and fussy!) by the end of the day because they did not have a nap. Before frustrations could escalate, we took the time to discuss this challenge with the families. They explained that following their cultural practices, the children never slept alone—which explained why the children wouldn't settle when staff moved away from them. We learned to recognize their cultural practices and planned for an extra staff member at nap time to stay near those children so the teachers could still use that time and the children would have that period to rest.

MEGHANN HICKEY is the senior manager of professional development at Hatch Early Learning, Inc. Previously, she worked for the Early Care and Education Consortium as a policy associate, at PBS as a professional learning developer, at NAEYC in the Early Learning Program Accreditation division, and as an infant through prekindergarten teacher in Massachusetts.

EQUITY Understand how children's cultural backgrounds and their cultures' values and ways of being and knowing might impact children's behavior in the classroom. Equity-focused educators involve children, family, and community in planning, and the naptime situation illustrates the value of this practice.

Personalized Professional Development

How Teachers Can Use Videos to Improve Their Practice

Rachel E. Schachter and Hope Kenarr Gerde

"In reflecting and in retrospect, [the children] are not real good with irregular plurals, and so putting 'mice' in was probably not a good choice on my part. I probably should have thought more about the pictures that I chose because [the children] still say 'mouses.' They don't say 'mice.'"

Jacki, a prekindergarten teacher, is reflecting as she watches herself lead a puzzle activity in which children match rhyming picture pairs. Considering the children's inability to find a matching picture for the word *mice,* she realizes that part of the problem was that the children had not yet learned many irregular plurals. A little later in the video, she sees that the children had difficulty labeling the word *mop.* Reflecting on that moment, Jacki suggests that her lesson might have gone better if the children had more background knowledge about what a mop is and how it is used.

By watching herself and the children participate in this activity, Jacki identifies a need in her teaching—to consider children's current background knowledge when selecting and using materials.

Engaging teachers in self-reflection by watching videos of their teaching is a powerful approach to professional development that can lead to meaningful changes in teachers' practices (Escamilla & Meier 2018; Sheridan et al. 2009). This chapter provides theoretical and research-based support for using videos for self-reflection to enhance teaching practice. It also offers practical guidance for engaging in self-reflection in classrooms and programs.

Personalized, Reflective Professional Development

To be effective, professional development must be ongoing and provide feedback on teachers' individual classroom practices. It seems that long-term, ongoing, classroom-based professional development is more effective for allowing teachers time to practice and refine new strategies (Desimone & Garet 2015). Importantly, teachers have reported that they prefer to engage in long-term, focused, and intense professional development (Garet et al. 2001). Yet these types of professional development programs are not the norm (Schachter, Gerde, & Hatton-Bowers 2019).

With a relatively small investment in video technology (as basic as a smartphone, tripod, and secure video storage), centers and schools can create their own highly effective, meaningful professional development centered on self-reflection. Using videos of practice provides an individualized approach to professional development, allowing teachers to take the lead in facilitating their own learning. Engaging in video-based self-reflection has been identified as an effective professional learning technique with the capacity to improve teachers' practice, which can promote children's knowledge and skills and enhance their social and emotional development (Downer et al. 2018; Landry et al. 2021). Videos allow teachers to critically evaluate their skills, test out variations in their practices, and consider how different strategies ultimately benefit the children.

Enhancing Prekindergarten Teachers' Practice

Viewing videos of their teaching across a range of instructional contexts provides opportunities for teachers to identify key areas in which practice can be enhanced. For example, while watching a video of herself leading a cooking activity, Amanda observed, "I probably didn't give them the opportunity to really answer my question. . . . I feel like I probably could have waited a little longer for them to answer that." Amanda made a powerful observation about her interactions with children, noticing that she needed to leave more wait time before giving them the answer to her question.

Engaging in self-reflection using video recordings can help teachers enhance practice by

> Providing the opportunity to think about what might not be working in the way intended and what could be modified. While watching herself lead group time, Amanda reflected, "I'm losing Wells. He's over it. . . . I need to get a fidget toy for him or something to keep him more on track." Although teachers attend to each child as much as possible when teaching, videos allow teachers to review an event repeatedly, focusing on one child at a time.

> Demonstrating teaching strengths. Recognizing their strengths can help teachers feel more confident, identify practices they want to continue, and consider how they can leverage these strengths as opportunities (Mills 2017). For example, when observing her morning meeting, Linda noted that she attended to each individual child in her classroom and included all of them in the conversation.

> Learning more about children's development. Watching children engage in conversations as they were involved in an activity showed Caitlin what the children were doing as she circulated around the room and helped her learn more about the children's abilities. Another teacher watching a video might recognize that a child needs extra support.

> Identifying needed changes to the classroom environment. When watching a morning meeting,

Abbey said, "There's so much extraneous noise. I had no idea—I'm so focused when we're there, but there's a lot of noise." This is critical, as noise can have negative impacts on both short- and long-term learning (Klatte, Bergström, & Lachmann 2013). This process allows you to make small changes to the environment that can have big, long-term impacts on practice and children's learning.

> Applying new knowledge or skills. Video self-reflection can also be a tool for practicing and extending content learned in other professional development offerings, like workshops or conference presentations. In response to an in-service training, Amanda had been trying to work more positive reinforcement and effective praise into her interactions and was able to see that progress in her teaching through video self-reflection.

The Reflection Process

At the start of the video self-reflection process, identify specific purposes for watching the video and goals for your teaching. Frequent, purposeful review of videos of the targeted practice, perhaps once a week, provides time to reflect on how things are going, improvements that have been made, and areas that need further development. Have questions to guide your reflection, such as the following:

> What do I notice about my targeted practice?

> How are children responding to my language or actions?

> What was successful about my teaching here?

> Is there something that I could do differently?

> Does the environment support my targeted practice and children's learning?

 EQUITY Teachers can watch for a variety of teaching strategies in the reflections, such as equitable practices. They can use the recordings to consider how they are meeting the needs of each child in terms of cultural and linguistic appropriateness and make adjustments based on what they observe.

A cycle of video, reflection, and refinement can continue until you feel you have mastered the strategies and accomplished the specific goals. Then, the reflection cycle can begin again by reviewing videos to identify new goals.

Engaging in meaningful reflection can occur only when a program allows teachers an atmosphere in which practice can be critiqued without judgment or punitive action. To grow, you must feel comfortable enough to take risks and try new skills. This can be a difficult process; as Beth observed, "Every time you think you got it down, there's something that screws it up." Teachers need time and support—with everyone understanding that meaningful change takes time.

It can be difficult to see oneself teaching and then to engage in a serious critique (alone or with others). Teachers and administrators should consider who is participating in the reflective process, especially in the beginning. If teachers are curious about their own practice, video self-reflection can be done individually with personal goals.

Reflecting can also be done as a collaborative professional development activity with coteachers or assistant teachers, other classroom teachers, specialists, coaches, and/or administrators. Working together as a community can be especially powerful for receiving feedback and working toward common goals (Clark 2019; Escamilla & Meier 2018). Teachers may feel more comfortable working in groups without administrators.

It is important to establish guidelines for the process in advance, to set parameters for discussions, and to ensure that everyone is comfortable (Schachter, Gerde, & Hatton-Bowers 2019). (For detailed examples illustrating the reflection process in action, see "Preparing for Evaluation with Video Self-Reflection," by Michelle Grantham-Caston and Cynthia DiCarlo, at NAEYC.org/dap-focus-preschool.)

Practical Considerations

There are many practical considerations for engaging in this type of professional development. Here are four of the most crucial considerations to help you get started:

› Focus the recording on the target teacher, not on children. Although this seems obvious, early childhood classrooms are busy, and children are often moving about.

› Plan recordings around learning goals. It is not efficient or realistic to record an entire day of teaching. Consider which strategies are being targeted and your professional learning goals. Then select which practice would be beneficial to reflect on and identify a good time to record it.

› Inform others about what you are doing. Children, families, and colleagues need to be told why and when you are recording instruction. Reassure families of their children's privacy and the benefits of recording. Check with program administrators on any program-based rules for the use of electronic devices and permission forms for families.

› Do not share videos. Recordings contain not only one person's teaching but the activities of children, colleagues, and others in the classroom, so take the same precautions with these videos as you take with child assessment data and anecdotal records. After reviewing a captured recording for reflection, delete the recording or store it somewhere secure.

Conclusion

Using video to reflect on practice is a powerful way to engage in personalized, ongoing, and intensive professional development, specifically targeting the needs of teachers and children in an individual early childhood program. This process provides opportunities to practice and receive feedback on skills learned in workshops or at conferences, which may improve the uptake of new ideas and strategies.

RACHEL E. SCHACHTER, PhD, is an associate professor in the Department of Child, Youth and Family Studies at the University of Nebraska–Lincoln. She studies ways to support effective professional learning for teachers that lead to improved outcomes for children.

HOPE KENARR GERDE, PhD, is a professor in the Department of Teaching, Learning, & Culture at Texas A&M University. Dr. Gerde's research focuses on the interrelations between early reading and writing skills among young children experiencing economic disadvantage, as well as the design and evaluation of high-quality teacher professional development delivered via distance learning approaches.

CHAPTER 31

Leading with LOVE
Leveraging Our Value Every Day

Chaz Simmons

As the owner of Kingdom Family Learning Center, a play-based community early learning program serving children from infancy to age 5, I understand the importance of professionalism in early childhood education. I prioritize exhibiting the characteristics, knowledge, and skills necessary to facilitate children's learning and support families. I feel it is my responsibility to communicate effectively, especially when providing information to the public about families' and children's issues. Therefore, I hold myself and our staff to high ethical standards, which helps build trust between the community and us.

I began my professional career as a customer service specialist in the financial industry, where I provided exceptional customer service for more than 10 years. Building rapport with and having empathy for each of my customers came naturally and transferred beyond my role. The mindset to listen for understanding helps you feel how someone else feels. As you discover where they are coming from and where they want to go, you can help guide them safely to where they need to be. To flourish, everyone needs to feel heard and understood, especially those whose voices sometimes go unheard because of their age or size. Ultimately, wanting to help meet that need led me to open an early learning program in my community. If every child in my community could participate in developmentally appropriate learning that recognized where they were physically, emotionally, culturally, and academically and provided the support needed for them to feel like valued members of the learning community, we would all benefit from the future leaders these children could become. To provide this type of learning environment for the children in our center, we focus on LOVE (Leveraging Our Value Every Day).

LOVE: Leveraging Our Value Every Day

Knowing each child personally helps educators build lasting relationships with trust and respect. We earn children's trust and respect by providing developmentally appropriate, equitable practices for each child that support their social and emotional, physical, linguistic, and cognitive development. Kingdom Family Learning Center is a faith-based community child care center, so we center what we do and who we are on LOVE. Love is patient, kind, and gentle, so it allows us to meet people where they are so they feel heard and seen, which is especially crucial for *young scholars*, the term we use for the children enrolled in our program to signal the importance of play-based, child-centered learning experiences in the early years. Having love for what you do or those you serve is a key characteristic of a true professional, and we use LOVE to put our professionalism into action every day.

L Is for Leveraging

We leverage our unique capabilities, resources, background experiences, and knowledge to maximize each child's development. Our educators strive to create a fun, loving, and safe environment that makes each child comfortable enough to share their feelings and ideas. These spaces help children learn and grow to be independent thinkers and problem solvers. The learning centers in our classrooms help develop social, emotional, and academic skills. We honor each child by including creative play at our learning centers and embedding science, technology, engineering, and math (STEM) activities to foster their curiosity and social and emotional skills. Playing with a stethoscope while pretending to be a doctor, building bridges and robots with blocks, and using the toy kitchen to open a restaurant are ways our children use their imaginations, language, and social skills through learning centers. The centers open their minds to a world of new possibilities.

I also make it a priority to leverage the knowledge of our families. To communicate with families, our educators use a mobile app to discuss important issues, milestones, and policies. In addition, we start each morning with smiles and personal greetings for every scholar and their family, helping to make sure they feel welcomed and wanted. By providing space for reciprocal dialogue with families, both in person and through the app, we are intentional about valuing and "drawing on families' expertise about their children for insight into curriculum, program development, and assessment" (NAEYC 2019b, 14).

We also leverage educational opportunities, supporting and encouraging continuous learning not only for young scholars but also for our educators. We have fostered a safe, collaborative environment for educators to share what is working in their classrooms as well as to seek guidance from each other about how to better serve the children they are working with. We seize any opportunity to learn more about educating diverse children with various learning styles. This commitment to learning helps us better reach all children of different ages and development levels.

O Is for Our

We champion inclusiveness, togetherness, diversity, and the "Kingdom Family way of learning" in our everyday routines at our center, intentionally creating a positive community where *our* children can be supported by us all. For example, teachers encourage children to be kind when they play to support them in building positive friendships. We practice togetherness by praying together before each meal as a family. Secular programs could adopt a before-meal ritual to foster a sense of cohesion as well. We focus on building good habits that children can carry on through their lives, including cheerful greetings and salutations each day. The Kingdom Family way of learning incorporates integrity and competence in a caring manner.

This safe and caring atmosphere is also felt by our families. As a program, we always share highlights of the child's day with their families at pickup time. We share what the child did well that day, the learning opportunities for the child, and what we can do together to work on those opportunities. We communicate these highlights using the sandwich technique: we share something positive, then a learning opportunity, and then another positive. For example, if Jimmy followed directions well but had also been hitting other children, we share the highlight in the following way: "Jimmy did a great job using his listening ears today! Although Jimmy used red (harmful or hurtful) choices several times today by hitting his friends, we are working on using green (safe and kind) choices to communicate his feelings without hitting others. With practice here at the center and at home, Jimmy will learn how to better communicate." This strategy promotes inclusiveness between our center and families by actively keeping families involved with aspects of their child's day, letting them know what their child did well and discussing how the center and the family can work together to act on any opportunities for improvement. While it can be challenging to master a professional communication strategy like the sandwich technique, we provide staff opportunities to practice as a part of our professional development.

V Is for Value

Early childhood professionals must establish supportive relationships with young children. Holding individual conversations that reflect a child's experiences and concerns; offering sincere, positive affirmations; and building on children's unique assets to support learning helps build self-esteem and exhibits how much we value the children. "Educators implement developmentally appropriate practice by recognizing the multiple assets all young children bring to the early learning program as unique individuals and members of families and communities" (NAEYC 2020, 5). Celebrating diversity is vital in helping children learn their own value, and that of others, because it helps highlight what each one contributes to the community. Practices that explore different cultures and languages and focus on the strengths and abilities of each child are essential. Our children feel valued and protected, which is essential for optimal learning and development. Embrace equity in your own practice by showing concern or care in your actions and words and paying attention to the details of the lives of the children, families, and educators.

I set standards that require teachers to be actively involved with each child and their family, building reciprocal relationships and showing compassion and concern for issues that affect them. I help them achieve this through targeted professional development opportunities aligned with NAEYC's Code of Ethical Conduct and professionalism standards, ongoing discussions, and routine recognition of educators' practices.

 DAP Connecting with families and showing empathy by attending to their concerns is a key component of developmentally appropriate practice.

E Is for Every Day

LOVE is an action word that requires work, and putting its elements into practice does not allow for taking a break. Patience is a virtue when trying to understand someone—especially a hungry, sleepy toddler at 7 a.m.—and educators must be willing to go the extra mile to meet the young scholars where they are, every day. One morning, one of our teachers sat down on the floor to talk with a scholar who was having a rough morning and did not want to participate in the morning routine. While engaging with the child on her terms, the teacher learned what the problem was and provided a solution: letting the child eat breakfast before the morning activity. Keeping the child's needs in mind each day offers you the opportunity to be an advocate for them. Actively engage with the children and model the behavior expectations with every interaction.

To consistently meet the diverse needs of young children, educators seek to manage "their own resilience, self-efficacy, mental health, and wellness" because they know that it "is critical to the effectiveness of their work, particularly when addressing challenging behaviors" (NAEYC 2019b, 25). So take care of your mental well-being. Know your limits and your boundaries. Understand what overwhelms you, what calms you, and what you can do to manage your stress inside and outside of work. Utilize what helps you be your best self daily, whether it's your morning coffee or your favorite afternoon snack. Make a conscientious choice to show up as your best self every day despite any obstacles or challenges you may face in your personal life.

Choose to be kind, not letting your emotions get the best of you, and remind yourself that children learn and watch everything you do, so do it well.

Conclusion

Exhibiting this LOVE daily with everyone we interact with ensures that joyful, play-based learning takes place at our center, on every level, with all ages and at all stages of life. When you do what you love, you will love what you do, which is a definition of success. I encourage early childhood educators to take the time to implement and support joyful, play-based learning with LOVE at the core of all they do, so young scholars are equipped with the tools, abilities, and resources they need to succeed in life.

CHAZ SIMMONS is the owner of Kingdom Family Learning Center in Fort Worth, Texas.

CHAPTER 32

Beginning (or Continuing) the Journey to a More Equitable Classroom

Janis Strasser and Llariley Coplin

Carly is preparing to read aloud her 4-year-old students' favorite book, *The Pigeon Finds a Hot Dog*, by Mo Willems. All except for Jamal are quietly sitting on the rug and waiting for her to begin. As she scans the group, her eyes stop on Jamal. She takes a breath and thinks, "Why is Jamal always interrupting, fidgeting, and bothering everyone while I read?" Just then, Jamal starts to make loud chewing noises and offers imaginary hot dogs to the children sitting next to him. "Why is he so difficult?" she ponders.

As many Americans become more aware of the many ways that bias permeates our everyday lives, things are changing. Companies (big and small), sports organizations, musicians, and other popular figures are reexamining—or examining for the first time—the words and images that they convey. In some cases, they are making changes to their products and advertisements to counter stereotypical, unfair, or hurtful representations of race, gender, and other aspects of identity. For example, the professional baseball team formerly known as the Cleveland Indians changed the team's name to the Cleveland Guardians, acknowledging the previous name's culturally insensitive origins. And to encourage gender identity inclusion, the Disney Channel has introduced more LGBTQIA+ visibility, including developing a nonbinary character, Raine Whispers, on their popular show *The Owl House*, which won a Peabody Award for its positive representation.

As educators, we too must take a look inward and evaluate our own thoughts, ideas, and practices as we acknowledge our past mistakes and strive for equity. Doing this kind of thinking, reflecting, and improvement can be overwhelming, uncomfortable, or upsetting. It is also a necessity. Here are just a few reasons why:

› Some White preschool teachers unconsciously feel that Black boys are more likely to misbehave and have lower expectations for Black boys than for other children. Black boys are much more likely to be suspended and even expelled from preschool than their White peers (Gaias et al. 2022; Wright 2019; see also Chapter 5 in this book).

› There are inaccuracies and gaps in how cultures, groups of people, and events are written about and represented in books, in the media, and in education. For example, Columbus Day and Thanksgiving are not celebrations for many Native Americans (Fleming 2006).

› Native American children have been prohibited from speaking their languages and practicing their cultural traditions in schools (Derman-Sparks & Edwards, with Goins 2020).

› Children from LGBTQIA+ families, or children who identify as gender fluid or gender nonconforming, may be bullied and marginalized (Espelage et al. 2019; Goodboy & Martin 2018; Kimura, Antón-Oldenburg, & Pinderhughes 2022).

These findings from research by no means represent the wide range of biased thinking, language, and behaviors that can occur in educational settings. Indeed, what research shows is that we all have implicit or unconscious associations and feelings that affect the way we make decisions and act. Sometimes we have these feelings even though they are contrary to our conscious or declared beliefs. They are the stories we unconsciously make up in our minds about people or groups without knowing or understanding the facts. Becoming aware of them can help us grow and change.

Several key NAEYC publications ask us to carefully consider how biases contribute to our work with children and families (see the position statement on advancing equity; the fourth edition of *Developmentally Appropriate Practice in Early Childhood Programs Serving Children from Birth Through Age 8*; and the second edition of *Anti-Bias Education for Young Children and Ourselves*). Biases can influence the verbal and nonverbal interactions and messages we send children and the way we look at particular classroom situations and children's behavior.

Knowing that we all have implicit biases and, simultaneously, have the capacity to change our thinking and improve our practices, we've outlined four steps that early childhood educators can take to understand their own biases and to advance equity:

1. Reflect on your current beliefs, attitudes, and practices.

2. Set goals that connect to or come from your self-reflection.

3. Identify steps to take toward achieving your goals, finding resources, and taking action.

4. Assess your progress and look ahead.

Early childhood educators are known for being lifelong learners and committed to continually growing as professionals. These steps can be a part of your overall professional development, and we suggest finding supportive colleagues and mentors to join you on this journey.

Reflect on Current Beliefs, Attitudes, and Practices

To begin, ask yourself a series of questions about your beliefs, attitudes, and experiences related to children, families, and the broader world around you. For example,

› Do you notice when a Black boy starts wiggling around on the rug more than when a White boy does this?

› Do you engage in one-on-one conversations with certain children much more often than others?

› Do you feel uncomfortable during a conference with two moms?

› Do you think that it is silly when you hear that some teachers don't want to have a Thanksgiving feast or teach the names of Columbus's three ships?

Set Goals

Based on your reflections, create one to two goals. Give yourself a timeline with at least one short-term and one long-term goal. For example,

› Find developmentally appropriate ways to acknowledge and support the positive behaviors of students who display challenging behaviors.

› Get to know each child and family in your setting.

› Understand the history and issues behind the LGBTQIA+ movement.

› Learn more about why Columbus Day and Thanksgiving are days of mourning for Native American people and how to accurately teach children about the history of these days.

Identify Steps to Take, Find Resources, and Take Action

After creating your goals, select and engage in activities that will help you make progress toward reaching them. These actions may include

› Reading books, articles, and blogs

› Watching videos online and listening to podcasts

› Attending workshops and conference sessions (in person or virtually)

› Trying out new strategies, activities, and materials in your setting

› Discussing your questions, learning, and progress with a trusted colleague and asking them to observe you

› Connecting with families to learn more about their experiences, hopes, and concerns

Assess Your Progress and Look Ahead

After giving yourself sufficient time to take action, it is important to gauge your progress, including

> Successes you've experienced

> Challenges or setbacks you've encountered

> How children's learning and your relationships with them have been impacted

> How partnerships with families have improved

> Questions that remain

> Evidence of your journey (writing, photos, video recordings)

Let's take a peek at Carly's journey as she used these four steps to understand more about her perceptions of Jamal and to grow as an educator and person.

Carly begins by reflecting back on her thoughts about Jamal. Is he *really* always engaged in negative behaviors, or does she notice his behaviors more than others'? Does she recognize and build on his strengths? Carly thinks about the fact that she has only one or two Black children in her class each year. She wonders whether she unconsciously has different opinions and expectations about children of color, and she wonders if she takes the time to connect with families of color as often as she does with White families.

So she sets goals for herself. Her long-term goal is to identify and understand her own biases. One short-term goal is to observe Jamal's behaviors during read-aloud and morning meetings for two weeks. She will then analyze her notes for any patterns in her words and actions and in Jamal's behaviors. Another short-term goal is to reach out to Jamal's family to learn about their expectations for him, his strengths, and any questions they may have.

 While Jamal's behavior during read-alouds may have been entirely age and individually appropriate, and only an issue because of Carly's heightened attention to his behavior, it may also have indicated that Jamal would benefit from support for developing self-regulation. Because play promotes self-regulation, offering highly engaging play experiences for children who are developing self-regulation skills is an excellent tool. Observing and recording a child's behavior and that of the teachers, as Carly did, helps illuminate the reasons behind a behavior.

After setting these goals, Carly identifies steps to take to support her efforts. She creates a form to record her and Jamal's behaviors and asks her assistant teacher to use it too so they can compare notes. Carly also begins using a journal for each child to send home a positive note about the child's day. Families can add to the journal too. Finally, Carly asks the director of the program if they can devote time during each staff meeting to discuss resources about understanding and countering bias, with each teacher having a chance to lead a discussion about one resource. (See "Resources to Begin [or Continue] Your Journey Toward Equity" on page 144 for some suggestions.)

Six months later, Carly looks back to assess her work with Jamal and her own growth. She notes successes. For example, she placed picture books and props into the dramatic play area and observed Jamal frequently acting out stories and creating puppet shows with the other children. She also notes that he likes to bring some of these materials home to perform for his family. After meeting with his family to share his strengths and challenges at home and at school, Carly started texting photos of Jamal's puppet shows to his parents. In response, his mom is now making sock puppets of favorite picture book characters for the classroom.

Her program's staff has also begun to engage in many meaningful, sometimes difficult conversations during their monthly meetings. Spurred by these powerful discussions, they plan to hold a book club next year focused on *Anti-Bias Education for Young Children and Ourselves*, and they will set goals, take action, and assess their progress in implementing anti-bias strategies and examining their own thinking and behaviors.

Having committed to this journey, Carly feels proud that she has started to confront her biases and reexamine how she interacts with students and families, to improve her classroom practices, and to move forward in a lifelong process of growing as an early childhood educator.

Conclusion

It can be intimidating to have conversations about race, gender, and other topics that you aren't comfortable talking about. But with dedicated planning, action, and reflection, your quest to understand and address your own biases will make a difference in young children's and families' lives—and yours too.

Resources to Begin (or Continue) Your Journey Toward Equity

Read Online
> Dena Simmons's "How to Be an Antiracist Educator" in *ASCD Education Update*, October 2019

> Dana Williams's *Beyond the Golden Rule: A Parent's Guide to Preventing and Responding to Prejudice*

> NAEYC's advancing equity initiative, advocacy resources, and content on equity and diversity from NAEYC's publications

> Learning for Justice resources (use the search word "preschool") and online magazine

Listen to These Podcasts
> NPR's *Parenting: Difficult Conversations*: "Talking Race with Young Children" (20 minutes)

> Harvard *EdCast*: "Unconscious Bias in Schools" (28 minutes)

> *The Early Link Podcast*: "Soobin Oh Discusses Anti-Bias Education in Early Childhood" (34 minutes)

> BBC Radio 4's *Analysis*: "Implicit Bias" (27 minutes)

Watch Online
> Chimamanda Ngozi Adichie's "The Danger of a Single Story" (18 minutes)

> Russell McClain's "Implicit Bias, Stereotype Threat, and Higher Education" for TEDxUMBaltimore (11 minutes)

> Alice Goffman's *How We're Priming Some Kids for College and Others for Prisons* (15 minutes)

> "Tyler Perry Speaks from the Heart About Racial Injustice and the World He Wants for His Son" for *People* magazine (9 minutes)

> "Native American Girls Describe the Real History Behind Thanksgiving" for *Teen Vogue* (2 minutes)

> "Why These Native Americans Observe a National Day of Mourning Each Thanksgiving" for *HuffPost* (5 minutes)

> "Columbus Day vs. Indigenous Peoples Day" for KARE 11 News (4 minutes)

JANIS STRASSER is professor emerita from William Paterson University. Prior to that she was a preschool and kindergarten teacher. She is coauthor of the NAEYC book *Big Questions for Young Minds: Extending Children's Thinking*.

LLARILEY COPLIN is a graduate of Boston University's College of Communications and an advocate for social justice.

CHAPTER 33

Incorporating Anti-Racist Approaches for Asian American Children

Shu-Chen "Jenny" Yen

Nine-year-old Emily and her 5-year-old sister Mei Mei (which means younger sister in Chinese) are waiting for their mom outside of a grocery store. They are playing rock, paper, scissors and laughing out loud when a man approaches and yells, "Stupid Asians! Go back where you came from!" Both girls are scared. Mei Mei starts to cry, and Emily doesn't know what to do. When their mom returns, they have a lot of questions: Why was he angry at them? Did they do something wrong? The girls' mother has questions of her own: How should she address this racist attack? What should she say to the girls? Should she talk to their teacher?

Conversations about race and racism are some of the most difficult conversations to have with young children. Many families and educators avoid talking about racism with young children because they are not comfortable with the topic or do not know what to say. However, in the aftermath of the murder of George Floyd and other Black Americans at the hands of police officers, the COVID-19 pandemic, the Black Lives Matter movement, and rising anti-Asian hate crimes, families and early childhood educators in the United States can no longer ignore discussing racism with children. The reality is that children experience issues of racism on a daily basis to different degrees. Some children may not experience a direct assault like in the vignette above but are exposed to frightening news, such as Asian elders being brutally attacked. Other children may hear about family members being detained and asked about their citizenship status. Although they may not understand the incidents, children may worry about their safety and their family's safety.

Why Discuss Race and Racism with Young Children?

Intentional parents often have questions about talking about such incidents with their children: Where should I start? How early should I start? Will they understand? When is a good time to talk to my children? How much is too much? While some adults initiate the conversation before children raise questions, others choose not to expose their children to conversations about racism too early for fear that children will not understand. Research, however, indicates that children start to have preferences around skin color and other facial characteristics early on. For example, while newborn infants show no preference for faces from their own or other ethnic groups, 3-month-old infants clearly show a preference for faces from their own ethnic group (Kelly et al. 2005). In addition, Perszyk and colleagues (2019) used implicit and explicit measures to assess the responses of 4-year-old children (children of color and White children) to target images of children of both race (Black and White) and gender (male and female). All children revealed a strong, consistent pro-White bias. Because of such findings, researchers and others strongly recommend that adults start talking with children about biases and race before kindergarten.

Undoubtedly, children in your classroom will bring up questions about race. Schools are reflections of our society, and as such, early childhood classrooms are spaces where racism is manifested (Husband 2012). Daren Graves argues that "whether we like it or not, race is happening in schools. Racism is happening in and around the school. Kids are forming racial identities in school, whether it's happening intentionally or not" (Tatter 2021). Scholars have called for anti-racist education to help teachers both examine their own beliefs and exposure to racism and challenge notions of racism in their classrooms (Allen et al. 2022; Husband 2012; Singleton & Linton 2006). Just like families, many teachers wonder if these discussions on racism are developmentally appropriate for young children and feel unsure about what to do (Sturdivant & Alanís 2019). This doubt often leads teachers to ignore the issues, minimize discussions, or implement a colorblind curriculum where teachers feel they do not need to discuss racial bias or inequities with young learners (Kuh et al. 2016). However, since young children are aware of racial issues at a very young age (Sturdivant & Alanís 2020; Winkler 2009)—this is often manifested in their drawings, conversations, and interactions with other children—it is critical that educators seek to understand what children are thinking about issues around race, how children are affected by racism, and how to engage children in anti-bias education.

I approached this chapter from my own sociocultural perspective and decades of work with young children, families, and early childhood educators. Consequently, the lens I bring focuses on the Asian American culture and seeks to address the issue of cultural competency in our field. In this chapter, I share some strategies for addressing issues of racism in the classroom setting, particularly as it relates to the Asian American community.

Examine Your Own Biases

Before talking with young children about racism, examine your own bias. We all have our own biases based on our social identities, including race and gender. These biases reflect cultural mindsets, stereotypes, and prejudices that are pervasive in our communities (Perszyk et al. 2019). Many educators, for example, believe in the myth of the "model minority," which stereotypes Asian Americans as smart and successful in education and accomplishing the American Dream (USC Pacific Asia Museum, n.d.). As a result, Asian American children often do not receive necessary educational intervention or assistance (Lee et al. 2017). As early childhood professionals, it is our responsibility to make sure that "every effort is made to help each and every

member of the community feel psychologically safe and able to focus on being and learning" (NAEYC 2020, 17).

 EQUITY Effective educators think critically about their own biases and how these may be reflected in their classroom environments, materials, and teaching practices.

Understand the Impact of Anti-Asian Hate Crime on Asian American Children

Since the onset of the COVID-19 pandemic, anti-Asian hate crimes have increased tremendously (Stop AAPI Hate, n.d.). For example, San Francisco police marked a 567 percent increase in reports of anti-Asian hate crimes in 2021 (*Washington Post* 2022). Many Asian American children, unfortunately, witness or experience anti-Asian hate at an early age. As an early childhood educator, you can help to combat the effects of these experiences by engaging in discussions and meaningful lessons about race (Cole & Verwayne 2018), integrating culturally relevant literature (Yenika-Agbaw & Napoli 2011), and adopting an anti-racist curriculum (Derman-Sparks, LeeKeenan, & Nimmo 2015).

Educate Yourself and Be Prepared

When tackling difficult conversations like racism, teachers must demonstrate cultural competencies, including understanding, appreciating, and interacting with people from different cultures. Preparation is the key to difficult conversations! As a professional, be emotionally and verbally prepared. Answer children's questions with respect, honesty, warmth, and objectivity. When you do not know an answer, assure children that you will try to find out. Acknowledge that these difficult questions are developmentally, culturally, and age appropriate for young children (Starnes 2022). It is equally important that you understand Asian American culture when planning to talk with children of Asian descent, especially under an anti-Asian climate.

Understand How Past Experiences Influence How We Think and Act

To better understand Asian American culture, seek information from families and communities about their cultural and linguistic experiences. Supplement your knowledge about communities' sociocultural histories. For example, in many Asian communities there is a "cycle of silence." When something scary happens, families do not talk about it. As a result, children think they should not ask any questions. This cycle of silence hurts children's social and emotional development and must be addressed, especially given the effects on the Asian American community of the unprecedented time of both the COVID-19 pandemic and rising anti-Asian hate. Learning more about these cultural beliefs and practices will help you understand how these experiences influence family dynamics and children's development.

 EQUITY Understanding a community's history can shed light on inequitable practices and help create culturally responsive educational programs.

The following resources may help you better understand Asian American culture and their experiences:

> *Minor Feelings: An Asian American Reckoning,* by Cathy Park Hong, is a collection of essays published in 2020 about the nuances of the Asian American experience.

> *Yellow: Race in America Beyond Black and White,* by Frank H. Wu, examines stereotypes such as the perpetual foreigner and the model minority myth and tackles affirmative action, immigration, and interracial marriage, among other issues.

> *Self Evident: Asian America's Stories* is a podcast that aims to challenge assumptions about Asian Americans.

> PBS's *Asian Americans* is a five-part documentary series on the history of Asians in America.

> *Asian American Stories in the Time of Coronavirus,* from the Asian American Documentary Network, is a YouTube documentary series exploring Asian Americans' experiences and challenges during the COVID-19 pandemic. #AsianAmCovidStories

Take Time to Learn About the Families with Whom You Work

It is important for teachers to understand that many Asian Americans come from a collectivist culture. This is quite different from the individualistic culture that is dominant in the United States. Collectivistic cultures emphasize restraint of emotion, parental authority, and social harmony. A value that is highly revered in Eastern cultures, collectivism means that the individual's efforts are made to honor the family and country, not to glorify the individual (Chao 1994). Many parents of Asian descent, for example, are concerned with maintaining social harmony; therefore, they teach their children to restrain their emotions so that they can maintain harmony with others (Fivush & Wang 2005). In contrast, individualistic cultures emphasize self-expression and autonomy (Wang & Tamis-Lemonda 2003). Many Asian American children come from families who practice collectivist culture but attend schools where an individualist culture is dominant. Effective teachers recognize and value attributes of both types of cultures. They help children understand and navigate the school culture while helping them maintain and see the value in their home culture.

Cultivate Community Resources

When families are seeking support, connect them to significant community resources such as local libraries, physical and mental health consultants, and government services. Think about how you can strengthen your own civic connections and contribute to the ongoing development of the community in which you work.

Speak Out Against Inequitable Practices

As an early childhood professional, you serve as an advocate for all young children and their families. Speak out against unfair policies or practices in your early childhood setting. Also, work with others who are equally committed to equity to change policies and institutional practices that might keep social inequities in place (Alanís & Iruka, with Friedman, 2021; Allen et al. 2022).

SHU-CHEN "JENNY" YEN, PhD, is professor of child and adolescent studies at California State University, Fullerton.

References

Alanís, I., M.G. Arreguín, & I. Salinas-González. 2021. *The Essentials: Supporting Dual Language Learners in Diverse Environments in Preschool and Kindergarten*. Washington, DC: NAEYC.

Alanís, I., & I.U. Iruka., eds. With S. Friedman. 2021. *Advancing Equity and Embracing Diversity in Early Childhood Education: Elevating Voices and Actions*. Washington, DC: NAEYC.

Allen, R., D.L. Shapland, J. Neitzel, & I.U. Iruka. 2021. "Creating Anti-Racist Early Childhood Spaces." *Young Children* 76 (2): 49–54. www.naeyc.org /resources/pubs/yc/summer2021/viewpoint-anti -racist-spaces.

Allen, R., D.L. Shapland, J. Neitzel, & I.U. Iruka. 2022. "Creating Anti-Racist Early Childhood Spaces." Viewpoint. *Teaching Young Children* 15 (4): 27–29.

Arreguín-Anderson, M.G., I. Salinas-González, & I. Alanís. 2018. "Translingual Play that Promotes Cultural Connections, Invention, and Regulation: A LatCrit Perspective." *International Multilingual Research Journal* 12 (4): 273–87.

Artiles, A.J. 2013. "Untangling the Racialization of Disabilities: An Intersectionality Critique Across Disability Models." *Du Bois Review: Social Science Research on Race* 10 (2): 329–47.

Bae, J.-H. 2004. "Learning to Teach Visual Arts in an Early Childhood Classroom: The Teacher's Role as a Guide." *Early Childhood Education Journal* 31 (4): 247–54.

Baldwin, J.A., R. Brown, & R. Hopkins. 1991. "The Black Self-Hatred Paradigm Revisited: An Afrocentric Analysis." In *Black Psychology*, ed. R.L. Jones, 28–44. Berkeley, CA: Cobb & Henry.

Bang, M. 2015. "Culture, Learning, and Development and the Natural World: The Influences of Situative Perspectives." *Educational Psychologist* 50 (3): 220–33.

Bates, L. A., & J. E. Glick. 2013. "Does It Matter if Teachers and School Match the Student? Racial and Ethnic Disparities in Problem Behaviors." *Social Science Research* 42 (5): 1180–90.

Bateson, K., Z.J. Darwin, P.M. Galdas, & C. Rosen. 2017. "Engaging Fathers: Acknowledging the Barriers." *Journal of Health Visiting* 5 (3): 126–32.

Bedore, L.M., & E.D. Peña. 2008. "Assessment of Bilingual Children for Identification of Language Impairment: Current Findings and Implications for Practice." *International Journal of Bilingual Education and Bilingualism* 11 (1): 1–29.

Bennett, S.V., A.A. Gunn, G. Gayle-Evans, E.S. Barrera, & C.B. Leung. 2018. "Culturally Responsive Literacy Practices in an Early Childhood Community." *Early Childhood Education Journal* 46 (2): 241–48.

Bennett-Armistead, V.S., N.K. Duke, & A.M. Moses 2005. *Literacy and the Youngest Learner: Best Practices for Educators of Children from Birth to 5*. New York: Scholastic.

Bird, E.K.R., F. Genesee, & L. Verhoeven. 2016. "Bilingualism in Children with Developmental Disorders: A Narrative Review." *Journal of Communication Disorders* 63: 1–14.

Bradshaw, C.P., M.M. Mitchell, L.M. O'Brennan, & P.J. Leaf. 2010. "Multilevel Exploration of Factors Contributing to the Overrepresentation of Black Students in Office Disciplinary Referrals." *Journal of Educational Psychology* 102 (2): 508–20.

Bresler, L. 1993. "Three Orientations to Arts in the Primary Grades: Implications for Curriculum Reform." *Arts Education Policy Review* 94 (6): 29–34.

Burchinal, M.R., A. Pace, R. Alper, K. Hirsh-Pasek, & R.M. Golinkoff. 2016. "Early Language Outshines Other Predictors of Academic and Social Trajectories in Elementary School." Presentation at Administration for Children and Families (ACF) conference, Washington, DC, July 11–13.

Cabrera, N.J., B.L. Volling, & R. Barr. 2018. "Fathers Are Parents, Too! Widening the Lens on Parenting for Children's Development." *Child Development Perspectives* 12 (3): 152–57.

Carr, M. 2001. *Assessment in Early Childhood Settings: Learning Stories*. Thousand Oaks, CA: Sage.

Carr, M., & W. Lee. 2012. *Learning Stories: Constructing Learner Identities in Early Education*. Thousand Oaks, CA: Sage.

Carr, M., & W. Lee. 2019. *Learning Stories in Practice*. Thousand Oaks, CA: Sage.

Carter, M. 2010. "Using Learning Stories to Strengthen Teachers' Relationships with Children." *Exchange* 32 (6): 40–44.

Castro, D.C., L.M. Espinosa, & M.M. Páez. 2011. "Defining and Measuring Quality in Early Childhood Practices that Promote Dual Language Learners' Development and Learning. In *Quality Measurement in Early Childhood Settings*, eds. M. Zaslow, I. Martinez-Beck, K. Tout, & T. Halle, 257–80. Baltimore, MD: Brookes Publishing.

Chao, R.K. 1994. "Beyond Parental Control and Authoritarian Parenting Style: Understanding Chinese Parenting Through the Cultural Notion of Training." *Child Development* 65 (4): 1111–19.

Chawla, L. 2015. "Benefits of Nature Contact for Children." *Journal of Planning Literature* 30 (4): 433–52. https://doi.org/10.1177 /0885412215595441.

Clark, K. 2017. "Investigating the Effects of Culturally Relevant Texts on African American Struggling Readers' Progress." *Teachers College Record* 119: 1–30.

Clark, M. 2019. "Edges and Boundaries: Finding Community and Innovation as an Early Childhood Educator." *Early Childhood Education Journal* 47: 153–62. https://doi.org/10.1007 /s10643-018-0904-z.

Clay, M.M. 1975. *What Did I Write? Beginning Writing Behavior*. Portsmouth, NH: Heinemann.

Cole, K., & D. Verwayne. 2018. "Becoming Upended: Teaching and Learning About Race and Racism with Young Children and Their Families." *Young Children* 73 (2): 34–43.

Curenton, S. 2006. "Oral Storytelling: A Cultural Art that Promotes School Readings." *Young Children* 61 (5): 78–89.

Dalkilic, M. 2019. "A Capability-Oriented Lens: Reframing the Early Years Education of Children with Disabilities." In *Disrupting and Countering Deficits in Early Childhood Education*, eds. F. Nxumalo & C.P. Brown, 67–82. New York: Routledge.

Dasgupta, N. 2013. "Implicit Attitudes and Beliefs Adapt to Situations: A Decade of Research on the Malleability of Implicit Prejudice, Stereotypes, and the Self-Concept." *Advances in Experimental Social Psychology* 47: 233–79.

DeHaney, F.L., C. Thompson Payton, & A. Washington. 2019. "Quality Includes Removing Bias from Early Childhood Education Environments." In *Advancing Equity & Embracing Diversity in Early Childhood Education: Elevating Voice & Actions*, eds. I. Alanís, I. Iruka, & S. Friedman, 26–34. Washington, DC: NAEYC.

Delgado-Bernal, D. 2001. "Learning and Living Pedagogies of the Home: The Mestiza Consciousness of Chicana Students." *International Journal of Qualitative Studies in Education* 14 (5): 623–39. https://doi.org/10.1080 /09518390110059838.

Derman-Sparks, L., & J.O. Edwards. With C.M. Goins. 2020. *Anti-Bias Education for Young Children and Ourselves*. Washington, DC: NAEYC.

Derman-Sparks, L., L.D. LeeKeenan, & J. Nimmo. 2015. *Leading Anti-Bias Early Childhood Programs: A Guide for Change*. New York: Teachers College Press; Washington, DC: NAEYC.

Desimone, L.M., & M.S. Garet. 2015. "Best Practices in Teachers' Professional Development in the United States." *Psychology, Society and Education* 7: 252–63.

Dewey, J. 1938. *Experience and Education*. New York: Collier MacMillan.

DiAngelo, R. 2016. *What Does It Mean to Be White? Developing White Racial Literacy*. New York: Peter Lang.

Dickinson, D.K., K.T. Nesbitt, & K.G. Hofer. 2019. "Effects of Language on Initial Reading: Direct and Indirect Associations Between Code and Language from Preschool to First Grade." *Early Childhood Research Quarterly* 49: 122–37.

Dickinson, D.K., & M.V. Porche. 2011. "Relation Between Language Experiences in Preschool Classrooms and Children's Kindergarten and Fourth-Grade Language and Reading Abilities." *Child Development* 82 (3): 870–86.

Downer, J.T., A.P. Williford, R.J. Bulotsky-Shearer, V.E. Vitiello, J. Bouza, S. Reilly, & A. Lhospital. 2018. "Using Data-Driven, Video-Based Early Childhood Consultation with Teachers to Reduce Children's Challenging Behaviors and Improve Engagement in Preschool Classrooms." *School Mental Health* 10 (3): 226–42.

Drummond, T. n.d. "Writing Learning Stories." Accessed December 27, 2020. https://tomdrummond.com /looking-closely-at-children/writing-learning-stories.

Durden, T.R., E. Escalante, & K. Blitch. 2015. "Start with Us! Culturally Relevant Pedagogy in the Preschool Classroom." *Early Childhood Education Journal* 43 (3): 223–32. https://doi.org/10.1007 /s10643-014-0651-8.

Durham, R.E., G. Farkas, C.S. Hammer, J.B. Tomblin, & H.W. Catts. 2007. "Kindergarten Oral Language Skill: A Key Variable in the Intergenerational Transmission of Socioeconomic Status." *Research in Social Stratification and Mobility* 25 (4): 294–305.

Eckhoff, A. 2013. "Conversational Pedagogy: Exploring Interactions Between a Teaching Artist and Young Learners During Visual Arts Experiences." *Early Childhood Education Journal* 41 (5): 365–72.

Escamilla, I.M., & D. Meier. 2018. "The Promise of Teacher Inquiry and Reflection: Early Childhood Teachers as Change Agents." *Studying Teacher Education* 14 (1): 3–21.

Espelage, D.L., A. Valido, T. Hatchel, K.M. Ingram, Y. Huang, & C. Torgal. 2019. "A Literature Review of Protective Factors Associated with Homophobic Bullying and Its Consequences Among Children & Adolescents." *Aggression and Violent Behavior* 45: 98–110. https://doi.org/10.1016/j.avb.2018.07.003.

Esteban-Guitart, M., J.L. Lalueza, C. Zhang-Yu, & M. Llopart. 2019. "Sustaining Students' Cultures and Identities. A Qualitative Study Based on the Funds of Knowledge and Identity Approaches." *Sustainability* 11 (12): 3400.

Evans, L.M., & A. Avila. 2016. "Enhancing Science Learning Through Dynamic Bilingual Practices." *Childhood Education* 92 (4): 290–97.

Farago, F., K.L. Davidson, & C.M. Byrd. 2019. "Ethnic-Racial Socialization in Early Childhood: The Implications of Color-Consciousness and Colorblindness for Prejudice Development." In *Handbook of Children and Prejudice*: 131–145. Cham, Switzerland: Springer.

The Fatherhood Project. 2015. "4 Steps to Engaging Dads in Schools." www.thefatherhoodproject.org /4-steps-to-engaging-dads-in-schools/#_edn1.

Ferreiro, E., & A. Teberosky. 1982. *Literacy Before Schooling*. New York: Touchstone/Simon & Schuster.

Fiore, L.B. 2020. *Assessment of Young Children: A Collaborative Approach*. New York: Routledge.

Fisher, D., & N. Frey. 2019. "Listening Stations in Content Area Learning." *The Reading Teacher* 72 (6): 769–73.

Fivush, R., & Q. Wang. 2005. "Emotion Talk in Mother-Child Conversations of the Shared Past: The Effects of Culture, Gender, and Event Valence." *Journal of Cognition and Development* 6 (4): 489–506. https://doi.org/10.1207/s15327647 jcd0604_3.

Fleming, W.C. 2006. "Myths and Stereotypes About Native Americans." *Phi Delta Kappan* 88 (3): 213–17.

Flurkey, A.D., & K.F. Whitmore. 2017. "Designing Curriculum in Response to Max's and Zachary's Learning." In *Reclaiming Early Childhood Literacies: Narratives of Hope, Power, and Vision*, eds. R.J. Meyer & K.F. Whitmore, 157–60. New York: Routledge.

Freire, P. 1970 [2000]. *Pedagogy of the Oppressed*. 30th anniversary ed. New York & London: Bloomsbury Press.

Freire, P. 1985. "Reading the World and Reading the Word: An Interview with Paolo Freire." *Language Arts* 62 (1): 15–21.

Gaias, L.M., D.E. Gal-Szabo, E.M. Shivers, & S. Kiche. 2022. "From *Laissez-Faire* to *Anti-Discrimination*: How Are Race/Ethnicity, Culture, and Bias

Integrated into Multiple Domains of Practice in Early Childhood Education?" *Journal of Research in Childhood Education.* 36 (2): 272–95.

Galdi, S., M. Cadinu, & C. Tomasetto. 2014. The Roots of Stereotype Threat: When Automatic Associations Disrupt Girls' Math Performance. *Child Development* 85 (1): 250–63.

Gardner-Neblett, N., E.P. Pungello, & I.U. Iruka. 2012. "Oral Narrative Skills: Implications for the Reading Development of African American Children. *Child Development Perspectives* 6 (3): 218–24. https://doi.org/10.1111/j.1750-8606.2011.00225.x.

Garet, M.S., A.C. Porter, L. Desimone, B.F. Birman, & K.S. Yoon. 2001. "What Makes Professional Development Effective? Results from a National Sample of Teachers." *American Educational Research Journal* 38 (4): 915–45.

Ghiso, M.P. 2016. "The Laundromat as the Transnational Local: Young Children's Literacies of Interdependence." *Teachers College Record* 118 (1): 1–46.

Gillanders, C., & S.Y. Sánchez. 2021. "Learning from Sociocultural Contexts: Partnering with Families of Young Bilingual Children with Disabilities." In *Language, Learning, and Disability in the Education of Young Bilingual Children*, eds. D.C. Castro & A.J. Artiles, 90–111. CAL Series on Language Education: 4. Bristol, UK: Multilingual Matters.

Gilliam, W.S. 2005. *Prekindergarteners Left Behind: Expulsion Rates in State Prekindergarten Systems.* FCD Policy Brief Number 3. New York: Foundation for Child Development.

Gilliam, W.S, A. Maupin, C. Reyes, M. Accavitti, & F. Shic. 2016. *Do Early Educators' Implicit Biases Regarding Sex and Race Relate to Behavior Expectations and Recommendations of Preschool Expulsions and Suspensions?* Research study brief. New Haven, CT: Yale University Child Study Center.

Gilliam, W.S., & G. Shahar. 2006. "Preschool and Child Care Expulsion and Suspension: Rates and Predictors in One State." *Infants & Young Children* 19 (3): 228–45.

Gillies, R. 2020. *Inquiry-Based Science Education.* CRC Focus Series: Global Science Education. Boca Raton, FL: CRC Press.

Goldenberg, B.M. 2014. "White Teachers in Urban Classrooms: Embracing Non-White Students' Cultural Capital for Better Teaching and Learning. *Urban Education* 49 (1): 111–44.

Gonzalez-Mena, J. 2010. *50 Strategies for Communicating and Working with Diverse Families.* Boston: Pearson Education.

González, N., L.C. Moll, & C. Amanti, eds. 2005. *Funds of Knowledge: Theorizing Practices in Households, Communities, and Classrooms.* Mahwah, NJ: Lawrence Erlbaum Associates.

Goodboy, A.K., & M.M. Martin. 2018. "LGBT Bullying in School: Perspectives on Prevention." *Communication Education* 67 (4): 513–20. https://doi:10.1080/03634523.2018.1494846.

Grande, S. 2015. *Red Pedagogy: Native American Social and Political Thought.* 10th anniversary ed. Lanham, MD: Rowman & Littlefield Publishers.

Grodsky, E., Y. Huangfu, H.R. Miesner, & C. Packard. 2017. *Kindergarten Readiness in Wisconsin* (WCER Working Paper No. 2017-3). Madison: University of Wisconsin–Madison, Wisconsin Center for Education. www.wcer.wisc.edu/publications/working-papers.

Hambly, C., & E. Fombonne. 2012. "The Impact of Bilingual Environments on Language Development in Children with Autism Spectrum Disorders." *Journal of Autism and Developmental Disorders* 42 (7): 1342–52.

Hamlin, M., & D.B. Wisneski. 2012. "Supporting the Scientific Thinking and Inquiry of Toddlers and Preschoolers Through Play." *Young Children* 67 (3): 82–88.

Hammond, Z. 2014. *Culturally Responsive Teaching and the Brain: Promoting Authentic Engagement and Rigor Among Culturally and Linguistically Diverse Students.* Thousand Oaks, CA: Corwin Press.

Heritage, M. 2010. *Formative Assessment: Making It Happen in the Classroom.* Thousand Oaks, CA: SAGE.

Howard, T.C. 2018. "Capitalizing on Culture: Engaging Young Learners in Diverse Classrooms." *Young Children* 73 (2): 24–33.

Husband, T. 2012. "'I Don't See Color': Challenging Assumptions About Discussing Race with Young Children." *Early Childhood Education Journal* 39: 365–71.

Ijalba, E. 2016. "Hispanic Immigrant Mothers of Young Children with Autism Spectrum Disorders: How Do They Understand and Cope with Autism?" *American Journal of Speech-Language Pathology* 25 (2): 200–13. https://doi.org /10.1044/2015_ajslp-13-0017.

Jessee, V., & K. Adamsons. 2018. "Father Involvement and Father-Child Relationship Quality: An Intergenerational Perspective." *Parenting: Science and Practice* 18 (1): 28–44.

Kelly, D.J., P.C. Quinn, A.M. Slater, K. Lee, A. Gibson, M. Smith, L. Ge, & O. Pascalis. 2005. "Three-Month-Olds, but Not Newborns, Prefer Own-Race Faces." *Developmental Science* 8 (6): 31–36. https://doi.org/10.1111/j.1467-7687.2005 .0434a.x.

Kimura, A.M., M. Antón-Oldenburg, & E.E. Pinderhughes. 2022. "Developing and Teaching an Anti-Bias Curriculum in a Public Elementary School: Leadership, K–1 Teachers', and Young Children's Experiences." *Journal of Research in Childhood Education* 36 (2): 183–202.

Kirkland, D. 2013. *A Search Past Silence: The Literacy of Young Black Men.* New York: Teachers College Press.

Klatte, M., K. Bergström, & T. Lachmann. 2013. "Does Noise Affect Learning? A Short Review on Noise Effects on Cognitive Performance in Children." *Frontiers in Psychology* 4. www.frontiersin.org /articles/10.3389/fpsyg.2013.00578/full.

Kostelnik, M.J., A.K. Soderman, A.P. Whiren, & M.L. Rupiper. 2019. *Developmentally Appropriate Curriculum and Best Practices in Early Childhood Education.* 7th ed. Upper Saddle River, NJ: Pearson.

Kuh, L.P., D. LeeKeenan, H. Given, & M.R. Beneke. 2016. "Moving Beyond Anti-Bias Activities: Supporting the Development of Anti-Bias Practices." *Young Children* 71 (1): 58–65.

Ladson-Billings, G. 2009. *The Dreamkeepers: Successful Teachers of African American Children.* San Francisco: Jossey-Bass.

Ladson-Billings, G. 2014. "Culturally Relevant Pedagogy 2.0: a.k.a. The Remix." *Harvard Educational Review* 84 (1): 74–84.

Landry S.H., T.A. Zucker, J.J. Montroy, H-Y Hsu, M.A. Assel, C. Varghese, A. Crawford, & E.G. Feil. 2021. "Replication of Combined School Readiness Interventions for Teachers and Parents of Head Start Pre-Kindergarteners Using Remote Delivery." *Early Childhood Research Quarterly* 56: 149–66.

Lee, D.M., L. Duesbery, P.P. Han, T. Tashi, C.S. Her, & V.O. Pang. 2017. "Academic Needs and Family Factors in the Education of Southeast Asian American Students: Dismantling the Model Minority Myth." *Journal of Southeast Asian American Education and Advancement* 12 (2). https://docs.lib.purdue.edu/jsaaea/vol12/iss2/2.

Levtov, R., N. van der Gaag, M. Greene, M. Kaufman, & G. Barker. 2015. *State of the World's Fathers: Executive Summary: A MenCare Advocacy Publication.* Washington, DC: Promundo, Rutgers, Save the Children, Sonke Gender Justice, and the MenEngage Alliance.

Licona, M.M. 2013. "Mexican and Mexican-American Children's Funds of Knowledge as Interventions into Deficit Thinking: Opportunities for Praxis in Science Education." *Cultural Studies of Science Education* 8 (4): 859–72.

Llopart, M., & M. Esteban-Guitart. 2018. "Funds of Knowledge in 21st Century Societies: Inclusive Educational Practices for Under-Represented Students, A Literature Review." *Journal of Curriculum Studies* 50 (2): 145–61.

Martinez-Hickman, O., & C. Amaro-Jiménez. 2018. "When Parents Get Involved, Things Just Get Better. Lessons from Latino/a Parents' Experiences in Public School." *NABE Perspectives* 41 (2): 9–12.

Masterson, M. 2022. "Planning and Implementing an Engaging Curriculum to Achieve Meaningful Goals." In *Developmentally Appropriate Practice in Early Childhood Programs Serving Children from Birth Through Age 8,* 4th ed., NAEYC, 215–51. Washington, DC: NAEYC.

McCarty, T.L., & T.S. Lee. 2014. "Critical Culturally Sustaining/Revitalizing Pedagogy and Indigenous Education Sovereignty." *Harvard Educational Review* 84 (1): 101–24. https://doi.org/10.17763.

McClure, M., P. Tarr, C.M. Thompson, & A. Eckhoff. 2017. "Defining Quality in Visual Art Education for Young Children: Building on the Position Statement of the Early Childhood Art Educators." *Arts Education Policy Review* 118 (3): 154–63.

McWilliam, R.A. 2012. "Implementing and Preparing for Home Visits." *Topics in Early Childhood Special Education* 31 (4): 224–31.

Mills, G.E. 2017. *Action Research: A Guide for the Teacher Researcher*. 6th ed. Harlow, UK: Pearson.

Moll, L.C. 2019. "Elaborating Funds of Knowledge: Community-Oriented Practices in International Contexts." *Literacy Research: Theory, Method, and Practice* 68 (1): 130–38.

Moll, L.C., C. Amanti, D. Neff, & N. González. 1992. "Funds of Knowledge for Teaching: Using a Qualitative Approach to Connect Homes and Classrooms." *Theory into Practice* 31 (2): 132–41.

Montessori, M. 2012. "Lecture 3: Education Based on Psychology." In *The 1946 London Lectures:* 13–22. Amsterdam: Montessori-Pierson.

Moquino, T.L., & K.M. Kitchens. 2021. "Remember, Reclaim, Restore: A Post-Pandemic Pedagogy of Indigenous Love in Early Childhood Education." *Occasional Paper Series* 46. https://educate .bankstreet.edu/occasional-paper-series/vol2021 /iss46/12.

NAEYC. 2011. "Code of Ethical Conduct and Statement of Commitment." Position statement. Washington, DC: NAEYC. www.naeyc.org/resources/position -statements/ethical-conduct.

NAEYC. 2019a. "Advancing Equity in Early Childhood Education." Position statement. Washington, DC: NAEYC. www.naeyc.org/resources/position -statements/equity.

NAEYC. 2019b. "Professional Standards and Competencies for Early Childhood Educators." Position statement. Washington, DC: NAEYC. www.naeyc.org/resources/position-statements /professional-standards-competencies.

NAEYC. 2020. "Developmentally Appropriate Practice." Position statement. Washington, DC: NAEYC. www.naeyc.org/resources/position -statements/dap/contents.

NASEM (National Academies of Sciences, Engineering, and Medicine). 2017. *Promoting the Educational Success of Children and Young Learning English: Promising Futures.* Washington, DC: The National Academies Press. https://doi.org/10.17226/24677.

NASEM (National Academies of Sciences, Engineering, and Medicine). 2018. *How People Learn II: Learners, Contexts, and Cultures.* Washington, DC: The National Academies Press. http://nap.edu /24783.

National Center on Early Childhood Quality Assurance. 2017. *Early Learning and Developmental Guidelines.* Fairfax, VA: National Center on Early Childhood Quality Assurance. www.childcareta.acf .hhs.gov/sites/default/files/public/075_1707 _state_elgs_web_final.pdf.

NCES (National Center for Education Statistics). n.d. "Racial/Ethnic Enrollment in Public Schools." Last updated May 2022. https://nces.ed.gov/programs /coe/indicator_cge.asp.

Neuman, S. 2011. "The Challenge of Teaching Vocabulary in Early Education." In *Handbook of Early Literacy Research*, Vol. 3, eds. S. Neuman & D. Dickinson, 358–72. New York: The Guilford Press.

Noltemeyer, A., & C.S. Mcloughlin. 2010. "Patterns of Exclusionary Discipline by School Typology, Ethnicity, and Their Interaction." *Perspectives on Urban Education* 7 (1): 27–40.

NRC (National Research Council). 2008. *Early Childhood Assessment: Why, What, and How.* Washington, DC: National Academies Press. https://nap.edu/catalog/12446/early-childhood -assessment-why-what-and-how.

Okun, T. n.d. "Divorcing White Supremacy Culture—Coming Home to Who We Really Are." White Supremacy Culture. www .whitesupremacyculture.info. Accessed March 4, 2021.

Paris, D., & S. Alim, eds. 2017. *Culturally Sustaining Pedagogies: Teaching and Learning for Justice in a Changing World.* New York: Teachers College Press.

Paris, S. 2005. "Reinterpreting the Development of Reading Skills." *Reading Research Quarterly* 402 (2)*:* 184–202.

Paulus, M., & C. Moore. 2014. "The Development of Recipient-Dependent Sharing Behavior and Sharing Expectations in Preschool Children." *Developmental Psychology* 50 (3): 914–21.

Perszyk, D.R., R.F. Lei, G.V. Bodenhausen, J.A. Richeson, & S.R. Waxman. 2019. "Bias at the Intersection of Race and Gender: Evidence from Preschool-Aged Children." *Developmental Science* 22 (3): e12788. https://doi.org/10.1111/desc.12788.

Pianta, R.C., B.K. Hamre, & A.P. Williford. 2011. *Banking Time*. Unpublished manual. University of Virginia.

Posey-Maddox, L. 2017. "Schooling in Suburbia: The Intersections of Race, Class, Gender, and Place in Black Fathers' Engagement and Family–School Relationships." *Gender and Education* 29 (5): 577–93.

Rector-Aranda, A. 2016. "School Norms and Reforms, Critical Race Theory, and the Fairytale of Equitable Education." *Critical Questions in Education* 7 (1): 1–16.

Riley-Ayers, S. 2014. *Formative Assessment: Guidance for Early Childhood Policymakers*. CEELO Policy Report. New Brunswick, NJ: Center on Enhancing Early Learning Outcomes.

Robertson, A. 2016. "The Radical Case for a Knowledge-Rich Curriculum." *Left History Teaching*. https://lefthistoryteaching.wordpress.com/2016/03/24/the-radical-case-for-a-knowledge-rich-curriculum.

Rodriguez, G.M. 2013. "Power and Agency in Education: Exploring the Pedagogical Dimensions of Knowledge." *Review of Research in Education* 37: 87–120.

Rogoff, B., B. Najafi, & R. Mejía-Arauz. 2014. "Constellations of Cultural Practices Across Generations: Indigenous American Heritage and Learning by Observing and Pitching In." *Human Development* 57 (2–3): 82–95.

Rosenblatt, L.M. 1976. *Literature as Exploration*. New York: Modern Language Association.

Salinas-González, I., M.G. Arreguín-Anderson, & I. Alanís. 2019. "Supporting Language Through Culturally Rich Dramatic Play." In *Serious Fun: Guiding Play to Extend Children's Learning*, eds. M.L. Masterson & H. Bohart, 35–44. Washington, DC: NAEYC.

Santiago, A. 2019. "NY Has the Richest, Poorest, Smallest, Most Unequal Congressional Districts." *City and State NY*. www.cityandstateny.com/articles/politics/new-york-state/ny-has-richest-poorest-smallest-most-unequal-congressional.

Sasaki, J.Y., & H.S. Kim. 2017. "Nature, Nurture, and Their Interplay: A Review of Cultural Neuroscience." *Journal of Cross-Cultural Psychology* 48 (1): 4–22.

Schachter, R.E., H.K. Gerde, & H. Hatton-Bowers. 2019. "Guidelines for Selecting Professional Development for Early Childhood Teachers." *Early Childhood Education Journal* 47 (4): 395–408.

Schickedanz, J.A., & M.F. Collins. 2013. *So Much More than the ABCs: The Early Phases of Reading and Writing*. Washington, DC: NAEYC.

Schindler, H.S., P.A Fisher, & J.P. Shonkoff. 2017. "From Innovation to Impact at Scale: Lessons Learned from a Cluster of Research–Community Partnerships." *Child Development* 88 (5): 1435–46.

Sheridan, S.M., C.P. Edwards, C.A. Marvin, & L.L. Knoche. 2009. "Professional Development in Early Childhood Programs: Process Issues and Research Needs." *Early Education and Development* 20 (3): 377–401.

Sims Bishop, R. 1990. "Mirrors, Windows, and Sliding Glass Doors." *Perspectives: Choosing and Using Books for the Classroom* 6 (3): ix–xi.

Singleton, G.E., & C. Linton. 2006. *Courageous Conversations About Race: A Field Guide for Achieving Equity in Schools*. Thousand Oaks, CA: Corwin Press.

Skiba, R.J., R.H. Horner, C.G. Chung, M.K. Rausch, S.L. May, & T. Tobin. 2011. "Race Is Not Neutral: A National Investigation of African American and Latino Disproportionality in School Discipline." *School Psychology Review* 40 (1): 85–107.

Skinner, D.G., V. Correa, M. Skinner, & D.B. Bailey Jr. 2001. "Role of Religion in the Lives of Latino Families of Young Children with Developmental

Delays." *American Journal of Mental Retardation* 106 (4): 297–13.

SLJ (School Library Journal). n.d. "An Updated Look at Diversity in Children's Books." Accessed June 19, 2019. www.slj.com/?detailStory=an-updated-look-at-diversity-in-childrens-books.

Souto-Manning, M. 2009. "Negotiating Culturally Responsive Pedagogy Through Multicultural Children's Literature: Towards Critical Democratic Literacy Practices in a First Grade Classroom." *Journal of Early Childhood Literacy* 9 (1): 50–74.

Souto-Manning, M. 2013. *Multicultural Teaching in the Early Childhood Classroom: Approaches, Strategies, and Tools, Preschool–2nd Grade*. New York: Teachers College Press.

Souto-Manning, M., & C.H. Mitchell. 2010. "The Role of Action Research in Fostering Culturally-Responsive Practices in a Preschool Classroom." *Early Childhood Education Journal* 37 (4): 269–77. http://dx.doi.org/10.1007/s10643-009-0345-9.

Starnes, L. 2022. *Big Conversations with Little Children: Addressing Questions, Worries, and Fears*. Minneapolis, MN: Free Spirit Publishing.

Steele, C. M., & J. Aronson. 1995. "Stereotype Threat and the Intellectual Test Performance of African Americans." *Journal of Personality and Social Psychology* 69 (5): 797–811.

Stop AAPI Hate. n.d. "Stop AAPI Hate." Accessed September 7, 2022. https://stopaapihate.org.

Sturdivant, T.D., & I. Alanís. 2019. "Teaching Through Culture: One Teacher's Use of Culturally Relevant Practices for African American Preschoolers." *Journal for Multicultural Education* 13 (3): 203–14. https://doi.org/10.1108/JME-03-2019-0019.

Sturdivant, T.D., & I. Alanís. 2020. "'I'm Gonna Cook My Baby in a Pot': Young Black Girls' Racial Preferences and Play Behavior." *Early Childhood Education Journal* 49 (2): 473–82. https://doi.org/10.1007/s10643-020-01095-9.

Tatter, G. 2021. "The Greatest Battle in the History." *Harvard Ed. Magazine*. https://www.gse.harvard.edu/news/ed/22/01/greatest-battle-history.

US ED (Department of Education). 2016. *The State of Racial Diversity in the Educator Workforce*. Report. Washington, DC: ED.

USC Pacific Asia Museum. n.d. "Debunking the Model Minority Myth." Accessed September 7, 2022. https://pacificasiamuseum.usc.edu/exhibitions/online-exhibitions/debunking-the-model-minority-myth.

USDHHS (United States Department of Health and Human Services) & ED. 2014. *Policy Statement on Expulsion and Suspension Policies in Early Childhood Settings*. Washington, DC: USDHHS and ED.

Vygotsky, L.S. 1978. *Mind in Society: The Development of Higher Psychological Processes*. Ed. and trans. M. Cole, V. John-Steiner, S. Scribner, & E. Souberman. Cambridge, MA: Harvard University Press.

Walton, G.M., & G.L. Cohen. 2011. "A Brief Social-Belonging Intervention Improves Academic and Health Outcomes of Minority Students." *Science* 331 (6023): 1447–51.

Wang, S., & C.S. Tamis-Lemonda. 2003. "Do Child-Rearing Values in Taiwan and the United States Reflect Cultural Values of Collectivism and Individualism?" *Journal of Cross-Cultural Psychology* 34 (6): 629–42. https://doi.org/10.1177/0022022103255498.

Washington Post. 2022. "San Francisco Police Mark 567% Increase in Anti-Asian Hate-Crime Reports in 2021." *Washington Post*, January 26. www.washingtonpost.com/nation/2022/01/26/anti-asian-hate-crime-san-francisco-covid.

Wasik, B.A, & A.H. Hindman. 2014. "Understanding the Active Ingredients in an Effective Preschool Vocabulary Intervention: An Exploratory Study of Teacher and Child Talk During Book Reading." *Early Education and Development* 25 (7): 1035–56.

Whitmore, K.F., P. Martens, Y.M. Goodman, & G. Owocki. 2004. "Critical Lessons from the Transactional Perspective on Early Literacy Research." *Journal of Early Childhood Literacy* 4 (3): 291–325.

Williford, A.P., J. LoCasale-Crouch, J.V. Whittaker, J. DeCoster, K.A. Hartz, L.M. Carter, C.S.Wolcott, & B.E. Hatfield. 2017. "Changing Teacher–Child Dyadic Interactions to Improve Preschool Children's Externalizing Behaviors." *Child Development* 88 (5): 1544–53.

Wilson, L., & J. Thompson. 2021. "From Breadwinner to Nurturer: Changing Images of Fathers in the Media." *Journal of Education and Social Justice* 7 (1): 73–91.

Winkler, E.N. 2009. "Children Are Not Colorblind: How Young Children Learn Race." *PACE* 3 (3): 1–8.

Worth, K. 2019. "Science in Early Learning Environments." In *STEM in Early Childhood Education: How Science, Technology, Engineering, and Mathematics Strengthen Learning,* eds. L.E. Cohen & S. Waite-Stupiansky, 3–21. New York: Routledge.

Wright, B.L. 2019. "Black Boys Matter: Strategies for a Culturally Responsive Classroom." *Teaching Young Children* 12 (4): 20–22.

Wright, B.L. 2022. "Creating a Caring, Equitable Community of Learners." In *Developmentally Appropriate Practice in Early Childhood Programs Serving Children from Birth Through Age 8,* 4th ed., NAEYC, 111–44. Washington, DC: NAEYC.

Yellowbird, M. 2021. "The Medicine Wheel: A Decolonizing Social Work Approach to Holistic Healing and Health." Presentation to First Nations Development Institute: Luce Indigenous Knowledge Fellows Inaugural Cohort.

Yenika-Agbaw, V., & M. Napoli. 2011. *African and African American Children's and Adolescent Literature in the Classroom: A Critical Guide.* 2nd ed. New York: Lang.

Yoshikawa, H., C. Weiland, J. Brooks-Gunn, L.M. Espinosa, W.T. Gormley, & M.J. Zaslow 2013. *Investing in Our Future: The Evidence Base on Preschool Education.* Washington, DC: Society for Research in Child Development. https://fcd-us.org/resources/evidence-base-preschool.

Yosso, T.J. 2005a. *Critical Race Counterstories Along the Chicana/Chicano Educational Pipeline.* New York: Routledge.

Yosso, T.J. 2005b. "Whose Culture Has Capital? A Critical Race Theory Discussion of Community Cultural Wealth." *Race, Ethnicity, and Education* 8 (1): 69–91.

Index

disability, definition of, 11
discipline
  exclusionary, 19–20
  implicit biases in, 20–21
  using guidance over, 15–18
  See also guidance, behavior
  documenting children's learning, 50–51, 57, 68, 118

E

early learning and development standards
  (ELDS), 109–113
English language with home language support
  model, 45
environmental supports, 9, 47–48
  timing and, 98
equity, 8–11, 92, 130, 139
  anti-racist approaches and, 145–148
  in the classroom, journey to more, 141–144
  promoting linguistic diversity and, 44–48
exclusionary discipline practices, 19–20
executive functioning, 128
expulsion practices, 19

F

families
  artifacts of, 32–34
  children's disabilities, views of, 42–43
  communication with, 26
  5 Rs for promoting positive engagement with, 26–29
  funds of knowledge of, 32–36
  ideas about bilingualism in, 41–42
  languages and interests interview with, 46
  with many languages engaged in one
    community, 30–31
  mealtimes in, 12–14
  as partners with educators, 105
  photographs of, 35–36
  reciprocal relationships with, 2, 24–25
  respect for, 26
  understanding everyday lives of, 41
  wanting a relationship with classroom
    community, 27–28
  wanting reassurance and responsiveness, 27
  wanting reciprocity, 28–29
  wanting teachers to reflect, 29
Family of the Week backpack, 26
fathers, engagement of, 37–39
fifty-fifty dual language model, 44–45
5 Rs for promoting positive family
  engagement, 26–29
formative assessment, 50, 55
funds of knowledge, 32–36

G

games, 35
goals, behavioral, 22

greetings, morning, 6–7
guidance, behavior, 15–18
guided exploration, 83–88

H

hate crimes, 145–148

I

implicit biases, 20–21
inclusion, 11
  in disciplinary practices, 20
index cards, for anecdotal records, 57
Indigenous approaches to developmentally
  appropriate practice, 126–129
individuality, x
Individualized Education Program (IEP), 8, 11
Individuals with Disabilities Education Act (IDEA)
  of 2004, 11
informal assessment of STEAM experiences, 52–54
inquiry thinking, 78–82
interdisciplinary teams, 11

K

knowledge-rich curriculum, 105–107

L

land-based childrearing, 126
Learning Stories approach, 68–71
  example of, 72–74
least restrictive environment (LRE), 11
length of structured activities, 99
life cycle in a box activity, 117–119
linguistic diversity and equity, 44–48
listening centers, 120–125
literacy-based mathematics, 89–91
LOVE: Leveraging Our Value Every Day
  program, 138–140

M

materials for children with disabilities, 10
mathematics
  mealtimes and, 12–13
  place-based, 114–115
  supporting positive racial identity with
    literacy-based, 89–91
mealtimes, 12–14
mealworms, 117–119
meaningful talk, 92–94
metamorphosis, 117–119
morning greetings, 6–7
motor and coordination skills and mealtimes, 12
multicultural learning spaces, 109–113
multidisciplinary teams, 11
multilingual learning spaces, 44–48